5,000 Years of Conflict

Over 50 Maps
Conflicts that Changed the World

Forward by

Earl H. Tilford, Ph.D.
Military Historian

Jay Kimmel

CoryStevens Publishing

5,000 Years of Conflict

First Printing, January, 2005

Copyright © 2005 by CoryStevens Publishing

Library of Congress Catalog Card Number (on file)

ISBN: 0-942893-05-0

Printed in the United States of America

CoryStevens Publishing
15350 NE Sandy Boulevard
Portland, OR 97230
www.corystevens.com

Dedication

In a most general way, this book is dedicated to the young people who lost their lives either directly or indirectly as a result of military conflict. It is their potential for a full life that was forever lost. In the Clint Eastwood film, *Unforgiven,* (written by David Webb Peoples) the William Munny character made the sweeping statement, "*It's a hell of a thing killing a man. You take away all he's got and all he's ever gonna have.*" In a more specific way, I want to thank the following people for their contributions in helping to make this book possible: My wife, travel partner and computer rescue source, Susan Kimmel, and copy-editors, Margaret Berson and Liz Nakazawa. Proofing assistance provided by Julie Westerman, Emily Kimmel, Rosemary Grover, Ray Maddix, Barbara Lambert, Rennie Carter, and Grant Schuler. Special thanks for additional contributions from Earl Tilford, Rusty Pickett and graphic designer Ken Manske

Author's Background

Jay Kimmel, B.A., M.S. was a certified Vocational Rehabilitation Counselor and office manager for over 12 years and a licensed Real Estate Broker for more than 10 years. Jay has authored a number of historical and financial articles and books including *REAL ESTATE INVESTMENT* (Cornerstone/Simon & Schuster); *U.S. NAVY SEABEES: Since Pearl Harbor; SAVAGE & STEVENS ARMS: Collector's History;* and *CUSTER, CODY & THE LAST INDIAN WARS* (CoryStevens Publishing). In 1965, during the Vietnam buildup, Jay's employment included work at the Armed Forces Examining Station but attempted naval enlistment at that time was denied due to the physical exam. Jay has traveled to all of the world's continents except Antarctica, Africa, and Australia. Travel to actual battle sites and being an active history buff continues to be one of his lifelong ambitions.

CoryStevens Publishing
www.corystevens.com

Contents

Foreword

Earl H. Tilford, Jr., Ph.D.
Professor of History
Grove City College

"A battle sometimes decides everything; and sometimes the most trifling thing decides the fate of a battle."

Napoleon, 1816

Of all the species, only humans kill for reasons other than instinctive drives for survival or food. People, unlike any other creatures, engage in legally-sanctioned killing to achieve political, ideological or religious ends; what we otherwise call war. Prussian general and philosopher Carl von Clausewitz, whose 1832 book *Vom Kriege* or *On War* remains the finest single volume ever written on war, wrote that "Battles decide everything."

Throughout the pages that follow, military historian Jay Kimmel, using a combination of descriptive narrative and illustrative maps, vividly recounts fifty of history's most important and decisive battles. *Fifty Battles: 5,000 Years of Conflict* does more than chronicle two score and ten of the countless thousands of battles fought from the Battle of Abydos in 3,050 BCE, which marked the unification of Egypt, to the series of sharply bloody engagements during the March 2003 "dash to Baghdad" at the beginning of the War in Iraq. In the pages that follow, Jay Kimmel brings each of these fifty battles to life with cogent commentary framed by insightful historical contextual commentary.

War operates at three levels from the strategic down through the operational to the tactical level where soldiers, sailors and airmen fight and die. Political leaders, whether kings, emperors, parliamentarians, presidents, generalissimos, or dictators, determine policies that set strategic goals. Purveyors of the opera-tional art then organize the forces, devise plans for their employment and move soldiers and equipment toward the fateful encounter known today as "movement to contact." It is there, at the tactical level, where soldiers, by killing and dying decide the fate of empires, political movements, religions and nations.

Battles serve as the unifying entity for hundreds, perhaps thousands, of tactical engagements. They are the bloody blender in which the visions of kings are animated by the heroics and sacrifices of soldiers and warriors fighting under the direction of men who may be as noble as Robert E. Lee, as bloody as Vietnamese General Vo Nguyen Giap or as depraved as Qusay Hussein. It all comes together in that bloody maul Clausewitz described as *"der schlacht"*…the slaughter.

Those battles that turn history, often turn on individual expressions of personal courage and brilliance…what the French call *"coup d'oeil"* or "the light of the inner eye." In battle, it is not unusual for a relatively minor engagement, like the desperate hand-to-hand fighting between Joshua Chamberlain's Twentieth Maine and the Fifteenth Alabama Infantry for Little Round Top on July 2, 1863, the key position anchoring the Union's left flank during the Battle of Gettysburg, to decide at the tactical level the outcome of a battle at the operational level that turns the strategic tide of war to determine the future of a nation. Because war is so quintessentially a human endeavor, the ways in which wars unfold…battles…reflect the very best and the worst of our human natures. Each battle covered in this rich volume serves as "capsulated history" due to the masterful manner in which Jay Kimmel has set the historical context. Leadership, weaponry, the lay of the land, and the morale of the forces come alive on every fact filled page.

Whether the reader is a seasoned professional soldier, a scholar steeped in military history, or simply a dedicated viewer of the History Channel, *Fifty Battles: 5,000 Years of Conflict* provides a rich and complete resource. So, batten down the hatches, strap yourself in and take point because much good reading is over the hill.

Earl H. Tilford, Jr., Ph.D., is a respected military historian who has published books on the U.S. war in Vietnam and the current Persian Gulf wars, in addition to more than fifty articles on military history. He is a professor of history at Grove City College in Grove City, PA. He has also served as the director of research and senior research professor at the Strategic Studies Institute of the U.S. Army War College.

PAX

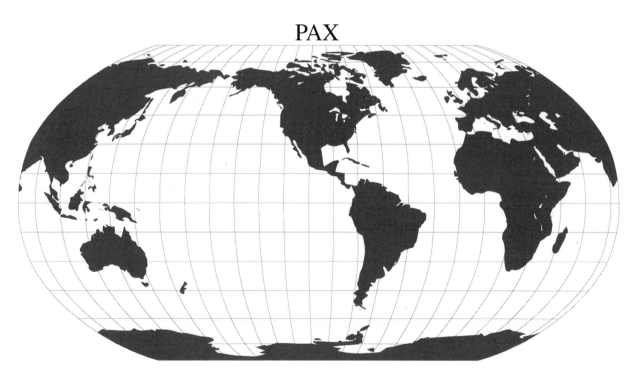

EL MUNDO

Introduction

Every battle has a huge emotional impact on the participants, their families, and friends. No matter what century or millennium the participants are individuals who ultimately account for their own actions in their own way. Battles have typically placed young men in the face of extreme danger against opposing young men. Whatever the original purposes may have been, reality comes down to personal survival and survival of those immediately closest at any given moment. The entire clan, tribe, or nationality will usually be secondary at best. In a fictional film scene in *Dances with Wolves,* the Kevin Costner character refers to a final battle scene between two rival tribes and how they fought for their lives and the lives of their families, not for deep, dark, psychological motives. Audie Murphy, the most decorated soldier of World War Two, authored the book *To Hell and Back* ©1949. His story was one of great courage as a common man on the field of battle. He wrote, "That's what it means to be a veteran—to be scared all the time."

This book is a chronological history of 50 battles that span over 5,000 years. The first and last battles, after five millenniums of technological change, were just a few hundred miles apart. Being killed or wounded by an arrow or a laser-guided missile controlled by a satellite still has much the same consequence for the soldier in the field. This book is about the context and consequences of specific battles that impacted the world, not the glorification of war. This book is dedicated to all of the young people whose lives were cut short due to battle circumstances beyond their control.

A statistical accounting of battles may be essential to evaluate what happened but is demeaning to the individual combatant's sacrifices and pain. Numerical counts are also irrelevant to the accelerated highs and lows of intense battlefield camaraderie. Surviving veterans often consider their time of service to be one of the most momentous times of their lives. The combatants that do not make it back home, for whatever reason, are foremost remembered for lifetimes and beyond by their buddies and their families. The same applies to the civilians caught in the conflict who became casualties.

Much of the history of battles has relied heavily on the frontal assault and digression to hand-to-hand combat. In the Battle of Cannae, for example, the Roman Legionnaires became so compressed there was almost no room to maneuver. In the Battle of Agincourt the French defenders in full armor were not only compressed but fatally weighted down by their armor. In other battles it was exhaustion and dehydration that were major factors such as the Battle of Carrhae, the Norman Conquest following the Viking invasion in 1066, the Battle of Manzikert, Little Big Horn, Little Round Top, and Dien Bien Phu.

Battles and wars have typically been times for rapid social change and technological innovation. It comes as some surprise just how little technological change occurred during the American Revolution. Communications tended to require days or weeks by horseback. Weaponry changed little. Dramatic social changes were made in the radical departure from being a subject of an absentee monarchy to being a voting member of a representative government. Like most revolutions, there were very divergent opinions and loyalties among the participants. For some, change was always too slow, or too fast, or they felt that things should be back the way it was, or that some impossible ideal should have been attained. Rarely did individual combatants have a major vote in the process except at the risk of their own life. Consider Peter the

Great's Russia, America's Yorktown, and France's "Storming of the Bastille."

The big picture was not what the typical soldier in the field was aware of, or maybe even concerned about. The war planners (the safe-in-their-bed monarchs and politicians) typically had a very different vision as they maneuvered little war models across big war maps. The primary U.S. decision makers for the decade-plus war in Vietnam rarely, if ever, spent any time in Vietnam and had little or no communication with the troops on the line. The Battle of the Little Big Horn was another example of a politically driven event that the soldier in the field saw very differently. Actually, the Little Big Horn was one of the last battles between radically different cultures that were "played on an even field." Weaponry and tactics were very similar due to the U.S. Army's non-use of cannons or Gatling guns. Communications, armaments, and mobility were similar on both sides. The real distinction was the overwhelming superiority in numbers of the defending Native Americans.

In 5,000-plus years battles have evolved on many different levels. Initial prehistoric battles, like group-coordinated hunting, probably relied heavily upon close observation of the environment and use of simple hunting tools. The same tools could function as blunt force weapons, bows and arrows, spears, or traps. Some elements of planning, physical gestures and oral communications were needed to meet their needs (food, clothing, and extras). Group coordination made it possible for the small clan or tribal unit to survive on something more than gleaning vegetation and carrion from animal kills. Rivalries over hunting grounds, water sources, or inter-clan offenses predisposed one group to battle with another. The discovery of copper and bronze improved their edged tools.

The evolution of defenses likely tended to take the form of concealment in wooded or brushy areas and possible dens or caves to reduce the chances of becoming the prey of predatory animals or humans. Early advances included the use of high ground to improve visibility for anything that might be approaching them and the use of gravity to more effectively throw objects down at the intruder. Rivers and large bodies of water were also natural defenses because they were hard to cross quickly and again made it more possible to see and attack an intruder before it was too late. Ultimately there was the use of piled up walls or barricades using available debris to slow down the intruder and to make the intruders more vulnerable as they attempted to climb over.

For many thousands of years the hastily assembled barricade evolved into the walled fortress. Archeological evidence is strong that rock formations and wood-based fortresses were common throughout much of the world and to some extent beyond the nineteenth century. Fire, of course, was one of the greatest threats to flammable structures. Therefore, whenever possible, fortresses tended to be coated with mud, cut stones, or stucco-like mixes to imitate stone such as was used throughout much of medieval Europe.

Walled cities during biblical times intentionally had small openings to limit the size and quantity of possible intruders. The expression, "It is harder for a rich man to get into heaven than it is for a camel to thread the eye of a needle," referred to the great difficulty of a warrior on a camel to charge through the small opening in the city wall. As fortress walls and their gates improved the primary offense was the siege. The enemy simply used force to restrict all new supplies of food and liquid until the besieged victims surrendered. The siege of Masada was a classic example. The siege of Troy reputedly lasted for ten years and was failing until the treacherous introduction of the famed wooden horse.

Lack of patience usually compelled the forces conducting a siege to try something different. Flaming arrows became one type of innovation. Ghengis Khan's troops sometimes captured domesticated birds, attached flaming debris to their legs and let them fly back to set fires. More commonly, the catapult was used by the Romans and others to launch large objects with or without flame (including diseased animal carcasses) into a fortress or a walled city. The heavy ram was another innovation for crashing gates. A defense for the ram was the artificial body of water around the outside walls (moot) that could be protected with a drawbridge, heated oil and archers along the notched top walls. An innovative offense for the moot that was used by Ghengis Khan was to march captives into the moot and create an impromptu bridge atop their bodies. Finally, it was the use of the cannon starting around the 1300's that marked the demise of the walled city, the feudal castle, the military fortress, and body armor. During World War Two General George S. Patton said if men can overcome oceans and mountains they can overcome man-made barriers. He referred to Hitler's Atlantic Wall of Fortress Europe and fixed fortifications, such as the Maginot Line and Siegfried Lines, as a "monument to the stupidity of man."

The American Civil War has been described as one of the first "modern wars." At one point or another that war included rifled barrels, centerfire ammunition, repeating firearms, the Gatling gun (machine gun), trench warfare, ironclad ships, rail-mounted siege guns, rail transport of troops, and aerial observation balloons. It was also a war of long range, 50-caliber weapons and no longer appropriate tactics from an earlier era. Frontal assaults quickly became obsolete during the cavalry and infantry charges of Napoleon against cannons that fired projectiles at the speed of sound. World War One had much the same idiocy of both infantry and cavalry charges against well-positioned artillery and machine gun fire. The Great War (1914-1918) also introduced the battlefield tank, the aerial fighter-bomber, reconnaissance planes, mustard and nerve gas, submarines, and mass killing on a scale unmatched in history at that time.

The transition between the beginning of World War One and the end of World War Two included some of the most innovative changes in the history of all wars. Changes included the torpedo bomber, atomic bomb, jet aircraft, V-1 and V-2 missiles, radar, sonar, asdic (British equivalent), enigma code machines, aircraft carriers, extreme long-range bombers, distinctly improved submarines, tanks, aircraft, penicillin, and mass killing on a worldwide scale estimated at over 55 million people.

Battles since World War Two, nine of which are detailed in this book, have been of the deep, dark, psychological variety. Technical innovations have been very sophisticated refinements of existing weapons, equipment, and methods of doing battle that would be somewhat familiar to the World War Two veteran in 1945. The current emphasis is upon doing everything possible to combat international, state-sponsored terrorism with loosely defined enemies who often have no border to defend and no ideology or standards of moral conduct except what they prescribe for themselves at the moment and seek to impose on others. The prospect that there will be a definitive resolution any time soon is not probable. The word "guerrilla" comes from the Spanish word for small war and the likelihood that fanatic individuals will perpetuate small wars is great.

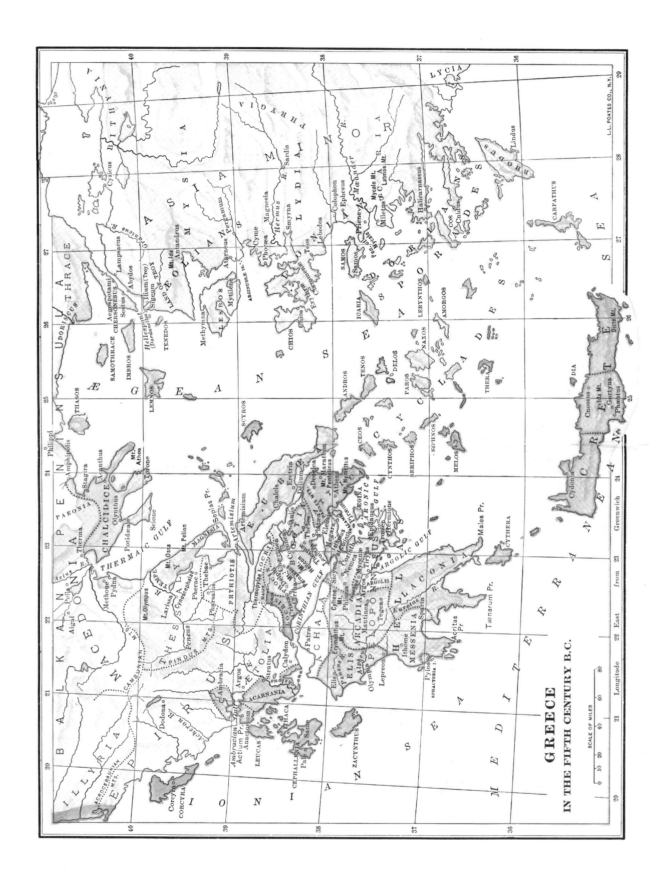

GREECE

IN THE FIFTH CENTURY B.C.

1
Scorpion King Unites Egypt, 3050 B.C.E.

"The Scorpion King," a Universal Pictures' film starring The Rock (Dwayne Johnson) and directed by Chuck Russell was released in 2002. A fictional story with great action scenes, special effects and original music score, the film has reignited substantial interest in ancient Egypt. This viewer's impression of the film, however, was that it was a great action film with little, if any, historical accuracy. Perhaps coincidentally, real documentation now exists that around the year 3050 B.C.E., there was a great battle just 300 miles south of Cairo that resulted in the unification of Upper and Lower Egypt. The victor was the Scorpion king whose realm was the ancient city of Abydos.

Abydos was once the most important city in Egypt. It lies about six to eight miles west of the Upper Nile River and roughly 100 miles downstream from the ancient city of Thebes. Archeological evidence suggests Abydos was also the holiest site in Egypt and, in mythology, the rumored birthplace of the Egyptian god-king, Osiris. The basic story is that Osiris married his royal sister, Isis, and transferred most of his royal duties to her as his queen. He then ventured further out into the world to expand the wealth and power of his kingdom. He had great successes because he was favored by the gods, or perhaps was a god himself. His jealous brother, Set, tricked Osiris into being sealed in a coffin that was then floated down the Nile. Isis learned of the betrayal and recovered her husband's body. The brother, Set, learned of the body's recovery and he secretly had it dissected and again floated down the Nile. In her grief and rage Isis recovered her dismembered husband, and mated with the divine corpse. The result was the birth of Horace (part falcon, part human) and Egypt's first mythological king. Every

pharaoh from that time forward had some association with the gods Osiris, Isis, and Horace. The spirit of Osiris eventually took on a mythological cult status as the god of transformation from life to death and as the overseer of eternal life in the world of the hereafter.

The non-mythological validity of a real Scorpion king appears to be beyond doubt. Hieroglyphic images in stone detail his existence and accomplishments as one of the earliest predynasty kings of Egypt. A burial place for the first kings of Egypt has been found near the ancient city of Abydos at a site called Umm el Ga'ab. There, a brick-lined tomb measuring 24' x 27' contained hundreds of ceramic storage vases from Palestine or Canaan, a crook-shaped scepter made of ivory, and 160 stamp-sized tags made of ivory or bone. Each tag was inscribed with basic hieroglyphs or picture symbols. The tags repeated reference to a scorpion definitely suggests the tomb was the burial site of the actual Scorpion king.

As indicated on the map, Abydos was situated from six to eight miles west of the Nile and north of the rival city-state of Naqada. The warriors of Naqada were depicted in rock etchings as longhaired primitive people with feathers worked into their matted hair. It can be inferred that hostilities resulted from competition for trade, for territory, for wealth, or any number of other factors as two rapidly evolving city-states competed for many of the same resources. The distinctions between the two groups of people were perhaps typical of classic power struggles between order and chaos, east and west, or good and bad where the strongest and most cunning generally prevails. The battle of Abydos against Naqada appeared to be one of heroic proportions and lasting outcome.

The apparent cunning of the Scorpion king was accomplished in organizing a surprise attack on Naqada through the desert, not the more anticipated assault along the west bank of the Nile. The Scorpion king's attack was a well concealed descent from the western mountains and across a forbidding desert. Abydos attacked the unsuspecting rear defenses of Naqada with overwhelming force. The battle was likely brief and deadly.

One of the essentials for a well planned and well coordinated attack was the need for good communications. Messages often had to be understood and transmitted from one location to another without reliance upon oral or visual communications. The problem was solved in this instance with the use of small ivory or bone tags about the size of postage stamps. Each of approximately 160 discovered tags contained about three hieroglyphs each that made up words, phrases or sound combinations to construct phrases or convey messages. It was as if the need for documented and transferable records was so great, that the king commanded that a system be developed that would accomplish that purpose. The result was that the first instance of verifiable use of written language has been traced to this specific place and time. This discovery preceded the cuniform language on clay tablets found in Mesopotamia several centuries later. Also, unlike cuniform tablets, the tags had a small hole at the top of each to be arranged in different sequences with a string-like material to express different combinations of words, thoughts, records, and general communications. This was a stunning first documentation of the use of written language. Necessity suggests that the first written language was mandated by the royal court for the purpose of war, recording the spoils of war, and perhaps for taxing the assets of the kingdom. Radiocarbon dating of the writing tags discovered in the apparent tomb of the Scorpion king placed the ivory and bone tags at approximately 3,200, B.C.E.

Command structure also has its needs for recognition of authority, focus, preparation and coordination of effort plus ongoing logistical supply. Again, much can be inferred from images etched into rock. Those images show a king's headgear that was later to be a part of the pharonic image for thousands of years of Egyptian history. Also, the macehead, the king's personal weapon for crushing the skulls of enemies was evident for the first time. This highly visual instrument of authority had its earliest recorded history at Abydos.

The evolution of Egyptian power and influence in the paradise-like region of the Nile Valley can possibly be traced back to the conquest of Naqada and the unification of both Upper and Lower Egypt under a powerful king. The Scorpion king had sufficient power to mandate the creation of the world's first written language—one of the world's greatest and most necessary inventions. Prehistory technically ended with the Battle of Abydos.

In addition to coordinating a surprise attack into an area of defensive weakness from an unexpected and improbable route, there is some evidence that the Scorpion king utilized information obtained from spies and assaulted the enemy with the intent of dividing their forces, and causing the most possible confusion. Smaller elements of the Naqada forces were likely overwhelmed by surprise archery assaults that were followed by quick cavalry assaults and then infantry assaults using swords, knives, and spears. The king likely used his macehead club to provide the final *coup de gras* upon select captives to instill fear in those who might oppose his power and authority.

The Battle of Abydos was one of history's first documented battles and was likely very comparable to succeeding battles for the next 4,000 years. Battles were typically fought face-to-face, or the distance that a spear or arrow could fly until the introduction of gunpowder.

Battles since the invention of gunpowder have especially accelerated cultural changes. Egyptian culture has likewise been evolving for at least 5,000 years. Currently, the rate of change continues to accelerate faster and faster.

Ancient map of Egypt courtesy of Royal Ontario Museum.

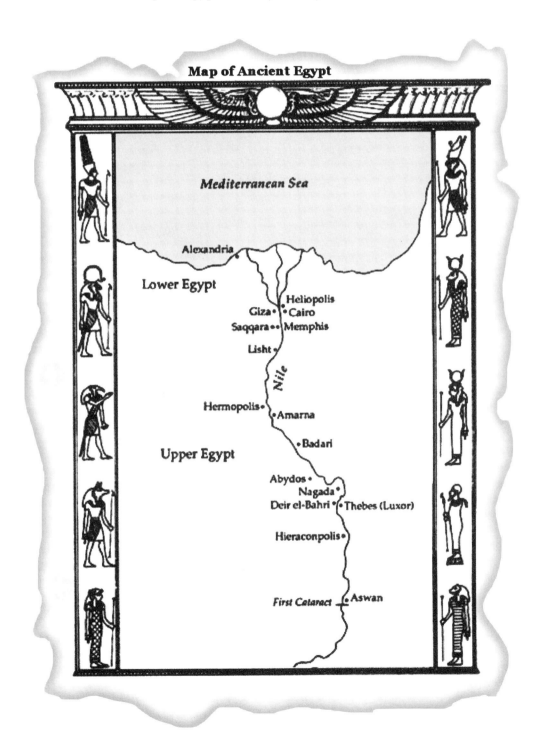

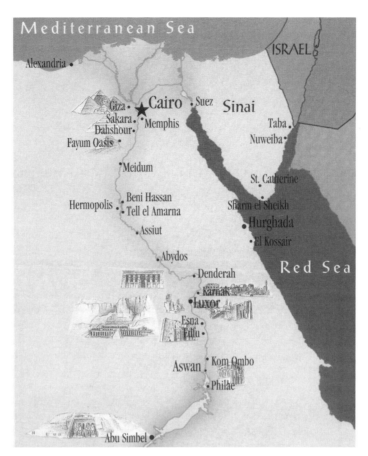

Modern Egypt

Capital: Cairo (Arab Republic of Egypt)
Population: Over 70 million
Area: Approximately 387,000 square miles
Religion: Muslim, Coptic Christian, Other
Climate: Dry desert, very hot summers and modest winter rainfall on northern coast.
Topography: Predominantly rolling hills of desert and areas of very arid mountains rising to maximum height of 6,500 feet. Northward flowing Nile River creates a fertile valley with "paradise-like" qualities that has been a continuous human habitat for at least 10,000 years.
Surrounded by Libya, Mediterranean Sea, Israel, Red Sea, and Sudan
Summary: Ancient Egypt was very much dependent upon the annual floods of the Nile to bring fertile new soil for their crops. Distances were such that the river valley was divided into Upper and Lower Egypt and may have been united for the first time by the Scorpion king about 100 years before Egypt's first dynasty in 3,100-3,050 B.C.E. The extremely dry climate has facilitated the preservation of much information about those early civilizations. The first step pyramid, for instance, was built in 2,780 B.C.E. and designed by a man named Imhotep. More to the present, the Suez Canal was completed in 1867 and is 120 miles long. The canal links the eastern Mediterranean with the Red Sea and access to the Indian Ocean. The Suez Canal has been the site of at least three recent wars: the Suez Crisis (1956), the Six-Day War (1967), and the Yom Kippur War (1973). The Nile River, basically parallel to the canal, is the world's longest at 4,145 miles and flows northward. The banks and delta of that river were converted by the ancient Egyptians into more than 10,000 square miles of arable land. The biggest single change in the flow of the Nile has been the construction of the Aswan High Dam that was inaugurated in 1970 by President Anwar Sadat. An old Arab proverd says, "Man fears time, yet time fears the pyramids."

2
Battle of Troy,
The Most Legendary War in History, 1250 B.C.E.

One of the world's longest enduring war stories dates back to the end of the Bronze Age (1600-1200 B.C.E.) and was long considered far more mythological than real. The actual conquest of Troy, with major embellishments, was immortalized by the famous Greek writer, Homer, in the *Iliad* and *Odyssey* about five centuries after the actual event. Centuries of detailed, oral storytelling of a great Mycean/ Greek city-state victory over Troy, a wooden horse, and the intervention of gods and goddesses has retained timeless appeal. Were the *Iliad* and *Odyssey* just literary fabrications? Were these ancient stories the entertaining work of many oral storytellers and finally committed to writing by a blind man named Homer? Current evidence continues to embellish these tales.

The Bronze Age layered sites of Troy are located at east-west and north-south crossroads of the Eastern Mediterranean. The ancient city of Troy sits in a natural position to have great influence upon active sea trading in the Aegean Sea and has virtual control of the Dardanelles and access to the Black Sea. Located in what is now a small site on the northwestern coast of Turkey, this walled and very prosperous city of ancient times was equally well-situated to benefit from the overland trade routes (Silk Road) connecting east and west. Recent, undersea exploration in that region has uncovered cobalt blue glass ingots from the region of current Syria and Palestine. Tons of copper ingots from Cyprus, Canaanite and Egyptian jewelry from the time of Akhenatan and a small number of swords from Mycenae were also found. Throughout the Bronze Age, the Minoans of the Island of Crete were skilled in working with gold and other metals yet lacked the raw materials without dependence upon trade such as offered by the city of Troy.

Troy may have been "an independent city-state" of the vast Hittite Empire that occupied much of the present nations of Turkey, Lebanon, and Syria. The same basic region was to later become the Ottoman Empire until the end of World War One. Bronze Age city states in the region that later became Greece probably had many reasons to come in conflict with the growing wealth and influence of Troy. Mycenae, Pylos, and Tiryns, in particular, joined forces to plunder such a rival source of power and riches. Myth has it that a ruthless king by the name of Agamemnon of Mycenae launched a war of revenge following the abduction of a beautiful Spartan princess, Helen. Legend said she was abducted by Paris, son of King Priam, the king of Troy.

Homer's account in *The Iliad* describes how King Agamemnon of Mycenae united other Greek city states by launching 1,000 ships against the well-fortified port city of Troy. The plan was to overwhelm Troy with a ratio of at least four to five warriors for each defender of Troy. According to legend, the assault became a protracted one lasting approximately ten years and became a stalemate despite the intervention of antiquity "superheroes" such as Achilles, Odyssey, and the Trojan hero, Hector. Other romantic or poetic deities, such as Aphrodite, also intervened. See "Digging Up Clues to the Truth Behind the Myth," *U.S. News & World Report,* May 24, 2004.

Realistically, it is not likely that assault forces contained within 1,000 ships could have sustained themselves for ten years by makeshift supply lines and foraging for all necessities in the surrounding countryside. *The Iliad* detailed only the last four days of the battle. Achilles had slain the popular Trojan hero,

Hector, and dishonored him by dragging his body outside the walls of heavily fortified Troy. Still, the decade-old stalemate remained. In desperation a new tactic was brilliantly hatched. A now fabled wooden horse that was placed outside the city's main gate with concealed warriors within is either a supreme act of treachery, or just good storytelling. The massive wooden gift-horse was supposedly moved inside the walled city of Troy. During the night, Greek soldiers hidden inside let themselves out and opened the impregnable gate as the Trojan's celebrated their apparent victory. The Greeks had staged a fake withdrawal but returned that night to destroy and plunder the city state of Troy. The power and glory of ancient Troy thus faded into history.

One of the first to confirm the true existence of legendary Troy was a wealthy eccentric named Heinrich Schlieman. In 1876 this amateur archeologist set out to prove key elements of *The Iliad* by hiring unskilled laborers to rapidly, if not recklessly, excavate various possible sites. The actual site that has since been confirmed by more accurate means including carbondating lacks the grand and heroic image detailed by Homer. The walled area of Bronze Age Troy was a surprisingly small city of only four to five acres. Most of the residents lived outside the walled area and were in part protected by extensive trenches dug into bedrock. Navigational conditions radically changed over the many centuries that elapsed. At the time of the actual Trojan War the sea level was higher and ships docked near the city.

One irony of Schlieman's dig and discovery of fabulous gold jewelry was that he had dug too deep. Ancient Troy, which occupied a prime crossroad for trade throughout the known world, was rebuilt, layer upon layer, over several thousand years. The battle site of Troy as described in the *Iliad* was actually two levels above Schlieman's claim. Archeological evidence of extreme, traumatic destruction has been confirmed by Manfred Korfmann of the University of Tubingen in various issues of *Archaeology*. The demise of Troy, however, gave rise to Greek (Hellenistic) culture and the concept of democracy that continues to impact much of the western world in particular to this date.

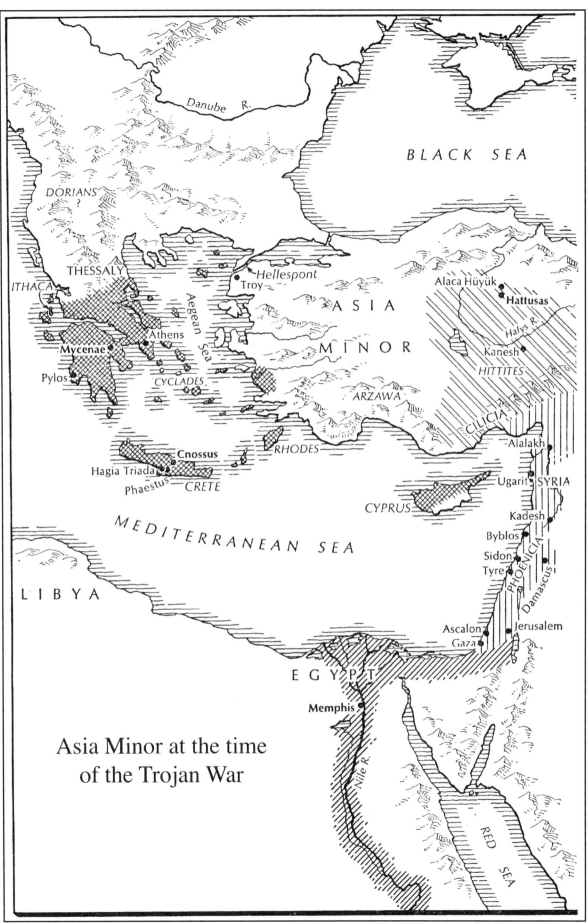

Asia Minor at the time
of the Trojan War

3
The Battle of Thermopylae, 480 B.C.E.

Sparta was the warrior-elite, city-state of the Hellenistic/Greek world. From birth, a male child was raised to be a warrior. No other pursuits were valued in the militant city-state that never exceeded approximately 10,000 citizens. All ordinary work was performed by captive slaves. The cultural orientation for young, adult Spartan males was summed up with the typical Spartan mother's admonition to an adult son, "You can come home carrying your shield, or upon it."

In place of the arts, religion, architecture, or sciences, the harshly disciplined Spartans evolved into a marginally literate, warrior society somewhat like the genetically-bred army ants of a typical ant colony. From early youth most Spartan males were groomed to be warriors. Although they were successful in most battles, they left little behind in the way of archeological evidence of their existence. The Spartan character has been epitomized as hardened discipline from birth and warrior preparation that accepts only victory or death.

It was in this militant context in the year 480 B.C.E. that 300 Spartan warriors defended a narrow mountain pass against a Persian army of invaders with over 800 times as many combatants. Initially, the Spartans were supported by 7,000 Greek defenders to help rebuild the wall that further reduced access through the narrow mountain pass. The Spartans, led by King Leonidas, and his 300 bodyguards volunteered to make a defensive stand against a massive Persian army of over 250,000 men. The ratio was so great that each Spartan defender knew the commitment was suicidal yet gave the rest of Greece some opportunity to build their defenses.

The young, ruthless, and ambitious Persian King Xerxes inherited his position upon the sudden death of his father, King Darius. The vindictive prince-turned-king ruled a vast empire from 486-465 B.C.E. He was a tyrant to his own diverse mix of people and he vowed to avenge his father for the humiliating defeat of the Persian army by 7,000 Athenian defenders at the Battle of Marathon. Therefore, Xerxes methodically assembled a force of well over 250,000 combatants to overwhelm and enslave his Hellenist (Greek) rivals to the west. Xerxes knew his forces had to pass through the Gates of Fire–the narrow mountain pass of Thermopylea just ninety miles north of Athens.

At the moment of first contact there were no surprises on either side. Each knew the relative size and strength of the other. King Xerxes, perched in a seat well above the battle, considered the Greek defenses in the mountain pass to be insignificant. He repeatedly issued orders for the tiny band of defenders to surrender their weapons. In frustration, he ordered wave after wave of captive slave warriors to assault the lightly held position. The first wave of Persian combatants repeatedly shouted for the defenders to lay down their weapons. In response, Sparta's King Leonidas, shouted back, "Come and get them."

In the extremely confined space, hand-to-hand battle raged from that point. The Spartans formed a tight phalanx and did what was necessary to hold the front lines in place. They also had heavier shields and longer spears that allowed them to kill thousands of the lightly protected invaders without losing ground. The Persian forces, with wickerwork shields and inferior weapons, simply could not penetrate the Spartan's heavy shields and defensive wall. Soon, there were massive piles of dead and wounded Persians that were also blocking the narrow mountain pass. The inability to maneuver prevented the Persians from conducting their style of warfare, or to flank the defenders. In extreme frustration, as the situation deteriorated without offensive progress, King Xerxes sent in his best troops. The select group of 10,000 elite warriors were known as the Immortals. Their success, however, was no greater than that of the enslaved pawns that had gone before them. The gap was too narrow to utilize the pressure of their numbers. Ultimately, about 20,000 Persians are believed to have been killed or severely wounded and after several days of fighting there was no sign of a breakthrough.

Elite Persian soldiers

An impasse might have occurred except for the betrayal of all of Greece by a local herdsman named Ephialtes. Perhaps due to insanity, he betrayed all of the Grecian people by showing the blockaded Persians a shepherd's trail to get above and behind the Spartans. When it was discovered that they were about to be completely surrounded, the Spartans insisted that the remaining Greek forces retreat southward to protect the Athenians.

Once in position on all sides Persian archers threatened to shower the Spartans with arrows until they blocked out the sun. The response of Spartan Captain Dienekes was, "Good, today we shall battle in the shade." Massive numbers of arrows were released and every last Spartan was killed. The one thing that the Spartans detested most was the arrow that kills from a distance, not face-to-face combat. King Leonidas' body was decapitated and a mockery was made of his proud head. To this day the name "Ephialtes" is another word for nightmare in the Greek language.

The Spartan force of 300 men held back the massive Persian onslaught for a full seven days. It ranks as the most lopsided defense in the history of warfare. The record may have been even more unmatchable in the days of hand-to-hand and face-to-face combat if it were not for the betrayal by one Greek shepherd. The delaying tactic did allow Greek residents to the south and in Athens to abandon their homes and retreat to the island of Salamis. The Persians soon experienced a massive naval defeat off the shores of Salamis and abandoned their quest to conquer lands and enslave people to the west of their existing empire. The disgraced and humiliated King Xerxes was claimed to have retreated to the royal brothel and was finally murdered after many years of debauchery. Europe was spared the crushing humiliation of Persian conquest. Hellenistic culture flourished and made significant cultural contributions to the Western World in particular.

Greece

Capital: Athens
Population: Nearly 11 million
Area: Just under 51,000 square miles
Religion: Greek Orthodox
Climate: Eastern Mediterranean, very mild to moderate temperatures, low rainfall
Topography: Extensive coastlines and mountains, over 2,000 islands (mostly uninhabited).
Surrounded by Albania, Macedonia, Bulgaria, Turkey, the Ionian Sea, Aegean Sea, Thracian Sea and Mediterranean Sea.

Summary: An ancient and very independent civilization near the center of active trade activities throughout the eastern Mediterranean world. Often a naval power because of huge amount of coastline and islands, they interacted with much of the known world and greatly spread their own cultural influences that are relevant to this date. One of the first documented conflicts outside of Greece was the Bronze Age war between Greek city-states and the Hittite city-state of Troy. The year 1193 B.C.E. has also been given as the date for the destruction of Troy by Greek forces. Conflicts with the bordering Persian Empire (established by Emperor Cyrus in 559 B.C.E.) included the Battle of Marathon and then the Battle of Thermopylae. The Peloponnesian Wars were essentially civil wars between the Athenians and the Spartans where the outcome was finally determined by Persian Empire financial intervention. The first Olympic Games were held in 776 B.C.E. However, weakness as one unified nation opened the way for Roman occupation. Greece was also occupied by Nazi Germany during World War II. A distinctly independent nation since that time, the timeless city of Athens—founder of democracy—was once again the home of the Summer Olympics of 2004.

4
The Peloponnesian War, 431-404 B.C.E.

Early Hellenistic states (Greece) included large numbers of islands as well as fiercely independent city-states. The most powerful of these cities possessed navies and, in varying degrees, had land-based armies. For reasons of security, power, wealth and prestige, the two most powerful cities—Athens and Sparta—formed either alliances or colonial control of other Greek-speaking (Ionic) cities and regions such as in the Table below.

Athens	Sparta
Hellespont, Samos	Corinth (chief ally)
Thessaly, Plataea	Delphi, Laconia
Halicarnassus, Euboea	Pelopennesus
Rhodes, Attica	Megalopolis
Delos, Amphipolia	Macedonia
Andros, Tenos	Thebes

Neutral States
Crete   Melos   Achaea
Argos   Aetolia
(others)

The Peloponnesian War spanned 27 years with distinct periods of peace in between. Mostly, it was a series of naval battles. Athens possessed the most powerful navy in the region by far, yet it was the Spartan navy that ultimately prevailed.

At the end of the protracted war Athens' resurrected navy was completely destroyed. It was also one of the first known wars in ancient history to be documented by a credible historian as it occurred—Thycidides. The war can be broken into five major periods:

Archidamian war Early (431-427)
Archidamian war Late (426-421)
Sicilian war (421-413)
Ionian war Early (412-404)
Ionian war Late (407-404)

The essential conflict related to Sparta's resentment of Athens' growing wealth and power in the diverse and very trade-sensitive region. To a major extent it was comparable to a trade war in which there were few rules. Athens, for example, once slaughtered the entire male population of the island of Melos and enslaved the women and children for refusing to abandon a neutrality agreement. The same Athens was also a model for early democracy, development of the arts, and ideals of freedom for the individual. It was Athens that had reached out to free Greek-speaking people of the region who were being oppressed by Persia (Battle of Marathon, 490 B.C.E. and Battle of Salamis, 480 B.C.E.). The Peloponnesian War, with many diverse battles, all but destroyed Athens as in some profound Greek tragedy.

Suspicious of Athens' aggressive motives, Sparta was almost the exact opposite in nearly every respect. The inland city-state was non-democratic, agrarian, conservative, militaristic, and a cultural backwater. With most of its power invested in the army, Sparta tried to maneuver Athens—the naval powerhouse—into a decisive land battle. Corinth, a major ally of Sparta, was also prepared to go to war against Athens because the same people who had built the Parthenon were trying to control the Corinthian Gulf. That seaway was a major trade route to Sicily, southern Italy, and other destinations within the Mediterranean. The very heavy-handed tactics that Athens applied to its non-allies had generated intense animosities in the region. Also, the previously battered Persian Empire was waiting for its opportunity to seek revenge upon Athens.

Pericles was the driving force behind much that is associated with the high points of ancient Athens. His efforts significantly contributed to

CENTRAL GREECE

proud fleet was reduced to twelve ships. Her democratic government was replaced with an aristocratic Committee of Thirty that was so corrupt that public pressure helped to bring back some democratic reforms within the first year. Athens was reduced to little more than a vassal state to Sparta. Athens' colonial empire was taken away. The foreign policy and political influence of Athens was thereafter grossly diminished.

Sparta, lacking a vision for the future except to maintain military strength, imposed heavy-handed tactics on Athens but failed to ever achieve greatness or a large empire. The continued disunity of the Greek states opened the door for conquest by Alexander the Great's Macedonians and later control by the Roman Empire. The stubborn independence of the Greek culture, however, has been especially famous for its contributions to the concept of democracy for the individual that survives to this date.

Athens's growth as the most powerful, most beautiful, and wealthiest city-state in the Hellenistic world. It was Pericles who was able to arrange a peace agreement with Persia in 449 B.C.E. It was Pericles' war strategy to maintain protective city walls and a naval powerhouse that protected Athens from a blockade siege. Within the first year of the war Pericles died of a plague introduced by continuous imports of grain from Egypt and the Black Sea area. His overall strategy to win a war of attrition against Sparta was successful at first but not in the end. Near the end, Sparta was heavily funded by Persia (Athens' old nemesis) to build a navy that overpowered Athens' navy and blockaded the daily importation of food to her citizens. As a result, Athens found itself in the position of unconditional surrender in 404 B.C.E. Sparta demanded the destruction of the city wall, and the seven-mile "Long Walls" from Athens to the docks. Athens' once

5
Alexander the Great at Gaugamela, 331, B.C.E.

The Battle of Gaugamela (Arbela) resulted in the defeat of the Persian Empire. Against overwhelming odds, Alexander the Great won three decisive battles against the Persian forces of King Darius III. The circumstances were different each time and the improbable victories established the youthful king and cavalry commander as one of the greatest tacticians of all times. For over two thousand years the details and consequences of what is known has been contemplated by historians and military planners alike. Misinformation about the number of participants, and embellishments related to mythological gods, have added mystery, but they do not distract from the significance of what actually occurred.

Alexander was the son of Philip of Macedonia. His father had been held as a privileged hostage in Thebes for many years. There, he acquired the military skills to call himself a general and, following various conquests, to proclaim himself as King Philip II of all of Greece except Sparta by the year 338 B.C.E. Further conquests and buildup of his forces led him to challenge Persia because of Spartan successes against that ancient empire and because of Persia's earlier attempts to control all of Greece. Philip, however, was assassinated in 336 B.C.E. as he made his preparations for the invasion of Persia. To the surprise of many, his 21 year old son, Alexander put himself in his father's place. With a vengeance, he implemented his father's plan to invade Persia and in the process he demonstrated his unmatched skills as a military leader.

Alexander's opponent, Persian King Darius III (336-330 B.C.E.) had little battlefield experience himself and had overcome an assassination attempt on his own life by Bagoas, the court eunuch that had raised him to the position of king. Darius had previously lost the

Battle of Issus (333 B.C.E.) to Alexander's forces and was intent to do all in his power to avoid another loss.

At Gaugamela, Darius had the distinct advantage of literally preparing the battlefield of his choice to make the most of his particular style of warfare. Unlike the Battle of Issus or the Battle of Granicus, where Darius was compressed along a narrow coastline, this site would be mostly level and made even more level to maximize cavalry and horse drawn chariot effectiveness. The site chosen was the broad Plain of Gaugemela (near Arbela in present-day northern Iraq). The area was sufficiently large to contain all of the Persian king's forces which were estimated to be at least four to five times larger than Alexander's forces. The levelness of the battlefield was important to Darius to maximize the effectiveness of his cavalry and roughly 200 horse-drawn chariots with extended axle blades to tear into the legs of opposing cavalry and infantry alike. Persia's power was in their numbers and fighting on their own land to preserve the fate of the Persian Empire.

Alexander was known to have about 40,000 infantry and 7,000 cavalry with Alexander leading the mounted forces. Darius, in contrast, occupied a command position behind the left flank of his cavalry. He also fielded ten elephants that, unlike Hannibal's war elephants, did not contribute significantly to the outcome of the battle. The Persian cavalry was mounted on excellent horses and was in nearly every respect comparable to Alexander's cavalry force. The critical difference in the battle's outcome was in leadership and tactics.

The massive face-off of Alexander's well disciplined forces was diminished by the shear size of the combined forces of Darius on an open plain. The element of surprise was not a factor. The expected outcome of this third attempt to defeat Alexander was likely decided in advance. The solution was simply to engage Alexander's forces, wear them down, completely encircle them and finish them off by shear weight of numbers. Just the opposite actually occurred.

As the inevitable confrontation began to fully take shape, Alexander's cavalry forces, on the right flank and personally lead by him, made a quick sprint to their right as if to reposition before charging into the left flank of Darius' cavalry. The surprise movement pulled a great many of Darius' left flank out of position as they rode to keep up. The momentary confusion produced a thinning of the Persian cavalry defense line. In another unexpected maneuver, Alexander pivoted his forces about 90 degrees to the left and straight into the brief weakness of the line. A fiercely concentrated charge at the fleeting weakness and confusion in the line quickly produced a disarray within the Persian's left flank. Alexander's abrupt cavalry moves caught most of the Persian defenders off balance.

Alexander's aggressive maneuver was followed by a second pivot of roughly 90 degrees that allowed his forces to attack the Persian's newly created flank and to charge down on the rear of the now "out of position" defenders. The slaughter that ensued was becoming apparent to Persian field commanders who also recognized that Darius himself suddenly risked capture or death at the hands of the enemy. The utter confusion, signs of critical weakness and panic produced by this radical change of fortunes completely undermined the field commanders. Decisions were rashly made that only contributed to the confusion and slaughter that was taking place throughout the battlefield. The charioteers were foiled when Alexander's infantry parted at the last instant and created great havoc by killing one or more

of the typically four-horse teams. The only plan that seemed to matter was the one being executed by Alexander's forces. Darius was escorted from the field for his own protection. The severity of the losses for the Persians in particular was so great that Darius was murdered by Bessus, a distant member of his family, once the results of the battle became fully known.

The power of the Persian Empire was forever broken. The Persian Empire had also ruled Egypt for 200 years and its people and territories stretched from the eastern Mediterranean across the current Middle East and into northern India and Afghanistan. The victories put a thirty-one-year-old Macedonian in control of much of the known world outside of the Far East. It stands to this date as the largest empire ever acquired by one man in the history of the world. Although his life was short, and definitely not the life of a deity, Alexander the Great accomplished most of what he set out to do. He contributed to a substantial imprint of Greek culture on the known world outside of the Far East. The brilliance of his hands-on military strategies and tactics have been studied by most succeeding generations of military planners. He set out to avenge his ambitious father's death. He did that in a way that is memorable to this date. Upon his early death the empire was divided up among his generals and slowly disintegrated as small empires.

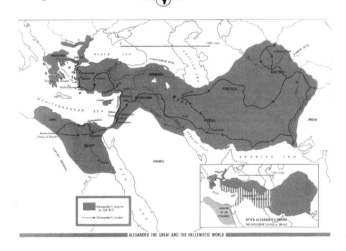

ALEXANDER THE GREAT AND THE HELLENISTIC WORLD

Macedonia

Capital: Skopje (Former Yugoslav Republic of Macedonia) Formed in 1991

Population: Approximately 2 million

Area: About 9,900 square miles

Climate: Northeastern Mediterranean and dry to cold depending on elevations

Topography: Mountainous inland country in southeastern Europe with peaks up to 6,500 feet. Contains Europe's deepest lake, Lake Ohrid, a site of many Roman and Byzantine ruins.

Religion: Mostly Orthodox Christians, some Slavic Muslims (Pomaks), others

Surrounded by Serbia and Montenegro, Bulgaria, Greece and Albania

Summary: The native land of Alexander the Great (Alexander III, King of Macedonia) and typically considered an extension of Greek culture. In 336 B.C.E. Alexander began his world conquest. It was the intention of Alexander to spread Greek culture throughout much of the known world in addition to restraining the aggressive expansion of the Persian Empire. Macedonia is a former Yugoslav Republic in southeastern Europe. Lacking an outlet to saltwater trading routes the region has relied heavily upon overland trade routes.

6
The Battle of Cannae, August, 216 B.C.E.

Known to antiquity as the Second Punic War, the Battle of Cannae [pronounced: can-eye, or cain-eye], was the Roman Empire's most serious and shocking defeat in its long history of almost continuous conflicts throughout the known world. Shortly after the battle, the citizens of Rome experienced a deep sense of panic that their invincible Legions had been virtually annihilated deep in Italian territory. An empire that had lived by the sword fully expected to be put to the sword. Rome, the Eternal City, survived.

The confrontation took place on a hot and dusty plain about two miles square and bordered by the Aufidus River (now the Ofanto River) to the northwest and the gentle, rolling hills of Cannae to the southeast. Conditions were ideal to demonstrate the effectiveness of hard-driving cavalry offense over tightly-packed infantry offense or defense. The First Punic war lasted 23 years and ended with a bitter defeat for Carthage. The Battle of Cannae lasted about four hours and was a major victory for Carthage. Hannibal's forces remained in Italy for the next 13 years. Roman insecurities led to the Third Punic War (149-146 B.C.E.) and the brutal destruction of Carthage, a North African city that once rivaled Rome.

Carthaginian General Hannibal Barca was intent upon fulfilling personal oaths to his father and his gods to take revenge upon the deeply hated Roman Legions. In doing so, he formed a mercenary army of many different nationalities. Made up of 40,000 infantry and 10,000 cavalry, they represented Carthaginians, Numidians, Spaniards and Gauls. Hannibal had demonstrated his seriousness and effectiveness by moving his army from Spain through the Alps and by defeating the Romans at the River Trebbia, the Italian town of Lucca, and again near Lake Trasimene.

The Battle of Cannae occurred without surprise on the east coast of Italy about 100 miles south of Rome. Two Roman consuls or generals, Paulus and Varro, had assembled roughly 80,000 infantry troops and 6,000 cavalry troops at the insistence of the Roman Senate. Supreme command of the Legions rotated between the two men on alternate days. The older and wiser Paulus cautioned against confronting Hannibal in a frontal assault. The advice was ignored by Varro. He considered his two-to-one superiority sufficient to crush the invaders. To enhance that crushing power, Varro ordered increased tightness and increased depth of his infantry forces. He formed compressed squares or rectangles resembling a checkerboard. The least experienced troops led as skirmish units. They were backed by more experienced troops with iron-tipped throwing spears (pilum), 20" Roman swords (gladius), and curved wood and iron shields weighing about 22 pounds each. Finally, the most experienced troops brought up the rear and did whatever was necessary for victory. The right flank was headed by Paulus' Roman heavy cavalry. The left flank of allied light cavalry was commanded by Varro.

Paulus' and Varro's forces had engaged in minor skirmishes for up to three weeks before the fateful battle on August 2, 216 B.C.E. Both major field armies were well aware of each other's presence and that a major confrontation was imminent. The Roman Legions were literally squared off to meet Hannibal's advancing force. The Cathaginian general was acutely aware of the much smaller size of his own forces and positioned them in a convex, crescent shape centered upon the advancing Legions. The inevitable point of contact with the most intensity was the center. Hannibal launched the battle by ordering his left flank cavalry to attack the Roman's smaller right flank cavalry. The Romans, using their shields as battering rams and short swords or spears for thrusting and jabbing began to seriously wear down Hannibal's forces. Several factors also began to make their presence felt. For one, the dust made ground-level visibility very difficult. For another, the summer day's heat began to take its toll on heavy shield-wielding troops. Finally, the urgency to push through the enemy caused the already tightened, Roman troops to compress themselves more tightly. Restricted in their ability to fight, they were in a prime position to be slaughtered.

It was at that moment, when a Roman breakthrough was almost assured, that Hannibal ordered the sweeping double envelopment of the Romans' flanks to compress them further. The original convex crescent was then taking the shape of a concave crescent. Combined with cavalry engagements on both flanks, the smaller army with better cavalry effectiveness was able to enclose the Romans on three sides and then hit their rear with another cavalry charge. The sudden result was realization that the Romans barely had any room to maneuver and fight. The fear of being slaughtered from all sides set in and fear and panic took over rather than a concerted breakout. The result was an estimated 50,000 to 70,000 Roman troops and their allies being killed on that field. Losses for Hannibal were about 6,000. Paulus, who lead the Roman cavalry, died from multiple javelin wounds after being knocked off his horse. His younger protégé, Varro, slipped away with a small remnant of his forces and returned to Rome with the devastating news.

Hannibal still lacked the strength to take on Rome so he did not do so. His own army had suffered tremendous losses. They faced dealing with injuries, extreme exhaustion and the need to sustain themselves in hostile territory. Hannibal lacked the numbers to maintain an effective siege of Rome and not be constantly confronted by guerrilla tactics throughout Italy. He was sufficiently powerful, feared and free to move about Italy for the next thirteen years before being called back to (Phoenician) Carthage to prepare for the anticipated next Roman offensive. The Third Punic War, over fifty years later, was from 149-146 B.C.E. In that battle Carthaginians faced a new Roman general, Scipio, who had learned the lesson of the effectiveness of cavalry over infantry. The Roman cavalry was also twice the size of the Carthaginian forces.

Carthage was leveled. Most residents were either killed or enslaved, and their fields were sown with salt. An estimated 150,000 survivors were sold into slavery. The Roman Empire continued as the undisputed power in the Mediterranean for many more centuries

In addition to Rome's brutality for all to see, the Romans were as intent upon building as they were upon destroying. Over the centuries Rome's typical political motive was to fight for expansion of empire in the name of "defense." Naturally, for those in power, the goal was also to enforce their brand of law, culture, and trade that was in the best interests of Rome. It was Latin culture, laws, and religion, not Phoenician, that impacted Europe for two millennia.

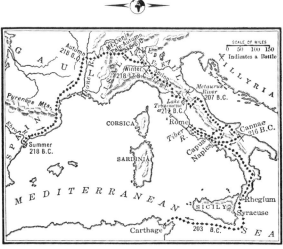

The route and marches of Hannibal from 218 to 203 B.C.E.

Italy

Capital: Rome (Italian Republic)
Founded in 753 B.C.E.
Population: Approximately 57 million
Area: Over 116,000 square miles
Religion: Roman Catholic, Other
Climate: Ideal Mediterranean, cool in the higher elevations and northern Alps
Topography: Roughly 500 mile long peninsula running from NW to SE. Extensive coastlines rise to central mountains and fertile valleys plus the northern Alps.
Surrounded by the Adriatic Sea, Ionian Sea, Tyrrhenian Sea, Ligurian Sea, Mediterranean Sea, France, Switzerland, Austria and Slovenia.
Summary: A major tourist destination since the late middle ages. Most famed as the origin of the Roman Empire that militarily occupied much of the entire region from roughly 500 B.C.E. to 500 C.E. The Romans made a major Latin imprint on much of Europe, Middle East, and North Africa. In 218 B.C.E. Hannibal led his army from Carthage through Spain, then over the Alps to invade Italy. By 312 C.E., Constantine became the first Christian emperor of Rome. In 410 the Western Goths sacked Rome and by 476 the Goths deposed the last western Roman Emperor, Romulus Augustus. The Middle Ages begin at that time. As the Roman Empire slowly disintegrated, Italy became one of the strongest proponents of Christianity in the eventual form of the Roman Catholic Church. In the year 1054 the Byzantine Empire split from the Holy Roman Church and by 1096 the first Christian Crusade was launched to take back Jerusalem from a radical new group of Turkish Muslims. Italian inventor, Rinaldo di Villamagna, was credited with creation of the first firing cannon in 1326. The Battle of Lepanto in 1571 was planned from Italy and helped to save the Catholic Church from an Islamic onslaught such as occurred with the Moorish invasion of Spain. During the Renaissance period Galileo Galilei introduced many physical laws of nature (1585) for which he was imprisoned by the Roman Catholic Church. By 1919, Benito Mussolini founded the fascist party of Italy and by 1936 his militant dictatorship conquered the impoverished African nation of Ethiopia. Mussolini was deposed on June 5, 1944, (the day before D-Day when 175,000 Allied soldiers assaulted Normandy).

7

Celtic Queen Boadicea vs. Roman Legion, 60 C.E.

Roman General Julius Caesar launched an assault upon the British Isles in 55 B.C.E. It was to be his most extended military campaign from his bases in Italy. As a result, he was never able to impose complete Roman domination over the Britons. The major exceptions were the Irish, Welsh, Scots and the northern England provinces.

Roman Emperor Claudius (41-54 C.E.) needed new military victories to reconfirm himself as a "manly" emperor. In the year 43 C.E. he demanded that a second attempt be made to subdue the Britons. The logistical issues related to great distances, unstable cooler weather, extreme limits on communication, and manpower problems continued to be the same as they were for Julius Caesar. The once tightly organized and overpowering Roman Legions were no longer what they had once been. The Welsh, in particular, had effectively used hit-and-run guerrilla tactics against the Romans for decades. Celtic Queen Boadicea proved to be another torment for the Roman intruders.

Boadicea was said to be a large, powerful, and fearsome-looking Celtic woman. She was the queen of the Celtic Iceni tribe of East Anglia. The Celts were very hardy pagan tribe members who were spread over much of Western Europe and the British Isles well before the Anglo-Saxon invasions that began in the sixth century C.E. The Celtic people are credited with construction of Stonehenge and many sites like it at approximately the same time that the early pyramids of Egypt were being constructed of similar massive stone. A Roman description of Queen Boadicea was contained in *The Rotten Romans* by Cassius Dio as follows:

"She was very tall. Her eyes seemed to stab you. Her voice was harsh and loud. Her thick, reddish-brown hair hung down to her waist.

She always wore a great golden torc [sic] around her neck and a flowing, tartan cloak fastened with a brooch."

Her husband, Pragsutagus, was king of the Iceni, a Celtic tribe that occupied much of present Norfolk and Suffolk counties in southern England. He was acknowledged by the Romans as a "client king" with no real power. It was understood that, in the face of Roman pressures and in comparison to Boadicea, her husband was a relatively weak monarch. He was further understood to have grave concerns about his health and his ability to leave his rich lands to his wife and two daughters upon his death. To accommodate these concerns, King Pragsutagus entered into an agreement that made the Roman Emperor, Nero (54-68 C.E.), a joint heir with his wife (Boadicea), their two daughters, and designated relatives to share his land. This document was prepared by a Roman notary. The "plot thickens" at this point. It was possible that the king was overly naïve about any possible business dealings with the distant Roman emperor. There was also the possibility that the Roman notary recognized an opportunity to profit from the situation. The result was clearly not what the king had intended. Upon his death in 60 C.E., Roman authorities seized all of the king's holdings. When Queen Boadicea protested the confiscation, she was humiliated in the extreme with a public flogging that was followed by the rape of her two daughters by Roman soldiers.

The Roman abuses of authority were a clear affront to all Celtic people who were subjected to the oppression of Roman rule. In that context, Queen Boadicea used her shame and rage to unite a Celtic army during the absence of the regional governor, Paulinus Suetonius. The governor was some distance away at the time attempting to suppress Druids in the Anglesey (Wales) region. The fire in

Boadicea's aggressive rhetoric ignited the hostilities that the native tribal groups had been suppressing. Her rage transferred to the rage of a very proud people with a long history as successful warriors. Their first act was the destruction of the town of Colchester and the defeat of the Ninth Roman Legion. Following the vengeful assault on the Romans in that town, Queen Boadicea regrouped to continue building her ragtag army of bitterly alienated Celts. She went on to sack Verulamium (now called St. Albans). Her next objective was the city of London.

The Roman governor, Suetonius, received word of the rebellion rushed back from Anglesey (Wales), and gathered additional forces along the way. As he approached the vicinity of London it became apparent that the rabble army now approached something like 200,000 combatants with cavalry support that was mostly composed of men. As victory was not certain, Suetonius withdrew and allowed the Romans and a great many citizens of both London and St. Albans to suffer the wrath of the queen's army.

Suetonius, being a professional warrior, continued to raise Roman troops and support wherever he could find it to successfully confront such a quickly organized army of virtual vigilantes. He chose the intended battle site with great care. He was aware of the Celtic tendency to make a massive, frontal attack while flanking the enemy on both sides. Suetonius therefore took up positions in a narrow valley where it was almost impossible for the Celts to use their outflanking tactics.

Prior to the actual confrontation, Boadicea used a horse-drawn Roman chariot to quickly move up and down the lines of her assembled army screaming out the humiliations of the Roman oppressors on the Celtic people. The rage was there, but the depth of experience to confront a professional army with centuries of experience was not.

The Roman governor made the most of his far smaller forces. He positioned them defensively as well as he could, using the physical defenses of his surroundings, and the discipline that he knew he could rely on. Another tactic was to encourage his men to hold and fight against a woman leader and an army that, he falsely claimed, contained more women than men. To defeat the Celts, the Romans had to call back most of their forces from Wales.

In the actual battle that followed, the Roman discipline made all of the difference. The Celts experienced an overwhelming defeat. Losses, according to some historians, ranged up to 80,000 killed while the Roman defenders lost only about 400 killed and a similar number of injured.

The proud queen who had united an incredibly large force against a common enemy had vowed never again to be captured by Roman authorities. Thus, as a result of the staggering defeat, she used poison to end her life. The rebellion ended and Roman authority was more firmly established than ever from 61 C.E. until roughly 410 C.E. The message of the rebellion that worked its way to a seriously declining Roman Empire was that subjugated people must be treated with reasonable respect and justice or more rebellions would be the result. Boadicea's defeat was the most serious rebellion that the Romans ever confronted in Britain. It has been estimated that as many as 70,000 Romans were killed during that rebellion. Rome nearly lost its outermost colony after barely one hundred years of occupation. Suetonius was replaced with a surprisingly effective governor, Julius Agricola, who consciously worked to reduce the tribute levied on Britons and expanded markets for trade. He helped to introduce a lasting level of prosperity, and legal reforms, as well as extending Roman authority further to the west and north of what Suetonius set out to ruthlessly accomplish.

Present day Britain

Britain during Roman rule

8
Masada: Defiance of Rome's Authority, 74 C.E.

As in many stories from antiquity, Masada may have different versions depending on who is telling the tale. Historically-based events of great emotional significance have a definite tendency to be embellished, self-serving and a bit loose with "hard facts." The possible myth of Masada is that besieged religious defenders of the Jewish faith (Zealots) held back a full Legion of Roman soldiers and then committed mass suicide rather than surrender their independence to Rome. The short and far less probable story is that Masada shielded thieves, bandits and renegades from the authority of Rome. In either instance, Rome could not afford to look weak, or risk losing the image of invincibility.

Historical and archeological evidence for the Masada story is very strong. The mountain of Masada has survived the ravages of time, intermittent wars, and 2,000 years of cultural changes. Masada is very isolated and a physical presence like Gibraltar. This natural fortress is situated in a very dry region opposite Mt. Moab in Jordan. It rises from the edge of the Judean Desert to a height of 160 feet above sea level. More impressively, it is actually 1,307 feet above the Dead Sea. From its mesa-like top it's possible to see most of the Dead Sea. This mesa-like plain is nearly 2,000 feet long, about 650 feet at its widest point and about 4,250 feet around. Historically, there were two and possibly three small, winding and very steep trails to access the summit. The "Snake Path" is on the east face and the "White Rock Path" (where the assault ramp was constructed) is on the west face. Masada represented one of the world's best, natural fortifications. Still, it had to be re-enforced with walls, stocked with weapons, rocks of all sizes, food, and clay jars to hold the rainwater that collected in 12 cisterns that were carved into the rock.

Twentieth Century archeology has been able to document some evidence of a probable early synagogue at the top of Masada. During the reign of Herod the Great, King of Judea (41 B.C.E. to 4 B.C.E.), the site was selected for its defensive qualities in the event of hostilities with Cleopatra's Egyptian border forces, or a Jewish uprising. About 37-31 B.C.E., Herod ordered the construction of two substantial palaces, storage and administrative buildings, defensive walls, and cisterns. Two parallel walls nearly 1,500 yards long with storage buildings in between were constructed. The palaces contained tile bathing facilities suitable for a king and had an unmatched, 360 degree view of the surrounding territory. The site was occupied as a Roman garrison from approximately the year six C.E. to 66 C.E. The site was reportedly captured after the beginning of the Jewish War. The leader of the Jewish rebels who captured Masada was Menahem, son of Judah the Galilean. His followers were a band of religious dissenters known as Sicarians (Zealots). In the chaos that accompanied the Jewish rebellion, Menahem was killed or assassinated by rivals within the city of Jerusalem. His nephew, Eleazar ben Yair, was able to make his way back to Masada and there remained as the Zealot leader until the tragic end in the year 74 C.E.

According to the writings of Jewish historian, Josephus Flavius (born 37 C.E. and died about 101 C.E.), the rebelliousness of the Sicarians contributed to the four-year, Jewish Revolt of Roman occupation (66-70 C.E.). . That rebellion resulted in the sack of Jerusalem, destruction of The Temple, and occupation of Old Jerusalem as barracks for Legion X Fretensis. The city would not be rebuilt for the next 60 years, and would not be the home of the Jewish people for the next 1,900 years.

According to Josephus, it was Roman governor/general Lucius Flavius Silva who led approximately 9,000 soldiers of Legion X Fretensis against Masada to restore Rome's authority. The recapture was not because Masada was a threat to Rome, but to preserve Rome's powerful image. Josephus also recorded that of the 966 defenders of Masada only one woman and five children survived. She was able to describe how the others drew lots to assist in the mass suicide rather than submit to Roman capture and probable heinous execution.

If accurate, the virtually impregnable site atop Masada allowed the defenders to withstand a continuous siege for much of one full year against 9,000 determined Roman soldiers and thousands of conscripted laborers. In 73 C.E., it was Roman governor Silva's task to lead the Tenth Legion of 9,000 soldiers. The numbers poised against the defenders therefore ranged from roughly 10,000 to 15,000 people when counting the conscripted laborers. Obviously, the Romans prepared for an extended siege in which the outcome would be certain. As the siege began to take hold, a total of eight base camps were established around the base of Masada. Extreme measures were taken to insure that no rebels would escape, and no one did.

An assault *en mass* was impossible due to the extremely narrow and precipitous access trails. Except for protracted starvation, success could be achieved only by building a final assault ramp. That process, under assault from the defenders at the top, would take many months to complete. Next, it was for the Romans to transport battering rams and other siege weapons into position to break through the walled defenses. The double wall at the top contained much earth, wood and rocks that made it very difficult to penetrate. Ultimately, the Romans had to resort to fire to actually breach the walled defenses. As the fire died down it was apparent that the Romans would swarm over the fortress interior on the following day. Martyrdom to deep religious and philosophical beliefs was clearly preferred to the justice that would have been imposed by the occupying forces

As in the parable that gives great delineation to a culture's moral history, the story of Masada is a very powerful tale of winning against terrible odds based on convictions and the desire to be free of external oppression. Masada has long been a Jewish model or symbol of the sacrifices which sometimes must be made to preserve cultural identity and freedom of beliefs. Masada literally stands as a symbol of courage for most people of the Jewish faith. In defensive terms, Masada is a classic example of the value of "holding the high ground." The Roman Legion at that time was a disciplined, coordinated and ominous fighting force and still required a ratio of 10 to 15 combatants to rout each defender. At the end, Roman general Flavius Silva said, "A victory? What have we won? We've won a rock in the middle of a wasteland, on the shores of a poisoned sea." The Roman Empire was just a few centuries away from extinction. Masada has remained as a monument to courage and freedom for almost 2,000 years.

Masada

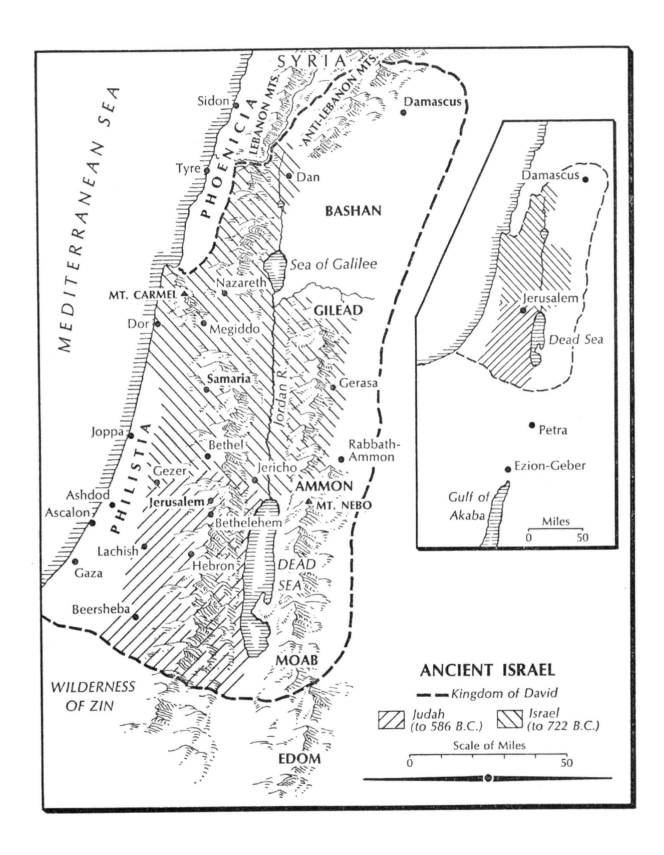

MEDITERRANEAN SEA

SYRIA

Sidon

Damascus

PHOENICIA

LEBANON MTS.

ANTI-LEBANON MTS.

Tyre

Dan

BASHAN

Sea of Galilee

Nazareth

MT. CARMEL

GILEAD

Dor

Megiddo

Samaria

Gerasa

Jordan R.

Joppa

Bethel

Rabbath-
Ammon

Gezer

Jericho

AMMON

Ashdod

Jerusalem

MT. NEBO

Ascalon

Bethelehem

Lachish

DEAD
SEA

Gaza

Hebron

Beersheba

MOAB

WILDERNESS
OF ZIN

EDOM

Damascus

Jerusalem

Dead Sea

Petra

Ezion-Geber

Gulf of
Akaba

Miles

0   50

ANCIENT ISRAEL

— — — Kingdom of David

Judah
(to 586 B.C.)

Israel
(to 722 B.C.)

Scale of Miles

0   50

9
Visigoth Sack of Rome, 410 C.E.

The various Gothic tribes of northeastern Europe were composed mainly of Teutonic or Germanic tribes with possible origins as far north as Sweden and as far east as the Ukraine. They first came to the attention of the Romans in the year 268 C.E. when they conducted a series of raids against the Roman Empire throughout the Balkans. Ultimately, and in part due to population explosions, they divided themselves into the Visigoths (west) and Ostrogoths (east) around 370 C.E. That was also the time when the Gothic people came into deadly conflict with the Asiatic Huns. The Visigoths sought protection through alliances with Rome and by crossing the Danube to the south. The Ostrogoths faired poorly against the Huns and were largely killed or absorbed.

A major foe of the Gothic people, Attila the Hun (406-453 C.E.) led a virtually unstoppable "horde" of Central Asian warriors who were ruthlessly expanding into Europe. Like Ghengis Khan almost 800 years later, "The Scourge of God," as the Huns were known in Europe, defeated everyone in their path including the Ostrogoths. By the fifth century they were a major threat to the Roman Empire and the Visigoths who joined forces to hold back the Huns. Well after the Visigoths departed from Italy, the Huns moved into Gaul (France) in 451 C.E. It was only due to famine and plague in Northern Italy in 452 C.E. that Attila negotiated a peace settlement with the Romans and then died the following year.

The Visigoths held the Roman province of Dacia for approximately one hundred years with little more than skirmishes against the Romans. During that time they accepted an early branch of Christianity known as Arianism. Their rough exteriors, "gross manners," and harsh-sounding language were deeply offensive to the Romans. The "mean-ingless" language to Roman ears was like the "bah, bah" sound of sheep and earned the Visigoths the condescending description of "barbarians." That stigma, and lack of social acceptance by Roman citizens, lasted until the actual sacking of Rome in 410 C.E., and far beyond.

By 364 C.E. Visigoths took over the Roman province of Thrace and surrounding areas. This affront to Rome brought about several battles in which Emperor Valens defeated the Goths. The real threat to the Gothic people came in 375 C.E. when they were first invaded by the ruthless Asiatic Huns. The Visigoths, under their leader, Fritigern, formed alliances with Rome against their common enemy, the Huns. Basically, the Goths were to receive lands, supplies, food, and to be paid for fighting with, not against, the already multinational Roman Legion.

The Goths were clearly the resented outsiders to the "civilized" and more urbane Romans. The result was often that promises were not kept and contempt for the "barbarian" intruders was shown in every way. By the year 378 C.E. there was a major rebellion against Emperor Valens because the Goths were literally starving. The rampaging rebellion became a decisive victory for the Goths. The Battle of Adrianople was Rome's worst defeat in 400 years. The battle scene was so grisly that Emperor Valens' body was never found. Up to 15,000 Roman soldiers were killed and their bodies were stripped of everything of possible value.

It was the year 382 C.E. before a peace settlement was worked out with the new Emperor, Theodosius I. The emperor knew that he no longer had the military strength to eliminate the Visigoth threat. The Visigoths honored their agreement, despite intense frictions between themselves and the Romans, at least during the life of Emperor Theodosius. Visigoth soldiers were being used as Roman shock troops on the front lines of every battle against Huns, Vandals, and others. The Goths lost almost 10,000 of their own soldiers on the first day of just one particular battle. However, when Theodosius died in 395 C.E., he divided the empire between his decadent and incompetent sons, Honorius (west) and Arcadius (east). Conditions for the Visigoths soon worsened to such a degree that pledges made to Theodosius were no longer considered binding.

395 C.E. was the same year that charismatic Alaric accepted the title of king among his Visigoth people, rather than clan chieftain as was typical in the past. Alaric and his forces continued to serve in the Roman Legion and he held a title equivalent to that of an army general. He learned everything possible about the Roman methods of fighting. His true loyalties, however, were to the Visigoth people, not Rome. By 401 C.E., Alaric made his first attempt to invade Italy, but was defeated by defenders under Roman General Flavius Stilcho. The Visigoths were thus forced to flee from Italy.

A second attempt to invade Italy was launched without sufficient rebuilding and reorganization of his army. Again, Alaric was defeated by Stilcho. The difference the second time, however, was that Alaric convinced the petty and self-serving Emperor Honorius to pay a large endowment to the Visigoths for not attacking a third time. Soon, as fate would have it, Honorius murdered his highly competent General Stilcho. A political faction took over Rome that opposed any payment to the barbarians. Honorius, lacking any personal honor, was thought to have ordered the execution of Visigoth wives and children of all those who served in the Roman army. An estimated 30,000 family members were ruthlessly killed.

As a direct result, serious retaliations in Italy by the Visigoths began in 408 C.E. The ultimate response was a third assault upon Rome in 410 C.E. The march on Rome began on April 24, 410. The city was surrounded and besieged and by August of that year Rome capitulated. Honorius agreed to appoint Attalus as the western emperor in exchange for lifting the blockade of the city. Forces friendly to Alaric had opened the gates to the city from within. Alaric and his troops were able to occupy and plunder the Eternal City for three days before evacuating on their own. The terrorized citizens of Rome, who had not been occupied by a foreign invader for at least 800 years, waited in total disbelief. The Visigoths took whatever they wanted and set fire to any obstacles in their way. Rome's long collapse into the relative anarchy of the Dark Ages was accelerated by that defeat.

Alaric, the Visigoths' most cohesive force at the time, died after a brief illness just a few months later in that same year possibly due to malaria or plague. As a result, there was no consolidation of power in Italy under the Visigoths and no expansion into Sicily or North Africa as had been planned. Instead, the Visigoths withdrew northward and settled into the region of present Spain. Ostrogoths (Eastern Goths) filled the Italian void for a few decades before being overthrown. A major part of the Visigoth legacy was to help preserve much of Roman culture and Christian religion in the coming Dark Ages. By 589 C.E. the Visigoths exchanged their Arian faction of Christianity for Roman Catholicism. Their influence on Western European culture, thought, and architecture for the next 250 years was a very real factor until the invasion of the Moors in 711 C.E. and the defeat of the Visigoths at a battle near Medina Sidonia, Spain.

Barbarian Invasions in Fifth and Sixth Centuries

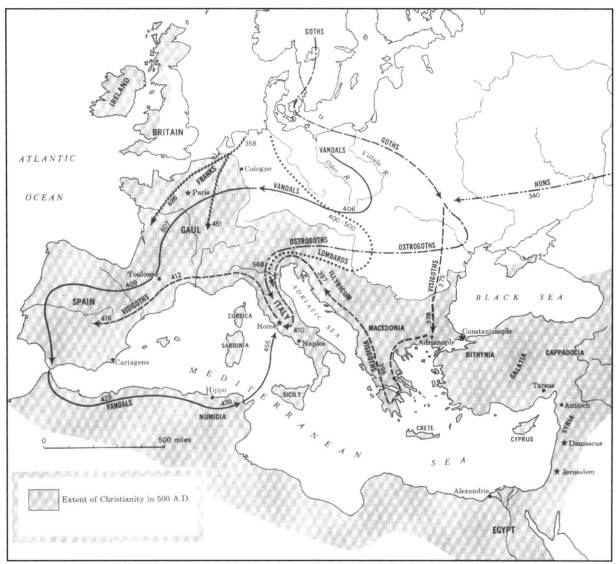

Source: Burns, Edward M., *Western Civilization*, 9th Ed. NY: W.W. Norton & Co.

10
Battle of the Talas River, Central Asia, 751 C.E.

The only known clash in history between Chinese and Arab armies occurred over 1,250 years ago at an obscure site within Central Asia. It was one of history's most decisive battles and one that spread technology still in use today out of China and into the rest of the world. The five-day battle was a major victory for Islamic Arab forces. It basically halted the westward expansion of the powerful Chinese Tang Dynasty (618-907 C.E.). Internal strife for the Islamic victors likewise dampened further eastward expansion of the Islamic faith.

The Battle of the Talas River was fought intensively for five days with many reverses and without a clear victory until the very end. Arab General Ziyad ibn Salih's army of approximately 30,000 Arab, Persian and Turkish troops was ultimately triumphant over Korean General Kao Hsien-chih's Chinese army of 30,000 along the banks of the Talas River (in present Kyrgyzstan) in July, 751 C.E.

This upset was just 39 years after the Arabs had taken possession of the city of Samarkand, Central Asia, which was famous as a destination along the Silk Road. The Battle of the Talas River ended China's hopes of moving further westward into Central Asia and of opening further trade routes to the West. For the Arabs, the military victory was an extension of their establishment of the Islamic faith in Persia (Iran), western Turkestan, and the republics of Central Asia. One tremendous spin-off of the Arab victory, that they apparently had no way of anticipating, was the revealed secret of making the world's most used commodity—paper. The discovery was revealed by various Chinese prisoners. The guarded secret of making paper had been known in China for at least 600 years without being exported to the rest of the world.

The prisoners were held in the central Asian city of Samarkand. This prosperous city along the Silk Road was a major destination for overland traders moving in either direction from China to Persia. This golden city was located in the fertile valley of the Zarafstan River and had been populated since at least the year 2,000 B.C.E.

A Korean general, Kao Hsien-chih (or Gao Xianzhi) was in the employ of the Tang dynasty emperor Hsuan-tsung. The Tang dynasty had been both prosperous and powerful for many centuries and sought the expansion of trading partners. Just four years earlier, the Chinese emperor had sent the army of General Kao Hsien-chih to forcibly eliminate the interference of Tibetans who were obstructing the Pamir mountain passes along the Silk Road. The task was aggressively handled and in the process opened the prospect of capturing Tashkent. This was another prosperous city of Central Asia and was located about 175 miles northeast of Samarkand.

General Kao Hsien-chih massed his forces for a march upon the Turkish king of Tashkent. It was a staged confrontation falsely accusing the king had not honoring trade agreements with the Chinese emperor in the past. The real motivation was to capture the wealth of Tashkent. With no chance to rectify the situation, Kao's forces beheaded the king and pilfered whatever they wanted in Tashkent. The impression was created that the Chinese emperor was either unaware, or had not authorized Kao's methods.

One omission that the emperor's army under General Kao failed to correct was the execution of the king's son as well. Instead, the escaped prince was able to get away and report what had happened to other Turkish tribes in Central Asia. Possibly there had been other conflicts. Either way, the enraged Turks sought the assistance of Samarkand. The desired help came in the form of Arab general Ziyad ibn Salih. His apparently mercenary forces were recruited by the regional governor to seek revenge and restore Tashkent to the former, royal family. Ziyad's army was drawn from troops as far away as Damascus.

Early on a day in July, 751 C.E., Ziyad positioned his army along the banks of the Talas River. The camp was near a small town of the same name and about 150 miles northeast of Tashkent. His allied forces were made up of Arabs, Persians and Turks. Being of comparable size, they confronted Kao's force of 30,000 Chinese soldiers plus a band of apparently mercenary Turks known as the Karluk.

The Islamic army attacked first using archers, well-armed cavalrymen and foot soldiers with both crossbow and swords. They weighed into the mostly Chinese forces. The battle raged for five days. Much of the fighting was hand-to-hand and by swords at proximities that were too close for effective use of crossbows, spears, and javelins. Most of the Arabian horses were downed by Chinese arrows. A major turning point occurred when Arabs on camels charged and at the same time made great noises with brass cymbals. The strange noise frightened the Chinese horses out of control and disintegration began to set in. About the same time, the Karluk forces learned of Kao's treacheries in Tashkent and turned on him. Kao's army was suddenly assaulted from both front and rear. Thousands died. Thousands of others escaped to the mountains, or were taken as prisoners. General Kao managed to escape. The decisive defeat ended China's aspirations to expand its domain further into Central Asia.

Among the captured prisoners were skilled craftsmen who knew the process of making paper. China had been producing paper for at least 600 years without revealing the secret

processes to the rest of the world. Once revealed, perhaps as a survival trading chip, the craftsmen prisoners were taken to the Turkish stronghold of Samarkand. Once there the prisoners established value for themselves by sharing the tightly guarded secret for making paper. Samarkand had ample water, fibrous flax plants and the labor necessary to make paper. Immediately, there was a demand for this product and it made its way to western markets along the established Silk Road and soon replaced Egyptian papyrus, clay tablets and animal skins as a lightweight alternative for written communications. Due in part to that windfall, Arabs were able to strengthen their Islamic influences throughout much of Central Asia. Arabs were no longer at a competitive disadvantage with the Chinese in the production and distribution of paper.

The powerful Tang dynasty had overcome threats from tribal groups in the region of Tibet and had established control as far west as Kabul and Kashmir. Continued expansion of China's interests to the west would have placed them in conflict with Islamic religion that was barely over 100 years old and was spreading like a wildfire. It was due to internal tensions that the Islamic victors did not make more of their success at Talas River. One immediate result was that Muslim shipping in the Indian Ocean improved as a result of suppressing the Tang dynasty's westward expansion. The decisiveness of the defeat inhibited the westward spread of Buddhism into the Islamic or Hindu regions of India and Central Asia north of India. The defeat at the Battle of Talas River also led to the An Lushan revolt in 755 C.E. which contributed to that dynasty's collapse about 150 years later.

Scarcely one century had elapsed after the death of Islamic prophet, Muhammad, in 632 C.E. Much of the Middle East, as far as parts of Afghanistan, had come under distinct Arab influence. Central Asia, however, was slower in converting to Islam in some regions, but came more and more under its influence by the year 705 C.E. It was in that year that Qutaiba ibn Muslim became governor of Khorasan. Later, the trade cities of Bukhara and Samarkand were under his control. Resistant to outside influences, the Central Asian city of Samarkand today has a mostly Islamic population of roughly 200,000. The residents continue to trade in silk, cotton, rice, gold, silver, pottery, and wine as was typical of the medieval period of the famed Silk Road. Relative isolation has its privileges in a world that is otherwise changing at record rates.

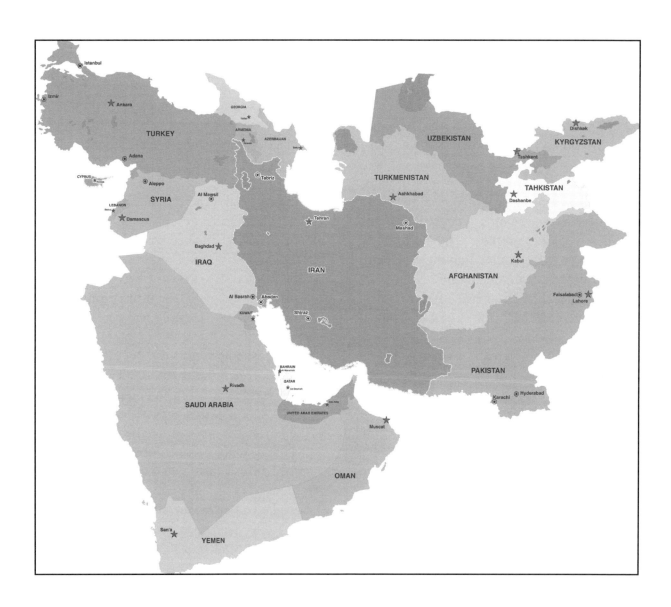

Kyrgyzstan

Capital: Bishkek (Formed 1991)
Population: Approximately 5 million
Area: Almost 77,000 square miles
Religion: Muslim 65%, Russian Orthodox
Climate: Minimal rainfall occurs in this Central Asian country on the old Silk Road.
Topography: Extensive deserts and mountains with little budget for roads or other infrastructure. Valleys are sufficiently fertile to not be dependent on other countries for food.
Surrounded by China, Kazakhstan, Uzbekistan and Tajikistan
Summary: The city of Tashkent existed in the first century C.E. Kyrgyzstan reluctantly became a part of Russia in the 1860's. It has existed as an independent country for not much more than a single decade. It is still one of the poorest and most isolated countries on the map but does have a good level of self-sufficiency that is typical of the area. Government tends to be repressive and the trend is toward greater Islamization that may be comparable in many ways to the Taliban of Afghanistan. Kyrgyzstan also has the distinction of being the site of the only military confrontation between Arab and Chinese forces at the Battle of Talas in 751 C.E. That battle limited the eastward expansion of Islam and the westward expansion of Buddhism.

11
The Last Major Viking Battle, 1066

When Edward the Confessor, King of England, died in January, 1066, he lacked a direct heir. The throne of England was ultimately passed to Anglo-Saxon Harold Godwin, Earl of Wessex. It was a time when there was immense rivalry for the throne of England. On September 25, 1066, Anglo-Saxon King Harold's disciplined army was prepared to confront a strong force of thousands of Viking raiders under the leadership of Norway's King Harald Hardrada. The Norse fleet landed at Riccall and planned to confront the English near the small town of York in northern England. The actual battle was near York and was focused on the wooded area that was approached by the Stamford Bridge.

It was a time when the successor to the English throne was chosen by a committee rather than by inheritance. Under this immense rivalry for the throne of England, William [the Conqueror] of Normandy issued his claim for the English throne as a second cousin to Edward the Confessor. Harold's brother, Tostig Godwin, Earl of Wessex also made claims to the throne for himself. It was Tostig who first conspired with William of Normandy to invade England, overthrow his brother, and share the throne. Rejected by William, Tostig conspired with King Harald Hardrada to invade England and divide the realm between them. When King Harold heard of his brother's treasonous plan to have King Harald Hardrada invade England, he reportedly said, "I will give him just six feet of English soil, or, since they say he is a tall man, I will give him seven feet!"

The ambitious, arrogant, and frequently cruel Harald Hardrada sailed from Norway with thousands of Viking raiders in roughly 300 long boats. Harald expected his reputation for ruthlessness to precede him and he fully expected that the vulnerable town of York would pay homage to him as well as provide him with hostages that he could sell in other markets. He was sure enough about this particular raid to leave a portion of his forces at the coast with the boats and to leave behind their protective leather jackets because of the hot weather. As they approached Stamford Bridge, probably the last thing the king expected to see was silvery reflections from the shields, helmets, chain-mail shirts, and swords of an English army rushing straight at his forces.

Harald attempted to rally his forces at the narrow Stamford Bridge. He shouted, "Carry your head always high where swords seek to shatter the skulls of doomed warriors." The rallying cry seemed to have some good effect as the outnumbered Norsemen began their clash with the English. There was a jam-up on the narrow, stone bridge and one Viking reportedly held back many of Harold's forces. The prepared English archers and swordsmen soon made their greater numbers felt as well. King Harald, who was in the midst of the fighting, received an arrow wound to the neck that proved fatal. The treacherous royal agitator, Earl Tostig Godwin, was also killed in that battle.

Leaderless, the battle turned more and more against the exhausted and outnumbered raiders without their protective leathers. Harald's reinforcements did arrive later in the day but all they found was the ruin of the battlefield. The remnants of Harald's force, knowing they were defeated, returned to Norway. The final outcome for the Vikings was that only 30 long boats returned to Norway.

There were scattered Viking raids over the next few decades, but never on the scale of Harald Hardrada's Stamford Bridge. After three centuries of ruthless, terror-inducing raids throughout most European waterways, it was inevitable that anti-Viking defenses would improve. Also, with time the Vikings assimilated more and more of their victims' and adversaries' behaviors and values. Most Vikings by 1066 had fused Christianity with their own pagan ideologies. Large numbers of Vikings had abandoned the smash and grab approach to looting in favor of active trading (albeit "stolen goods") for what they actually wanted. Many used their acquired wealth to settle into farming communities with good soil and weather, not the hard-scrabble farms of their ancestors in the north.

A classic example is the Norman French whose ancestors had been Vikings. Those Normandy "Vikings" were the same forces, lead by William the Conqueror, that invaded southern England just two days after Hardrada's defeat. On September 27, 1066, William's forces landed unopposed at the beaches of Pevensey. Two weeks later, William's forces would confront King Harold at the Battle of Hastings, October 14, 1066.

King Harold's exhausted forces were defeated. Harold and his other brothers were killed. On Christmas Day, 1066, William, the illegitimate son of the Duke of Normandy, and a duke in his own right, was crowned as king of England.

The Viking scourge of terror, since its first massacre of the Lindisfarne Monks in 793, had a major impact in opening medieval European markets to trade (including the slave trade). Viking "tradesmen" opened markets throughout Western Europe as far east as Kiev, Russia, and as far west as Newfoundland. The Vikings' skill in both river and ocean-going boat design and navigation was far superior to their European contemporaries. Their success as cold-blooded predators and sociopathic thieves pressed agrarian Europe into economic growth and mobility that did much to move Western Europe out of the Middle Ages.

King Harald Hardrada was not the typical Viking. His claim to the royal family was dubious. At age fifteen Harold's half-brother, or perhaps his uncle, Olaf Haraldsson, was killed in his efforts to regain the throne. That was the year 1030. Harald was injured in that attempt but managed to escape with his life. He lived in exile in parts of Russia and later in Constantinople. He worked his way through the ranks of the Vanangian Guard, an elite unit of mostly Swedish Viking mercenaries who provided security services to the Byzantine empress, Empress Zoe Porphyrogenita (1028-1050).

His nephew, Magnus the Good (Olaf's son), was placed on the Norwegian throne in Oslo, 1042. Being aggressive to the bone, Harald had acquired great wealth, and due to his wealth, he persuaded his nephew to share the position of king. Then, probably to no one's surprise, the nephew "died" in 1047. Harald succeeded his nephew to the throne. However, as a result of his death and total defeat of his forces at Stamford Bridge, the "Viking Empire" never occupied other parts of Western Europe as King Harald had intended. The French Normans, of Viking ancestry, instead became the ruling force in Medieval England. The northern Viking raids into Europe also ended within the next few decades.

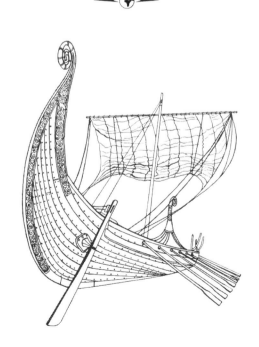

Norway

Capital: Oslo

Population: Approximately 4.5 million

Area: Over 149,000 square miles

Religion: Lutheran, Protestant, Roman Catholic

Climate: A land of northerly and coastal weather reaching up to the arctic circle, yet ice-free year round due to the warm Gulf Stream.

Topography: A somewhat vertical country extending from north to south and a region of ragged coastlines and islands with deep fjords and mountains reaching to 6,600 feet.

Surrounded by the Atlantic Ocean, Sweden, Finland, Russia, and the North Sea

Summary: An oil-rich nation that for centuries depended upon marine activities, hardscrabble farming in very short and cold growing seasons, forestry and the grazing of domestic animals such as cattle, sheep and reindeer. The early Vikings made their presence known to the rest of Europe as sea raiders beginning in the year 793 with the raid upon the Lindisfarne Monks of northern England. The Viking raids did not end until a few decades after the last major Viking assault into England in the year 1066. Relative isolation helped to preserve Norway as a relatively neutral region until being occupied by the Germans early in World War II. Norway hosted the 1994 Winter Olympics in Lillehammer and continues to be a major tourist destination.

12
The First Christian Crusade, 1099

The split between the Roman Catholic Church and the Greek Orthodox Church of the Byzantine Empire was a severe blow to Pope Gregory VII (1085-1088). His successor, Pope Urban II (1088-1099), faced a major crisis in 1095 when the Byzantine Emperor Alexius Comnenus appealed for help in taking back territory in Asia Minor that had recently been lost to the Seljuk Turks. The Islamic Seljuk people who captured Jerusalem in 1076 were from Asia Minor, but very different from the tolerant Islamic people before them. They were equally hostile toward both Christians and Jews and essentially cutoff access to the Holy Lands for the first time. Stories of their atrocities against Christians and Jews soon filtered back to Europe.

Jerusalem had been essentially "an open city" since its capture by the Caliph Omar's Islamic armies in 637. Religious pilgrims were allowed to visit holy sites on the condition that new churches were not built and crosses, or other religious symbols, were not displayed in public. The pilgrims paid a modest toll for these privileges. However, this new branch of Seljuk Turks from the region of present-day Iran, captured Jerusalem and from the year 1076 religious intolerance of outside groups was ruthlessly practiced. Storics of every imaginable brutality soon made their way back to Europe.

The Byzantine emperor was likely anticipating assistance in the form of mercenaries who could be paid to confront the Seljuks. Pope Urban II, a non-pacifist like Gregory VII, called for a Council of Clermont (France) to seek combatants for this eastern Mediterranean crisis. To everyone's surprise, the appeal brought forth a religious fervor and frequent chants of "God wills it." Instead of small bands of mercenaries, huge numbers of people (nobles and impoverished alike) volunteered

to take Jerusalem and the holy sites back from Islam. The inspired reaction opened the potential to reunite the Catholic Church, to diminish the authority of Germany's King Henry IV, and to establish a new European peace settlement while taking back Jerusalem. Suddenly having up to 100,000 dedicated crusaders for a religious cause was not anticipated by anyone. The huge force of volunteers was unique to the European experience at that time.

Pope Urban II was French and had carefully chosen Clermont, France, to recruit as much of the French nobility as possible for his grand plan to reunite the church and hold back the Islamic tide. The imminent threat of the Moors to the south of them was a sufficient reminder that the danger was real. He appointed Adhemar de Le Puy to be the leader of this religious force. Le Puy had been the bishop of Puy-en-Velay since 1087. He was often in conflict with Raymond IV, count of Toulouse, over leadership, but was able to keep the spiritual campaign mostly on track. Le Puy was able to communicate effectively with Emperor Alexis Comnenus and has been given much credit for the successes at Antioch. He died in August, 1098, yet his "spirit" contributed to the capture of Jerusalem in the following July.

The Seljuk Turks came to political prominence in the late eleventh century from the region of present Iran and were only recent converts to Islam. There had been roughly a century of both good and bad faith dealings between them and the assorted representatives of the Byzantine Empire. At a low point in their relations, Byzantine Emperor Diogenes and his forces crossed the Euphrates River in 1071 to destroy the much smaller forces of Seljuks at the Battle of Manzikert. The Seljuks feigned a retreat until the Byzantine Christian forces were exhausted in the heat and then saturated them with arrows before coming at them from three sides with their curved swords. Diogenes was later released for a huge ransom and the two forces actually allied themselves during the thirteenth century against the Mongol invasions. Both Christians and Muslims were put to the Mongol sword at the Battle of Anatolia. Surviving remnants of the Seljuk people would eventually go on to form the Ottoman Empire that became a powerful force in the region until the Great War (WWI).

The appeal to organize the First Crusade was so great that following Pope Urban II's words, very large numbers of impoverished citizens of Western Europe assembled and began the great march along the Mediterranean coast to the Byzantine capital of Constantinople. They continued onward, virtually leaderless, and possessed little more than their own bodies and devout spirits. Many died along the way. The rest were put to the sword by Turkish defenders as they crossed the Bosporus into Asia Minor.

In contrast, the equally fervent nobles throughout Western Europe recruited far more disciplined and equipped armies to confront their Islamic adversaries. They followed much the same routes as the wretched poor who preceded them on their way to Constantinople. Regrettably, the religious zeal of the moment was such that many of the innocent Jewish people along the way were brutally murdered. By the spring of 1097, an estimated 100,000 religious crusaders had consolidated their forces on the east side of the Bosporus. The medieval knights were a sufficient fighting force to hold back the Turks and to seize Antioch, Turkey, on June 5, 1098. Most of Syria was also captured. They moved southward along the Mediterranean coast until they reached Jerusalem in June, 1099. By early July the Christian warriors were greatly reduced in numbers and sometimes both barefoot and starving outside the fortress walls of the city. The bare footedness has also been described

as a deception to imitate the biblical story of the surrounding of the walls of Jericho.

The disjointed mass launched their final assault on the Muslim defenders of Jerusalem on July 13, 1099. Within days the crusaders were victorious and proceeded to massacre all Muslim and Jewish inhabitants who resisted them. The religious zeal that had driven them to such an alien part of the world, the Holy Lands, was mostly forgotten in the brutality and imperialism of doing what they did because they could do it. The grand success of the First Crusade was that they did capture Jerusalem as they had set out to do. Subsequent crusades typically met with failure. The treatment of Jews in Western Europe after the First Crusade typically worsened for reasons that defy any rational explanation

The First Crusade temporarily helped to build up the respect and power of the papal monarchy. Mostly, it helped to reduce fears throughout Western Europe of an Islamic onslaught such as had been experienced by Visigoth Spain. Strong fears of Asiatic Huns from the mostly unknown East, and the later pressures from the Mongols from that same dreaded East, kept most Europeans on edge. The sense that powerful forces from the East could be held in check contributed to a revival of religious spirit and general optimism that could be seen in much of twelfth century Europe. Exposure to new ideas, luxuries, new cultures and trade goods between east and west was encouraged for the first time in centuries. Venice and Genoa, in particular, began to prosper. A common threat had forced many different people to work together, yet did not excuse savage slaughter of innocents and imperialistic land grabs. The religious vitality of the high-medieval period that followed helped to encourage reforms and broader ways of viewing the world and the diverse people within it. The exception was the irrational prejudice toward persons of the Jewish faith.

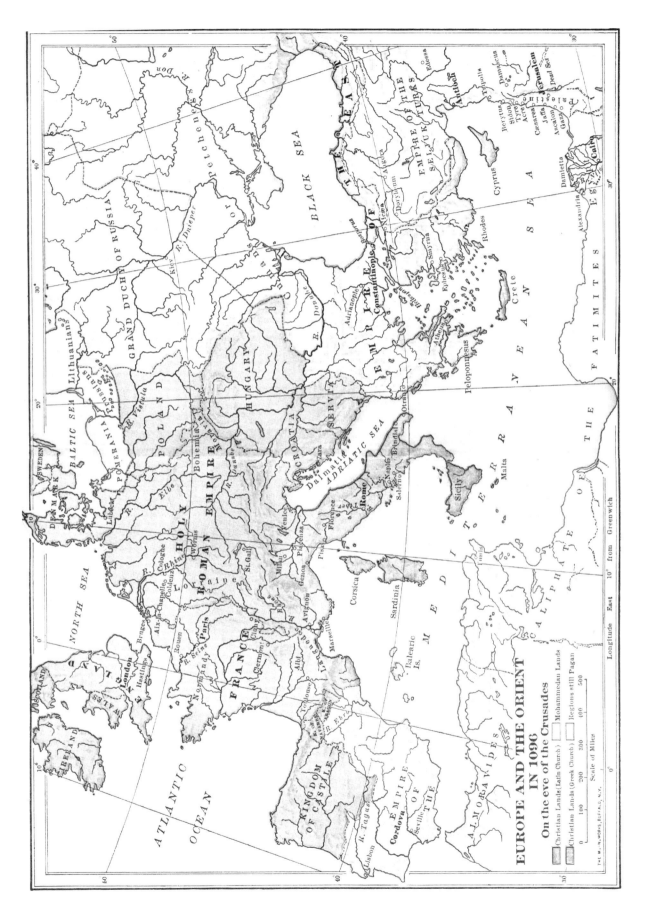

EUROPE AND THE ORIENT
IN 1096
On the eve of the Crusades

Christian Lands (Latin Church)
Christian Lands (Greek Church)
Mohammedan Lands
Regions still Pagan

0   100   200   300   400   500
Scale of Miles

THE M. N. WORKS, BUFFALO, N.Y.

49

13
Ghengis Khan vs. the Kwarezm Empire, 1218

The "scourge of mankind," Ghengis Khan (c. 1162-1227) was far "bigger than life" in many respects. He has been credited with acquiring the world's largest empire within the lifespan of one man. He survived and overcame extreme adversities at many different points in his life. He united diverse clans and tribes of

Ghengis Khan

mostly Mongolian herdsmen into the most feared and most successful conquering force in the history of the world. As king (khan) he ordered the codification of tribal law (Yassa) that was probably based on the harsh experiences of living on the Mongolian steppes. That rigid and apparently absolute code of conduct put a life-and-death emphasis upon right and wrong as well as concepts such as obedience and loyalty. It was the implementation of that code of honor in the harsh realties of high deserts and barren, northern steppes that filled Ghengis Khan with a lifelong vengeance.

Born with the name Temujin ("iron worker") in approximately 1162 C.E., he was the son of

a Mongol chieftain, Yesugei, and his wife. Few details of his childhood have survived until he was about 13 years of age. At that time his father determined it was time to arrange for Temujin's bride from another tribal village. A few years later, following marriage and the birth of his first son, Yesuaei, the future khan of khans learned that his father had been poisoned by a group of Turkish Tartars—arch rivals of the Mongol people. Because of his inexperience the adolescent Temujin's claim to assume his father's position was flatly rejected. For his audaciousness, his small clan was essentially abandoned on the unforgiving steppes of Mongolia either to make it on their own, or to starve. Under such severe conditions, Temujin became aware that food was being stolen. He captured and killed one of the thieves who turned out to be one of his half brothers. By acting upon his sworn vengeance against "food thieves," plus the Tartars who had killed his father, and the Mongol band that forced his family into starvation, he continued to gain a respected name for himself among Mongol tribes.

Later, when Temujin was off hunting he was captured and held prisoner by members of an enemy tribe. He managed to escape and, in the process, he killed one of the guards. He survived all attempts to recapture and kill him. News of his exploits circulated and further enhanced his reputation for bravery and survival skills. A subsequent raid on Temujin's small clan reportedly left them with one horse and little of anything else. He pursued the thieves relentlessly but was successful only in recovering the stolen horses. Again, the rumors circulated and the Mongol teenager was elevated to almost mythological status.

Along with physical toughness and great charisma, the adolescent son of a "murdered" chieftain perhaps felt an early destiny to deal with the enemies of his people. By roughly 1179, at the age of 17, Temujin began to organize tribal members against the rival Tartars and rogue elements within the Mongol tribes. He teamed with his father's close friend, Togrul and others, such as Borgurchi and Subodai. They were soon able to build a force of thousands to face their common enemies. The first real difference between this early group and a band of vigilantes was the very strict structure and leadership by example that the future khan was able to put in place. Groupings were eventually organized in 10's, 100's, and 1000's as if by the decimal system. Each combatant provided his own horse, weapons, clothing, and the sparse food that would sustain them. Resupply came from raids.

Ruthlessly successful raids were such that in the year 1183 Temujin was declared a Mongol khan and given the name, Ghengis ("spirit of light," or "precious warrior"). It was during that period that Ghengis Khan ordered the codification of the unwritten laws of the Mongol steppes (Yassa). Compliance with the Yassa and Ghengis' strong leadership were major factors in holding Mongol tribal groups together. Still, it took two years to eliminate the Tartar threat. Of the Tartar survivors of one particular battle, all who were taller than the axle of a wagon were executed.

Almost always outnumbered, the Mongols made major incursions into the three primary regions of China before Ghengis would be named Khan of Khans (king of kings) in 1206. In 1201 Ghengis had to defeat the rival Mongol tribe of Keraits before the remainder of the Mongol tribes could be united. The Keraits were led by his boyhood friend, Jamuga, and were nearly destroyed to the man. Jamuga, however, escaped and was able to rebuild his forces for a major confrontation at the Battle of Mount Jeir'er in 1203. By the following year this last rival within the Mongol tribes (Keraits) was finally defeated.

The new focus by 1207 was to extend the Mongol Empire into the three Chinese regions that were divided as follows: Chin and Tangut in the north, and Sung in the south. The Tangut's were quickly subdued in 1209. Two years later, following a buildup of Mongol forces, a campaign was begun against the Chin Empire that included the present city of Beijing. That city was laid to waste.

Most of the Chinese empire came under the control of Ghengis Khan by approximately the year 1212. Often, much larger Chinese forces were first defeated and then virtually annihilated. The constant drums of the Mongol hoard actually drove some people mad with fear. If needed, the Mongols actually marched captives into protective moots until they could cross over on their dead bodies. The goal of uniting all of China, however, was not realized until the reign of his grandson, Kublai Khan in 1279.

Not a sentimental man, Ghengis Khan did recognize that trade along the Silk Road could be a benefit to his own people. Camel caravans in particular were often filled with riches. In the year 1218, however, the Mongol Empire received information that a group of Mongol traders and merchants had been executed by a local governor within the Kwarezm Empire. It was in the region of the ancient Silk Road and a part of the Persian Empire that included parts of present Afghanistan, Turkestan, Uzbekistan, and Iran. The affront was met with a Mongol demand that the responsible governor be handed to them or that war would be declared. Representatives of Shah Mohammed II refused and the Mongols were true to their promise. Ghengis Khan therefore led an army of 90,000 to attack the Kwarezm Empire from the north and ordered a force of 30,000 men to attack from the east.

The ferocity and effectiveness of the very mobile and disciplined Mongol forces was grossly underestimated by the Shah's force of roughly 400,000 men. A campaign that appeared to be recklessly launched quickly became a decisive victory for the ruthless, light cavalry forces of the Khan. At its conclusion, Ghengis Khan ordered 20,000 men to pursue the Shah and to kill him. They chased him westward across the remnants of the Persian Empire only to discover that the Shah had died on an island in the Black Sea. Roughly a dozen years after the death of Ghengis Khan, the Shah's son rebuilt the Kwarezm forces only to be utterly destroyed a second time by the Mongols. It was during that campaign that the Mongol forces first became aware of "the fire that flies" (flaming arrows).

Besides the aggressiveness of small clusters of Mongol cavalry that would charge into the heart of significantly larger numbers of opponents, the Mongols had several advantages. They were probably the best horsemen of that time. They used saddle stirrups and short, composite bows that allowed them to launch large numbers of arrows without using one hand to control the horse. They wore one or more layers of silk shirts that kept them cooler in battle and often allowed them to remove an arrow without tearing large quantities of flesh. Once close in, they were probably as effective with sword, dagger and sometimes assorted weapons as any combatant on the field. They were masters at exploiting the probable and sudden weakness of their opponent. In subsequent battles the advanced notice of their extreme ruthlessness in killing all who opposed them sent waves of panic and confusion. Their actual deeds and apparent lack of interest in most skills and knowledge of their captives helped to project the image that there would not be one survivor to shed a tear for the vanquished.

For the unsuspecting and the naïve, the Mongol light cavalry in particular, with brilliant leadership, forged itself into a weapon that was all but unstoppable except for the death of

Ghengis Khan in 1227. Except for the 20th Century, the Mongol "Horde" killed more people and destroyed more cities than any other event in world history. Oddly, DNA studies suggest the Khan and his immediate descendants may have impregnated more women than any identifiable source in world history. The Christian notion during the Crusades that a great horde from the East would descend upon the Moslem World and destroy it proved to be false.

Victories of Ghengis Khan, his sons and grandsons include the conquests of Tartars (Turks), and rebel Mongol tribes, Chin Empire, Tangut and Sung Empires, Hsia-hsia (Korea), Kwarezm Empire (Persia), Abassid Caliphate, the Alans, Georgians, Kipchaks (Turks), Ghuzz, Seljug (Turks), Volga Bulgars, Samarkand and Bukhara, Russian tribes, Polish tribes, Germanic tribes, Hungarian tribes and into present Southeast Asia. The Lithuanians were defeated in a major battle against the Golden Horde in the Crimea of Russia, 1399. It was word of Ghengis Khan's death that turned his armies back from within a few hundred miles of Vienna, and resulted in cancellation of invasion plans for Egypt and Syria. Upon Ghengis Khan's death his empire was divided among his sons.

"All who surrender will be spared;
Whoever does not surrender but opposes with struggle and dissension, shall be annihilated."

Ghengis Khan

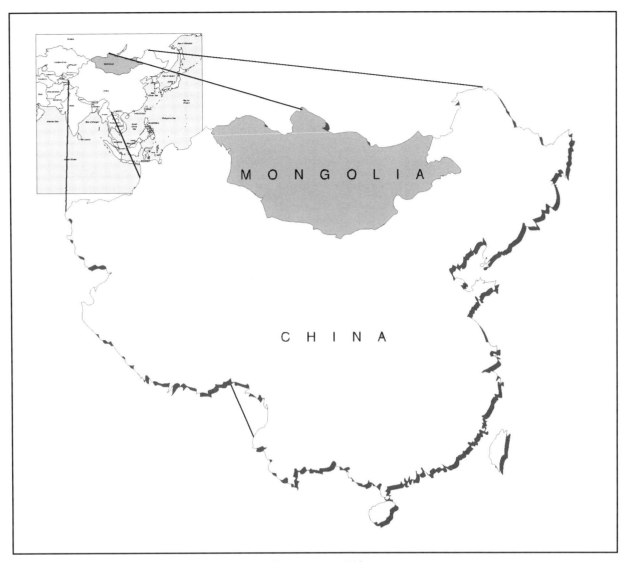

Mongolia

Capital: Ulan Bator
Population: Over 2.5 million
Area: Over 604,000 square miles
Climate: Extremely cold winters to -50°F, dry desert (Gobi) and steppes
Topography: Rolling hills of desert and steppes in Central Asia. Few distinguishing features.
Religion: Tibetan Buddhist, Muslim
Surrounded by Russia, China and just touches Kazakhstan
Summary: A landlocked area of Central Asia. Harsh conditions and relative isolation has typically meant subsistence lifestyles for most of its inhabitants over the centuries. It was in 1179 that Ghengis Khan first organized the various nomadic tribes into a cohesive fighting force that terrorized much of the known world. The Mongols invaded China by 1210 and by 1227 Ghengis died and left his vast empire to his three sons. His descendants captured Moscow and Kiev by 1240. The Mongolian dynasty in China ended in the year 1368 and was followed by the Ming Dynasty. Mongolia was occupied by the Japanese during World War II and has since tried to build up the economy based on mineral riches in addition to coal and oil reserves. The end of communism in 1990 has opened the way for economic reforms and democratic politics in this very isolated sector of the world.

14
Kublai Khan and the Divine Wind, 1274 & 1281

Kublai Khan (1215-1294) was the fourth son of Ghengis Khan's fourth son, Toluia. He succeeded his brother, Mongke, and was elected by the Mongols as "Great Khan" in Northern China in 1260. He was the first foreigner to rule China in many centuries. From 1251 to 1259 he actively assisted emperor Mongke in military and administrative campaigns to complete the conquest of China. It would take another 20 years of campaigns to subdue the Sung dynasty of Southern China. He estab-

Kublai Khan

lished his lavish capital in what is now the city of Beijing. He cultivated a strong relationship with Venetian adventurer, Marco Polo, over a 20 year period of East/West exchange.

As the conquest of China became a reality, Kublai Khan was able to refocus his attention and his armies to the conquest of Koryo (Korea). A decade long conflict with bitter reverses on both sides ended with the monarchy of Koryo agreeing to be a subject state of the Mongols and to allow the crown prince to be held as hostage as a personal guarantee. When Koryo's king died in 1274, Kublai Khan arranged to have one of his daughters marry the

crown prince and return to Koryo with a Mongol entourage that was the equivalent of a full *coup d'etat*. And with that issue settled, the Great Khan could indulge his ambition for conquest of Japan as well as Burma, Thailand, Java and the rest of Southeast Asia. The Mongol conviction for three generations was that they had a "...Mandate of Heaven to become the Master of the Universe."

In 1274 the virtually unstoppable, land-based military of Kublai Khan sought to complete the conquest of the Far East. He used emissaries to deliver written orders to the Kamakura Shogunate of Kyoto, Hojo Tokimune. He could either pay the demanded tribute or face the consequences of invasion and total defeat. The shogun, who wanted little to do with foreign partners except possibly some trade and religious exchange with Zen Buddhist Monks in southern China, ignored the demands. Japan had clear intentions of maintaining its feudal isolation and unique, cultural distinctions. The lack of a response, however, infuriated the Great Khan and he set about to creating an invasion fleet in Southern Koryo

The total fleet constructed and armed with cannon, gunpowder and supplies totaled approximately 900 vessels and included up to 300 large transports. Approximately 32,000 Mongol, Koryo and Chinese troops made up the assault force. The allied force included about 6,700 Koryo sailors, rowers and helmsmen. Their departure from the southern tip of Korea on November 2, 1274, was no surprise to the militant Japanese. The Mongol fleet soon captured the outlying islands of Komota, Tsushima, and Iki as staging points for the invasion of mainland Japan. The mostly uncontested assault landed on the big island of Kyushu between November 18 and 19. They were met near the town of Hakata by less than four thousand Japanese samurai defenders who were ill-prepared for their first exposure to cannons, exploding gunpowder projectiles, and synchronized cavalry attacks. Japanese defenders were on the verge of defeat. Apparently, however, resistance remained stronger than expected and the expedition returned to their ships on the 19. A violent typhoon suddenly destroyed about half of the Mongol fleet and caused the death of at least 13,000 men. At that point the venture was abandoned and the survivors returned to Koryo (Korea).

The Great Khan accepted that the failure of the first expedition was due simply to an act of nature. By 1291 he had assembled a grandiose second fleet of more than 900 vessels with a total of 42,000 men that would sail and row from Koryo. A far larger force of 3,200 vessels with closer to 100,000 men delayed their departure from the Yangtze River in China to join the northern fleet. The two fleets were expected to join forces at the islands of Iki and Tsushima before assaulting Kyushu as one unstoppable body.

The smaller fleet from Koryo departed on May 22, 1291. They reclaimed the outlying islands as before, but rather than wait for the Yangtze fleet, the Koryo fleet pressed on to Kyushu and arrived on June 21. Their arrival near Shigashima was significantly impeded by the improved defenses of the Japanese, who were not so naïve the second time. Small, highly mobile Japanese vessels pounded away at the much larger Mongol vessels with effective nighttime guerrilla tactics. The Mongol fleet finally withdrew to the outlying islands, and, when further attempts to land were mostly unsuccessful, the Koryo fleet commander decided to wait for reinforcements.

The far larger Yangtze force departed from the mouth of the Yangtze River on July 5, 1291. By mid-August the two forces were finally massed off Tsushima Island for an overwhelm-ing assault on Japan. To everyone's surprise, except Japan's "true believers," a major typhoon developed on the night of August 15, 1291. That kamikaze ("divine wind") that the Zen Buddhist Monks had prayed for destroyed much of the huge, Mongol fleet and killed over 10,000 of the Khan's forces. Small Japanese vessels landed on Tsushima Island right after the storm and managed to kill many more thousands of their enemies. It has been estimated—perhaps mythologized—that only five to ten percent of the combined fleet of over 4,000 vessels returned to the Asian mainland. The research of Lee Wha Rang suggests that only 10 to 15 percent of the Mongol fleet was actually destroyed by typhoons. The "myth of Japanese invincibility" remained powerful until 1945 and was a major factor in their desire to expand throughout the western Pacific. The ancient fear of being absorbed by the vast numbers of Chinese diminished after Kublai Khan's two failed invasions and confidence in Japan's Code of Bushido was greatly reinforced.

Kublai Khan died a seriously depressed and obese alcoholic at the age of 79. The death of his favorite wife and his designated heir in 1281 was compounded by constant strife religiously and politically. The failed attempts at conquest and lavish extravagances as China's foreign emperor helped to bring down the Yuan dynasty he founded within decades after his death. Still, his many positive contributions had a lasting effect on China. He governed in a way that showed respect for the Chinese people. He was remembered as the "Great Khan." The Divine Wind, that completely frustrated the khan, gave the Japanese people an enormous, if false, sense of invincibility. That sense of never being defeated contributed to their ruthless ambitiousness in seeking to become a colonial power in the Far East as a part of events leading up to World War Two.

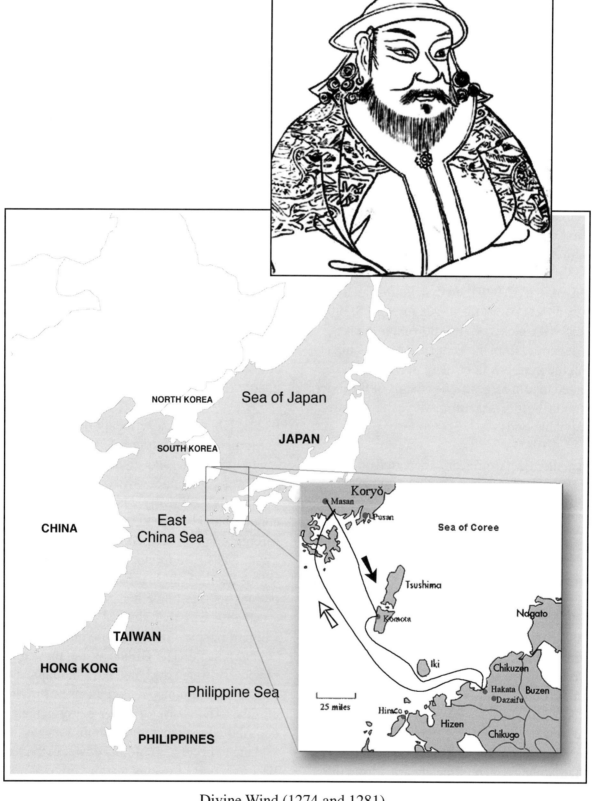

Divine Wind (1274 and 1281)

15
The Battle of Agincourt, France, 1415

The battlefield of Agincourt was little more than an agricultural crossroad in northwestern France around the beginning of the fifteenth century. Periodic wars between France and England were not uncommon following the Norman invasion of England in 1066. The significance of Agincourt was that a maximum of 7,000 under-funded English troops of King Henry V confronted and defeated at least 20,000 affluent French defenders who typically represented the noble classes. The French troops possessed full body armor made of steel. The steel armor was a recent and distinct improvement over the lesser quality and lighter gauge of iron. Archeological discoveries from the battlefield included a well embellished spur with ornate finish work. The implication, backed by historical record, was that the French were far better funded, better equipped for battle, and were defending their own soil. Everything totally favored the French.

Henry's army was about seventy-five percent composed of archers because the English king was near to bankruptcy. Logic, in the king's mind was clear, he could recruit two archers (the artillery equivalent of the age) for the price of one infantry soldier. To raise the money for his ill-equipped force, he was rumored to have pawned the royal jewels. A dramatic victory against the French nobility appeared to be against all odds. A decisive victory in favor of the English, however, did occur but was wrongly attributed to the English longbow. With about 5,500 archers able to launch up to ten arrows per minute, the air could be filled with 55,000 arrows every minute and normally produced a devastating effect. For centuries the lopsided victory of this reckless gamble was attributed to the success of the longbow. For approximately one century after Agincourt there was relative peace between England and France. Filling the air with arrows was a good strategy if it worked. It did not. The iron bodkin arrowhead has been tested and found that it would not typically penetrate steel armor. The historical explanation for the extremely one-sided victory against overwhelming odds had to be explained by other means.

For one thing, the affluent French forces assembled before the English archers were not trained soldiers, but a large remnant of continental nobles and knights. They had been massed at the request of France's King Charles VI and were convinced that they were superior to the English in every respect, especially in numbers and equipment. The aristocratic French were undisciplined and indifferent to the lessons of the battles of Crecy and Poitiers. The event was more of a sporting hunt than a real military confrontation. In fact, the English had difficulty drawing them into battle at first. Sporadic French cavalry charges were driven back in a state of confusion. The dismounted men-at-arms soon discovered that their movements were tedious and the churned fields of mud all but impassable.

The solution to the mystery of such an improbable victory was contained in the battlefield itself. The thick, clay-like soil of the region has changed little since 1415. For weeks prior to the battle there had been severe downpours of rain that made the soil in that region an especially sticky bog. Further testing showed that both horses and heavily armored foot soldiers would not only sink into the water saturated soil, but would also have great difficulty in extracting a foot once caught in the suction of the mud. Fully armored soldiers who fell onto the ground were unable to get themselves up, and instead were prone to cause others to fall. To make matters worse, the pressure of the excited troops pressing forward from the rear only compounded the problems of collisions and of being trampled. Full armor face masks likely impaired visibility and the ability to respond to directions from a remote command. The unarmored Englishmen were far more mobile and for that reason they were far more effective with their swords, hatchets, arrows, and spears that pulverized the sluggish knights.

The terrain of a battlefield is generally not apparent from a map. At the Agincourt battlefield the terrain was shaped somewhat like a funnel. As the French moved forward, they became compressed into a tighter and tighter area that quickly caused the over-weighted French troops to bog down in the sticky mud soil. Armored horses, in particular, were especially prone to sticking in such churned up mud as well as being far more vulnerable to arrows. Once in motion, the compressed forces to the rear exerted intense pressure on the forward lines. Very large numbers of otherwise well-prepared French knights were literally trampled to death in the mud. Death by the

force of arrows would have been a secondary factor. The French forces actually defeated themselves to a far greater extent than the English won the Battle of Agincourt.

The "failure" of the improved steel armor to protect the French forces likely contributed to its sudden disappearance as a defensive shield. An additional irony of Agincourt is the absence of cannon fire and musket fire that would have made the steel body armor of the day obsolete with the very first shot. The Battle of Agincourt was completely lacking in surprise innovations except those provided by Mother Nature. The impact of the English longbow was a major factor, but was distinctly overrated due to the introduction of heavier steel armor. Crowding, pushing, shoving, and just plain getting stuck in a wickedly muddy battlefield shaped like a funnel was the real undoing of the French forces. The English victory, even if for misunderstood reasons, did contribute to a sustained period of peace for warlike Western Europe.

France

Capital: Paris

Population: Approximately 60 million

Area: Over 212,000 square miles

Religion: Roman Catholic, Protestant, Jewish, Muslim

Climate: Many regional variations, sufficient rainfall to be mostly arable, generally mild temperatures without extreme highs or lows. Snowfall in mountainous regions

Topography: Mostly low-lying pastures and gentle hills leading to mountains near the eastern and southern borders.

Surrounded by Atlantic Ocean, English Channel, Belgium, Luxembourg, Germany, Switzerland, Italy, Monaco, Mediterranean Sea and Spain

Summary: Known as Gaul in ancient times France, like Spain, has evidence of cave dwellers dating back 30,000 to 40,000 years. Once the last Ice Age had passed the low-lying fields of Western Europe were especially attractive for subsistence living and agricultural development. The Franks and then the Romans were among the first to occupy and to control the native people living in that area. The absence of major barriers had made it especially attractive to aggressive Celtic and Germanic tribes, Huns, Mongols, and even the English. Charlemagne attempted to restore elements of the former Roman Empire starting in 768 C.E. The Battle of Agincourt in 1415 followed the Seven Years War between the two nations 25 years before. Western European land wars have long been commonplace. The Hundred Years War lasted from 1337 to 1453. The French Revolution and the Napoleonic Wars were a part of the somewhat continuous wars. By the end of World War I a total of 1.4 million French soldiers were lost. World War II and Dien Bien Phu also had tragic results for the French people. Currently, France is the largest agricultural producer in the European Union (EU) and excels in both the arts and technology.

16
Spain's Defeat of the Moors, 1492

The Iberian Peninsula of Western Europe is the site of present-day Spain and Portugal. Historically, it has been a residence for diverse groups of people who dated back to the earliest cave dwellers around 35,000 B.C.E. The Iberian people emigrated there from North Africa around 4,000 B.C.E. The areas near the Pyrenees were settled by Celts, Basques, and Franks. Phoenician traders established colonies along the Spanish coast, especially at Cadiz. Early Greek traders were followed by Carthaginians. The 600 year settlement by the Romans was followed by a 250 year settlement by Germanic Visigoths. Imposed on those diverse cultures was an almost 800 year occupancy by Arabic/Berber Moors from North Africa. Defeating and ejecting the Islamic Moors in 1492 restored Catholicism as the national religion. Coincidentally, 1492 was the year Christopher Columbus discovered Caribbean islands in the New World. As a result, Spain, which was the poorest and most battle-torn nation in Europe, became the wealthiest nation by far in just a few decades.

Following the Visigoth sack of Rome in 411 C.E., Italy was abandoned in favor of mass emigration to the Iberian Peninsula. Suddenly, without a strong Roman opposition, the Germanic Visigoths were able to settle much of present Spain except for the northern areas held by Basques, Franks, and kindred groups of independent mountain people. The rugged, mountainous terrain and stretched supply lines from North Africa blocked the efforts of the Moors to capture that region as it had for the Gothic invaders.

For many centuries the Gothic people were nomadic tribes in northeastern Europe. The Goths who migrated to the west were known as Visigoths. Those who remained in the east were known as Ostrogoths. They typically had individual clan chieftains rather than a strong, central leadership. That form of political structure routinely broke down as their numbers and problems continued to grow. As a result, in their 250 year occupancy of Spain, there were frequent feuds and conflicts among the basically tribal groups. A long succession of typically weak "kings" ruled without possessing central, unifying power.

By the year 711 the weaknesses of intertribal feuds and conflicts reached an extreme crisis. One Visigoth clan sought outside help to settle disputes and increase power in a rebellion against the current Visigoth monarch, King Roderick. The door to revolutionary change was opened when a disgruntled clan invited a North African Muslim army to come in and settle their feud with Roderick. The North African army led by Jabal Tariq ibn Ziyad did

Moorish Castle

cross over to Spain from Morocco and killed Roderick. The following year a force of 20,000 Arabs led by Musa ibn Nusair pushed into Spain and used the old Roman road system to quickly establish control of many regions. The far larger population of Visigoths was ineffective in stopping the invasion because they were so poorly organized. There was little or no support from the indigenous populations that had been overrun by the Visigoths centuries before.

The Islamic invaders were able to control territories as far north as the Pyrenees but were defeated by the Franks at Battle of Tours in 732 C.E., and did not move into Western Europe as was likely intended. With some exceptions, the Islamic Arabs and Berbers maintained an uneasy peace in much of Spain for most of the next 800 years. The Moors, a mix of Arabs and Berbers, imposed their cultural, architectural, and religious stamps, but were reasonably tolerant of the Catholic and Jewish people within their domain.

Shortly after the Moorish invasion there was a religious rebellion known as *La Reconquista.* A Muslim force was defeated by Visigoth King Pelayo in an area known as Covadonga in the year 718. In 1090 Alfonso VI briefly defeated the Moors and captured the city of Toledo. In the same year, El Cid put together a force of Christians and Muslims to capture and briefly hold the province of Valencia. A decisive Christian victory in 1212 at the Battle of Navas de Tolosa marked a significant reduction in Moorish power within that region.

Typical of the decentralized character of the Visigoths, there was little coordinated effort to drive out the Moors until the capital of Cordoba was briefly defeated by Ferdinand III of Castile in the year 1216. The internal strife of the Muslims was compounded more and more by pressures from the independents in the north and waves of new powerseekers coming out of North Africa. Ferdinand III recaptured Cordoba in 1236 and Sevilla in 1248. A twenty-five-year-long rebellion against forces coming out of North Africa was started by Alfonso XI and ended with the defeat of the Moors at the Battle of Rio Salado in 1337.

The final stage of the Christian Reconquest began with the marriage of Queen Isabella of Castile and King Ferdinand of Aragon in 1469. Their shared monarchies brought together the two most powerful, Spanish Christian kingdoms. Following a ten-year siege of Granada they succeeded in defeating the Moors for the last time in 1492. They became known as the Catholic monarchs and initiated a fanatical purge to establish Catholicism as the dominant if not the sole religion of Spain. The obsessed and intensive efforts to purge Spain of its Moorish occupancy for almost eight hundred years took on the nightmarish features that became known as the Spanish Inquisition. One of the peculiarities of history is that Tomas de Torquemada, who was descended from Jewish converts to Catholicism, became the most notorious of the Inquisition's heinous prosecutors. Unknown thousands of Islamic Moors, Protestant Christians, and Jews were tortured and typically killed in horrendous ways for not having the "correct faith."

One of the most memorable dates in Spanish and American history—1492—also marked the beginning of Spain's Golden Age. By chance, and certainly one of the worst possible times for "man's inhumanity to man," was Christopher Columbus' discovery of islands in the present Caribbean with some gold, raw materials, and "lightly defended" native peoples, as described by Columbus, to be used for slave labor if not "immediately converted to Catholicism." The three basically empty-handed voyages of Columbus to the New World were followed by Hernan Cortes' confiscation of Aztec wealth in 1519. By 1534, Francisco Pizarro's small force would confiscate the wealth of the Inca peoples. The immediate result was that Spain suddenly became Europe's wealthiest nation. The world's greatest treasure trove of wealth, however, was soon squandered on rebellions, losses to "pirates," a zealous Inquisition, internal conflicts, and the loss of the Spanish Armada.

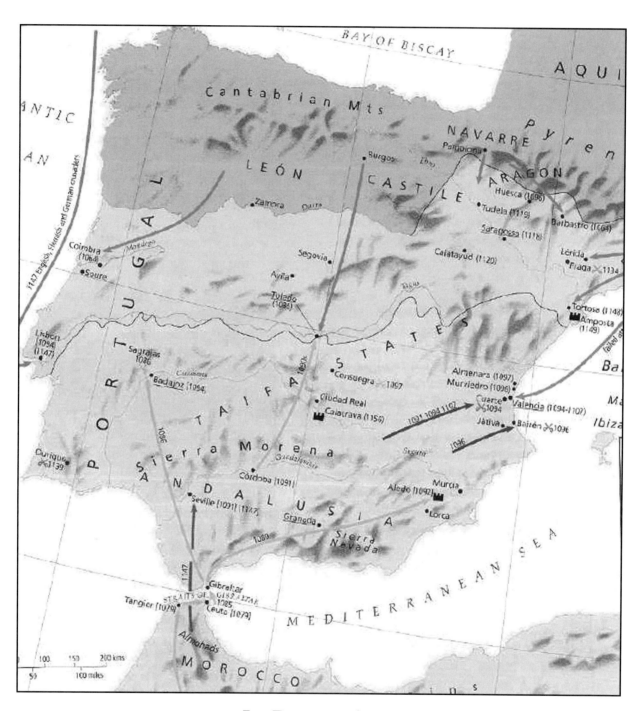

La Reconquista

Spain

Capital: Madrid

Population: Approximately 40 million

Area: Almost 195,000 square miles

Religion: Roman Catholic

Climate: Much drier than France despite exposure to Atlantic Ocean. Very hot and dry summers. Wetter in the north than in the south. Coastal areas are milder and share the ideal Mediterranean climate

Topography: A high plateau in the central regions with many mountainous areas

Surrounded by the Atlantic Ocean, Portugal, the Mediterranean Sea, and France

Summary: The earliest inhabitants are believed to be from the North Africa area and to date back as far as 35,000 B.C.E. The early Iberian people were later mixed with Phoenician traders, Greeks, Romans and others who used the Mediterranean as the highway of the ancient world. The Romans occupied Spain for approximately 600 years before being displaced by the Visigoths in 410 C.E. The Islamic Moors began their invasions of Spain in 711 C.E. and made a huge impact upon that Catholic nation for the next 800 years. The Moors were finally ousted in 1492 just as discoveries of the New World were beginning to take place. Those discoveries gave Spain the wealth to launch a vast armada of warships against England's Anglican Queen Elizabeth I in 1588. The defeat that followed was a major factor in Spain's return to relative impoverishment. In exchange for relatively high dependencies on imported oil and gas, Spain continues to emphasize its tourism industry and is making progress in technological areas as well.

17
The Battle for Aztec Gold, 1519

The history of new discoveries is often replete with ironic turns of events. The discoveries of Christopher Columbus, Vasco da Gama, and even Ferdinand Magellan, first to circumnavigate the globe, did not immediately profit Spain in major ways. Within little more than half a century (1519-1588), the impoverished nation of Spain became the world's wealthiest nation. Spain suddenly controlled an empire that spanned much of the globe. Hernan Cortes, like Francisco Pizarro a few years later, had a tremendous effect upon redistribution of the world's wealth and power in the early sixteenth century.

Christopher Columbus, who made four trips to the New World, and Governor Diego Velasquez, who was assigned to Cuba by 1511, soon learned that there were severe limits on arable land and slave labor in the New World to meet the growing demands of European consumers. New sources of land, labor, wealth, and converts to Catholicism had to be found. Pope Alexander VI set up a north-south "line of demarcation" in 1493 that granted new discoveries east of the Azores, Cape Verde Islands, and present-day Brazil to the Portuguese, and everything to the west was "given" to Spain. The purpose was to avoid war between those two countries, and preserve their loyalty to the Catholic Church at a time of Protestant revolution in much of Western Europe.

Caribbean Governor Velasquez had commissioned several expeditions to the Yucatan area between the years of 1516 and 1518. Rumors from local natives were strong that very large and very wealthy cities were to be found west of the Gulf of Mexico. In 1518 Governor Velasquez commissioned Hernan Cortes to further explore the Yucatan in search of potential converts to Catholicism and to confirm the elusive stories of great wealth to be had. A

resourceful young man, Cortes was something of a skilled adventurer and had served as Velasquez' clerk during the 1511 settlement of Cuba. He was commissioned to make a third venture to the Yucatan, but rumors started that Velasquez no longer trusted the young man to do only what he was instructed to do. Thus, before the commission could be withdrawn, Cortes rushed preparations and set sail for the Yucatan area on February 18, 1519.

He had hastily recruited about 400 assorted soldiers from the Cuban territory. His provisions included some musketry, a few small cannon, and sixteen horses. Cortes flaunted the authority of the crown by founding a city on his own that he named "Villa Rica de la Vera Cruz." He proceeded to order his small fleet destroyed to pressure the weak army he had formed to accept his authority. He rejected the commission to explore, form trade alliances, and to seek captives for either conversion or forced labor. Instead, he set out to conquer much of present-day Mexico and Guatemala in his own name. He intended to petition King Charles V that he was making a just war on heathen natives who served a godless ruler. By that time he had sufficient knowledge of the Aztec civilization to anticipate a favorable response from the king on the basis of claiming new territory in the name of Christianity and to bring great wealth to the Spanish crown.

By joining forces with small tribes who were bitter enemies of the Aztec people, Cortes and his curious ensemble were able to greatly expand their forces and knowledge of the territory enough to proceed toward the Aztec capital of Tenochtitlan. With the indispensable support of large numbers of native allies, guides and interpreters, the expedition of Cortes struggled for three months to make the arduous, 185 mile crossing from the coast. Advance notice of the peculiar intruders was received as fulfillment of an Aztec prophecy that these men must be descendants of the fair-skinned god, Quetzalcoatl, who was expected to someday return from the east. With that bit of good fortune, Cortes and his followers were positively welcomed by the Aztecs and their emperor, Montezuma II. The Spaniards were treated with great respect and presented with many gifts. In a short time, however, relations between the two groups disintegrated rapidly. Following his own personal agenda, Cortes seized Montezuma and held him for a ransom suitable for a powerful emperor. The incredulous Aztec court began to collect the demanded objects of gold.

Cortes had to face the wrath of a very disgruntled Governor Velasquez, who had sent out an expedition to bring the rebellious captain back under his control. Cortes was successful in neutralizing the Spanish soldiers sent against him and returned to Tenochtitlan. There, he discovered that his own unruly soldiers had killed many Aztecs during a religious ceremony and had provoked a massive uprising against Cortes' people.

Cortes played his best high card by displaying the captured Montezuma to a large crowd of the incensed populace. In the commotion that followed, a rock was hurled and struck the emperor's head. Within three days the emperor was dead. The only option remaining to the Aztecs was to make a hasty retreat in which heavy losses were sustained. Cortes and his survivors reached the safety of Tlaxcalan villages. He aggressively sought to reorganize the remnants of his following and large numbers of native allies to return to Tenochtitlan and besiege the temple-rich city in 1521. The Spaniards and their allies were successful in blocking food and fresh water from getting into the city. Finally, and unexpectedly, a smallpox epidemic weakened or killed about 100,000 of the city's defenders. Cortes and his allies were able to force their way into the city of Tenochtitlan which surely felt the gods had betrayed them. The victorious Spaniards torched the city and further stripped it of its wealth and glory. The gold and other forms of wealth, and new territories placed in the name of the Spanish crown were sufficient for Cortes to vindicate his name before the Spanish crown and Governor Velasquez. By 1540, Mexico City would start to be erected upon the ruins of Tenochtitlan. The defeat of the one-hundred-year-old confederation of the Aztec people marked their almost immediate cultural demise and tremendous windfalls of wealth and power for a small, impoverished country on the Hispanic isthmus of Western Europe.

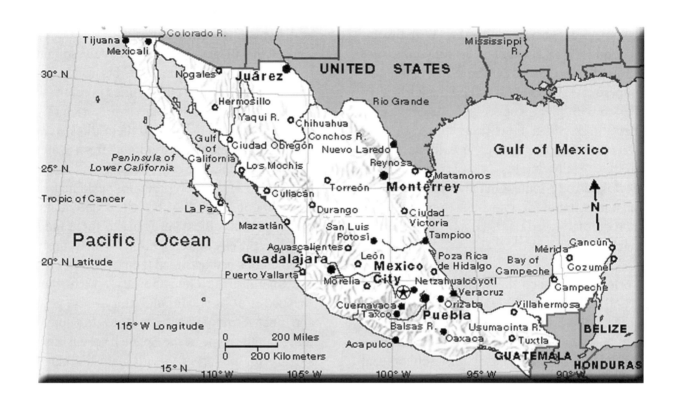

Mexico

Capital: Mexico City

Population: Approximately 100 million

Area: About 756,000 square miles

Religion: Predominantly Roman Catholic

Climate: Subtropical and from ideal coastal to hot and dry deserts to high mountains

Topography: Extensive areas of high desert and rugged mountains. Subtropical coastal areas

Surrounded by the United States, Gulf of Mexico, Caribbean, Guatemala, & Belize

Summary: A land of diverse Native American tribes that were typically small in numbers due to the relatively harsh physical environment except for the confederation of the Aztecs, Olmecs, and other Pre-Columbian tribes. First discovered by Spaniards in the early 1500's. It was Hernan Cortes' small band of adventurers and alliances with tribes hostile to the Aztecs that defeated that affluent empire in the year 1519 following a smallpox epidemic that killed approximately 100,000 of the Aztec people. Mexico is one of those rare countries that has not had major military designs on other countries. Following centuries of occupation by Spain, the country was briefly governed by France and later lost much of its original territory in conflicts with the United States. Under the current leadership of President Vincente Fox there have been many positive reforms that are helping to build the economy of that nation. Major investments are being made in tourism, manufacturing, and agricultural pursuits.

18
Inca Empire Destruction in Seven Years (1532-39)

The collision of the Inca Empire with a band of Spanish adventurers in the 1530's could not have occurred at a worst time for the people of the high Andes. The Inca people at the time of contact with Spaniards were in the early phase of a civil war. The Inca Empire extended approximately 2,000 miles from the northern borders of present-day Ecuador, and included most of Peru and much of present-day Chile on the South American continent.

The term "Inca" referred to the very highest social classes, but the word evolved to represent the principal group of Andean mountain people who ruled a highly civilized empire with absolute authority for many centuries. The principal language spoken was Quechua, but many other languages were also spoken as the Incas captured or absorbed more and more surrounding tribal groups.

The Inca, as the Spaniards thought of them, were highly advanced for the time in medicine, astronomy, and high-elevation construction. The government was a totally rigid theocracy with nearly every decision emanating from the Inca emperor, who was considered a direct descendant of the immortal sun god. The Inca's pedigree was monitored carefully and he was groomed to be the head of the priesthood, the military, and the ultimate authority regarding all taxes and all laws.

It was an extraordinary accident of history that Inca society was in a state of civil war at the time of discovery by the Spaniards. What had been a very cohesive and powerful empire was especially vulnerable following the death of Emperor Huayana Capac from smallpox. Upon his deathbed he divided his empire between his two sons, Atahualpa and Huascar. The political situation was ripe to be exploited by the small band of Spanish conquistadors. With a band of 168 men, about 12 musket fire-arms (harquebuses), a few small cannon, about 27 horses, and support of rival tribes, Francisco Pizarro forever altered many centuries of Inca culture and history.

Francisco Pizarro was the illegitimate son of an infantry captain. He was basically an illiterate in a rigid class-conscious society. One of his alternatives to change his life circumstances was to become a maritime adventurer, and he did. He sailed to the New World in November, 1509, and was actually a part of the discoveries of present-day Venezuela and Colombia. He was also with Vasco Nunez de Balboa in battles with various natives of the region (some using poison-tipped arrows) and a part of the first European crossing of Central America's (Panama) isthmus and the discovery of the Mar del Sur (Pacific Ocean). By 1515 Pizarro was a part of other expeditions to seek gold and anything of value from the natives along the Pacific coast.

By 1522 he became aware of the astounding success of Hernan Cortes in conquering the Aztecs of Mexico with a very small force of his own. In 1524 Pizarro created a partnership with Hernando de Luque (a Spanish priest), Diego de Almagro, and Gaspar de Espinoza to raise money for explorations south of present-day Panama. The rights to explore these new regions had to be obtained as well. Usually, this was in the form of a share of profits from the expedition, if any. Some gold was returned to compensate the main sponsor, territorial governor Pedrarias, but overall, the expedition was only minimally successful.

A new territorial governor, D. Pedro de los Rios, agreed to help sponsor a second expedition, which was launched on March 10, 1528. The partners purchased two ships. Together, Pizarro and Almagro set sail for the San Juan River (Colombia). That was the furthest point

Almagro had reached on the previous voyage. The experience was a near disaster. Sponsorship was cancelled when poor results were reported. Pizarro, however, refused to return. He proceeded southward to the northern part of present-day Peru and founded the city of Trujillo on its coast. His orders to his men were strictly to befriend the natives encountered and to learn enough of their language to create interpreters and gather information about gold. He remained there approximately 18 months.

Pizarro returned to Panama with dramatic stories of gold treasure and a goodly amount of actual gold, but it was not enough for the territorial governor to sponsor another expedition. The alternative, as encouraged by his partners, was for Pizarro to return to Spain and obtain the sponsorship of King Charles V. The king was ultimately convinced of the expedition's merits and signed a formal charter on June 26, 1529. Pizarro now had the authority and sponsorship to set sail from Spain on January 18, 1530, with approximately 250 soldiers who included his brothers Hernando, Juan, and Gonzalo.

Pizarro returned to Panama and with great effort was able to reenlist his two former partners, Almagro and Luque. One of the issues was that the partners were barely mentioned in Pizarro's new charter from the king. By the following January, 1531, Pizarro was able to depart from Panama with three ships, 180 men, and 27 cavaliers.
He made camp at the mouth of the Santiago River and sent back three ships for more reinforcements. Limited exploration of that area was unproductive and resulted in an attack by hostile natives. Weathering the attacks, they were met many months later by two returning ships from Panama that increased their expedition forces by roughly 100 men and a small number of horses that were commanded by Hernando de Soto.

With the additional men and supplies, Pizarro was able to proceed further south. In 1532 the Spaniards reached Tumbes and from there ascended the Andes and by November, 1532, they reached the Inca city of Cajamaraca. Intelligence gathered from rival natives in earlier voyages was sufficient to set one of history's greatest ambushes in place. The technologically superior Spaniards were initially viewed as very powerful, almost godlike forces that might intervene on one side or the other of the Inca's civil war. The invitation was made to meet with Atahualpa in an act of friendship. The meeting was a pre-planned betrayal. The great Inca was abruptly held as a captive and a ransom demanded for his release. The ransom was to be a room measuring 17' by 22' filled to the 8' ceiling with gold. The stunned followers of the great Inca complied with the demands of the Spaniards.

Atahualpa, however, was strangled on June 24, 1534, for showing apparent disrespect for the invader's religion. In a classic error of translation from one radically different culture to another, the great Inca had been led to believe he could "hear" the word of God in the bible presented to him. Atahualpa held the book to his ear and, hearing nothing, threw it to the ground. The act of sacrilege, at the height of the Spanish Inquisition, was such that the great Inca was given the choice of being burned alive, or of being strangled to death. He chose the latter. Without one of the two god-like leaders, the disintegration of a complex empire in the midst of civil war was thus well under way.

The conquest of the Peruvian area was virtually complete with the capture of the Inca capital of Cuzco. Pizarro took steps to consolidate his improbable conquest by founding new settlements, especially near the present capital of Lima. Spoils were crudely divided as they had been done in the past. Efforts by Pedro de Alvarado to claim the city of Quito were interrupted by Sebastian de Benalcazar and Diego de Almagro. Pizarro in exchange offered Almagro the opportunity to seize Chile for himself. When that promise failed to materialize, Almagro attempted to seize Cuzco. In the process, Pizarro sent his half-brother, Hernando Pizarro, to Cuzco. In the resulting battle Almagro was defeated and put to death. By 1539, Pizarro had appointed his brother, Gonzalo Pizarro, as governor of Quito. The cunning, deceits, and atrocities of those early years were extreme even for greed-driven conquistadors. A rival faction from Almagro's followers surprised Pizarro at a dinner. He was overpowered and killed.

The confiscated wealth of the Aztecs and the Incas suddenly poured into war-torn Spain like a raging torrent of liquid wealth. At the height of the Spanish Inquisition there was the distinct impression of divine intervention that heathen wealth could be used to restore Catholicism in Western Europe. The Spanish monarchy in particular felt an obligation to stem the Protestant revolution. However, most of that astonishing wealth was soon lost to bad management, military and civil conflicts, and especially due to the defeat of the Spanish Armada (1588). The formerly isolated world of the Americas was suddenly and drastically changed forever.

Machu Picchu

69

South America

19
The Naval Battle of Lepanto, 1571

Located a few miles east of the Little Dardanelles, the harbor of Lepanto forms the narrows that closes the Gulf of Corinth. It was also the site of one of the most decisive naval battles in history. The area, off the western coast of present-day Turkey, has steep cliffs overlooking the harbor and a long history from ancient times as a major trading port on the Ionian Sea. It was controlled by the Athenians around 450 B.C.E. At issue in 1571 was the potential for the Ottoman Empire to control the Mediterranean and to perhaps spread Islam to the remainder of Europe. A powerful myth had been in place for centuries that the Ottomans could not be defeated. The Battle of Lepanto ended that myth.

Lepanto was purchased by Venice in 1407. The region was occupied by the Turks in 1498. It was the spreading power and influence of the Islamic Ottoman Empire that was of concern to the Vatican in particular. The Protestant Reformation had placed great strains upon the Catholic Church and had helped to inspire the Inquisition to help preserve the Catholic faith. It was a time for extreme actions, not just words. "New worlds" and the potential for new converts to Christianity had only recently been opened up. The Vatican's great fear as the end of the sixteenth century neared was the potential that the Ottoman Empire might take over the Mediterranean Sea as their personal lake. To prevent that from happening, St. Pius V, a Dominican pope (1504-1572), was instrumental in persuading major city-states of Italy (Venice, Genoa, Papal State, Savoy-Piedmont), Spain, and elements of France and Poland to build and arm a Christian fleet that could stop the Ottoman Turks. The result was a fleet of over 200 vessels and up to 80,000 combatants including sailors and oarsmen.

The commander selected to lead this fleet of 200-plus vessels was 26 year old, Don John of Austria (1547-1578). He was the illegitimate son of the Holy Roman Emperor, Charles V (1488-1576), who was in part famed for his "Hapsburg jaw." Don John was also the half-brother of King Philip II of Spain. He was raised in Spain, well educated, given a title by his half-brother, and encouraged to choose a military career. He successfully fought against Moorish pirates in 1568. Later, he headed Spanish forces against Morisco rebels in Grenada. Philip II appointed Don John to be the Spanish admiral/general of the Holy League navy. The fleet was being assembled at the port of Messina, Sicily. Admiral Don John was a choice that Pope Pius V would not regret.

Sultan Selim II's Ottoman (Turkish) fleet at the Gulf of Lepanto was under the command of Uluc Ali Pasha. His sail and oar-powered fleet was comparable to that assembled by the Christian Holy League. Uluc, however, seriously underestimated the strength of Don John's fleet. The Turks were both outmaneuvered and out-gunned (1800 guns to Uluc's 750 guns). In the broader world view, the Ottoman Empire had actually started a period of decline with the death of Sulayman the Magnificent (1494-1566). The decisive loss at the Battle of Lepanto further accelerated that decline on both land and sea. The Turkish fleet was rebuilt the following year but was no longer a major threat in the western Mediterranean. The psychological edge of fear was no longer the same.

For more than one month the Turkish Armada had been anchored inside the fortified harbor of Lepanto. Upon word of the approach of the Christian fleet, Uluc began to move his fleet westward and into the Gulf of Patras. On October 7, 1571, the two roughly comparable fleets met near Patrasso. The Ottoman (Turkish) fleet was just enough outside the vicinity of Lepanto that they could not take advantage of defensive artillery pieces at the fortress. The major distinction between the two fleets was that the Turks had underestimated the strength of the Christian fleet. The superior firepower of the Christian fleet soon resulted in the sinking of 17 ships and capture of approximately 117 of the 208 Turkish vessels. The Turkish galleys that were not burned, sunk, or grounded ashore were boarded and captured in ferocious, hand-to-hand fighting. Also, there was the capture of Turkish artillery and stores. About 15,000 galley slaves (mostly Christians) were rescued. A majority of the Turkish combatants were killed or severely injured. From 5,000 to 15,000 Turkish combatants were captured. Most were executed. Both fleets had been reduced by about one-half, but the Christians had captured far more of everything. The Christian crusaders lost 17 galleys and about 8,000 combatants. Uluc Ali Pasha narrowly avoided total defeat by escaping with between 40 to 50 galleys.

This battle is considered the biggest sea battle between sail and oar navies since early Roman times. With 208 ships plus 66 other vessels, the Turks had allowed themselves to become bottled up toward the harbor of Lepanto in such a way that there was little room for maneuver. The intense fighting was in part decided by the Christian fleet's greater firepower and the Spanish swordsmen. A massive and largely symbolic naval battle between the forces of Christendom and Islam began in the morning and was ended by 4 p.m. of the same day. The worlds of both religion and politics were forever changed. Miguel de Cervantes (1547-1616), who would later become world famous as the author of *Don Quixote de la Mancha,* described the Battle of Lepanto as "…the most important event in centuries." He was an actual combatant and his left hand was severely injured during that battle.

News of the dramatic victory reached Venice first and from there was communicated throughout a grateful Catholic world. A tremendous veil of fear was suddenly lifted. It was said that Pope Pius V had a vision of the battle and its victorious outcome as it was occurring. Upon confirmation it was said he fell to his knees in tears and exclaimed that his life's work was complete. Pope Pius V, who had earlier excommunicated Queen Elizabeth I, died several months after the Battle of Lepanto. The event resulted in the production of hundreds of songs, poems, and works of art throughout Western Europe to commemorate the great victory. It was the first great defeat of the Muslim navy. The Roman Catholic Church had one of its greatest historical moments. The Mediterranean was no longer threatened with becoming a Muslim lake. In few places has the word "Lepanto" remained a household word. However, the results of that one-day naval battle have endured for more than four centuries.

Battle of Lapanto courtesy of US Naval Institute

Turkey

Capital: Ankara
Population: Over 73 million
Area: Over 297,000 square miles
Religion: Muslim
Climate: Mediterranean coastal areas with dry mountainous interior that is hot in summer and cold in winter
Topography: A very mountainous area with elevations up to 9,900 feet. A distinct crossroad of the ancient and modern world and gateway between east and west.
Surrounded by Mediterranean Sea, Aegean Sea, Greece, Bulgaria, the Black Sea, Georgia, Armenia, Iran, Iraq, and Syria
Summary: A region of spectacular mountains, warm coastlines, and archeological sites dating back to the earliest civilizations. Important during the Bronze Age for its mineral deposits and crossroads location (cf. Troy, Silk Road, link to east-west). The Turks conquered Asia Minor in 1390 and remained the center of a Mideast empire for many centuries. Turkey was founded in 1923 following World War I and the collapse of the Ottoman Empire. In earlier times the region had been the seat of the eastern Roman Empire that came to be known as the Byzantine Empire. Along with the change in name from Constantinople to Istanbul in 1931 has been a major change in religious focus from Eastern Orthodox to Muslim. Due to history and warm sunny beaches, tourism is now a major growth industry in Turkey due to many millenniums of history and warm, sunny beaches.

20
The Spanish Armada, 1588

Phillip II, King of Spain (1527-1598) was an extraordinary monarch in many respects. His long reign included many of the richest exploits from the colonies in the Americas. The stunning wealth moved Spain from a mostly impoverished nation to one of the wealthiest and most powerful nations in the world at that time. Instead of using that wealth and power to contribute to royal decadence, Phillip was determined to use it to restore Catholicism to its once exalted position in Europe. He was especially determined to reverse a Protestant revolution that had been in part expanded by Henry VIII (1509-1547) of England. Phillip II gave meticulous attention to the details of state. His typically understated style of dress was so ordinary that international visitors often mistook him for a staff member of the king, not the king. His consuming determination was to launch a huge fleet of soldiers against England to replace the Protestant queen, Elizabeth I, with a Catholic monarch, not to control England.

Early news that Phillip II had commissioned the construction of a huge invasion fleet reached Queen Elizabeth I (1558-1603). The fleet was being constructed in the port of Cadiz, Spain. In response, bold and forward-thinking Queen Elizabeth commissioned privateer Sir Francis Drake to destroy the unfinished fleet while still in the harbor. Drake successfully destroyed many of the unfinished Armada ships by drifting incendiary ships into the harbor with winds and tides in his favor. The setback did not reduce Phillip's determination to invade formerly Catholic England. He simply used his immeasurable wealth to continue the construction of his armada of ships. The huge loss of supplies, however, severely haunted the rebuilt armada. A shortage of good barrels severely limited Spain's ability to preserve sufficient food and water for such a long voyage.

The Spanish Armada set sail from Lisbon in May, 1588. On board approximately 130 warships there were 7,000 sailors and 19,000 soldiers. The assault plan on paper included coordination with the Duke of Parma's 27,000 troops located within the Spanish Netherlands. The size of the armada and good weather from the west all favored the Spanish fleet. The invasion plan was not well coordinated with the Duke of Parma. The next major failure was adhering to King Phillip's meticulous master plan and not striking the English while low tides held them in the Portsmouth harbor.

The English, though greatly outnumbered, were not without their own resources. Elizabeth's forces had twenty years of experience in provoking Spain. There was the execution of Catholic Mary, Queen of Scots, following her abortive efforts to marry Phillip II and restore Britain to Catholicism. Elizabeth had no standing army. The Spaniards had two, but England's defense was its Royal Navy. Ship design was being radically altered in the time of Elizabeth's reign from top to bottom. Warships were typically smaller than their Spanish counterparts but were more streamlined, more race-built, and had improved rigging designs. English cannon were built for longer range, but had limited impact upon the heavy ships of the armada.

In legend, at least, Admiral Drake took the time to complete a game of bowls before launching his fleet from the Portsmouth harbor. Escaping a possible trap due to Spanish inaction, Drake was able to get upwind of the enemy. There he was in a position to attack, or not. The Spanish fleet immediately went into the defensive with a crescent formation. The expectation was that close-range fighting would follow and the English would be completely outnumbered. The English, however, had heavier gun batteries on their smaller ships and wanted a long-range assault.

The English Coberon cannon ("the snake") was advanced gunnery for its day, but sixteenth-century gunnery was still an obscure art. A replica has been demonstrated to be accurate at approximately 600 yards at zero elevation and to travel at 400 meters per second, or faster than the speed of sound. At a time when math and scientific methods were at real low points, it required an aggressive barrage of accurate and consistent fire to sink a large warship.

Before going into battle, the Duke of Parma and his troops had to be picked up in Flanders. Medina Sedona, a reluctant fleet commander, soon discovered that there was no suitable port. Therefore they turned into the open seas with the Duke as the weather turned against them. Strong tidal flows worked against the Spanish. The English, ever quick to exploit an ad-

The British meet the Spanish Armada

vantage, sailed five flaming ships into the Spanish fleet. The English moved in close where it was expected that they would be at a great disadvantage. The English were able to get off cannon fire much more rapidly than the Spaniards, but lacked the right munitions to sink Spanish ships. By closing to within 50 meters the English were more likely to miss than to make effective hits. The English nearly

ran out of ammunition and their "superior cannon" did not work as well as expected. The Spanish were not defeated and remained both intact and a formidable force.

Admiral Sedona, still intent on carrying out his plan, now blew out to sea. His intent was to escape to the North Sea, sail westward, and then return safely to Spain. The intent was to make a large counterclockwise swing into the Atlantic and then to sail southward. The problem came in not understanding the strength of the North Atlantic Gulf Stream, which is still a powerful force on sailing ships that far north. The result was that navigational calculations were off by a significant amount and at least 3,000 men crashed upon the rocky western shores of Ireland. Admiral Sedona executed one captain for not following his strict navigational orders. The reality was that one third of the Spanish fleet was shipwrecked on the Irish coast. Bad weather continued to block the southward progress of the remaining Spanish fleet. Spanish ships, being larger and more cumbersome, typically did not sail well against the wind. Crews were severely battered, weakened by injuries, and ultimately starving. Many could no longer fight off being pounded by storms, being lost, and were no longer sea worthy due to battle damage. As a result about 50% of Spain's great armada never returned. Phillip II had exhausted his New World wealth and was to die a miserable and impoverished death. Queen Elizabeth had placed her faith in God, Sir Francis Drake, and the Royal Navy commander, High Admiral Lord Howard of Effingham. Phillip's failure was a tremendous boost for the Protestant revolution and Britain's emergence as a great, international sea power, and disseminator of British culture and language.

King Philip II

21
Peter the Great's Defeat of Sweden, 1709

Peter the Great (1689-1725) co-inherited one of the largest, most pastural, feudal, and down-trodden empires of all times. He was born May 30, 1672, into the reigning family of Alexis Romanov (1629-1676) and Natalia Naryshkina. To protect the boy from assassi-nation, Peter's youth was mostly insulated from the grinding poverty and ethnic strife that marked much of still-feudal Russia. He was raised at a country estate outside of Moscow. He managed to escape the classical education of most European heirs to a throne by force-fully indulging his three great passions. These were war games, sailing, and all things West-ern. From staff and others who could be drafted, young Peter formed two opposing regi-ments that he could drill and actually use to play war games. His sailing was done in an old recreational English sailboat and most im-portantly, he exposed himself to everything about modern Western Europe that he could absorb. His indulgent and "driven" life was traumatized by the death of his thirty-one year old father on January 29, 1676.

The premature, royal vacancy produced an in-tense power struggle between the family of the czar's first wife (the Miloslavskaias) and Peter's maternal family (the Naryshkinas). Ultimately, a partial solution was attained by installing Peter's half brother, Feodor III, on the throne from 1676 to 1682. The agreed upon plan was that Peter and his other half brother, Ivan V, would be designated as co-czars once they reached the age of maturity. It was Ivan's sister, Czarina Sofia Miloslavskaias, who was the actual holder of power until she was over-thrown in 1689. It was believed that she had twice tried to murder her brother's rival, Peter. She was exiled to Siberia and forcibly confined to a nunnery for the remainder of her life.

Peter began his reign of sharing power with his physically and mentally weak half brother,

Ivan V, in 1689. By that time, Peter had ac-quired the extraordinary height of six feet and seven inches. He had a very progressive ori-entation about the potential for his grossly un-derdeveloped country and almost unlimited ambition to do something about it. In 1695, Peter disguised himself as a Russian diplo-mat and traveled throughout Western Europe to learn all he could about bringing his own country into the modern world. After several years of getting information for himself in-stead of depending on subordinates, he took on the full responsibilities of being the czar in 1698 with a vengeance. He pushed for re-forms, including dress codes that discouraged wearing long robes and of wearing beards. He initiated a number of military campaigns, and did all within his power to push a reluctant country into a new role as a leading European power. He modified the Russian calendar to match the one in use throughout most of con-temporary Europe. He increased the Russian military from 30,000 men in 1695 to almost 300,000 by 1725. He also created the Rus-sian navy and pushed for additional outlets to warmer year-round harbors. He began mass conscriptions of young nobles as well as men of the lowest social classes. He moved the capital to St. Petersburg and made many re-forms within the government. Among the re-forms were major increases in taxes to sup-port these ongoing new ventures. He brought in Western advisors to train people and to in-troduce new technologies and industries.

His military venture to acquire seaports on the Black Sea in 1697 was the first time Czar Pe-ter put his newly formed army against a for-eign power. In desperation for a warm water seaport, his army seized the Black Sea port of Taganrog and the town of Azov on the Don River. It was the first time in centuries that a Russian army had struck outside of its borders and was intended to also demonstrate a level of equality with the current monarchs in Europe. The czar's detailed planning, ample artillery, and the fading glory of the Ottoman Turks and (Turkish) Tartars of the Crimea combined to produce Peter's first great victory.

Peter the Great

The most significant expansion of Russian lands came from the defeat of Sweden following 20 years of battle known as the Great Northern War (1699-1721). The battles lasted throughout much of Peter's reign. It was Peter who initially declared war on Sweden based on Swedish conquests of the Baltic States at least fifty years earlier. There was also a thread of animosity that could be traced back to the Scandinavian Viking raids into Russia many centuries before, but not forgotten.

At the beginning of the Great Northern War, Sweden was a major military power in Eastern Europe. The leadership of their young king, Charles XII of Sweden, was often considered brilliant and a huge challenge to the determination of Peter the Great. The exhausted Russian army at the beginning of the war, however, was not well prepared to take on the very seasoned Swedish forces. The Battle of Narva on the Baltic coast in 1700 was a disastrous defeat for the young czar. But it did give him time to prepare for later offensives and to begin the construction of a Russian navy. Russia had no ships on the Baltic when the war commenced. Sweden, on the other hand, had 39 ships-of-the-line and large numbers of cannon.

King Charles' confidence was extremely high after his decisive victory at Narva. He launched an offensive into Poland against Peter's ally, King Augustus II. That battle raged for eight years and resulted in Augustus being deposed by the Swedish forces. The Swedish king was not so successful in trying to control and destroy Russia's only Baltic port of Arkhangelsk in 1701. A Swedish fleet of seven warships under Commodore Karl Lewe relied on captured Russian river guides to lead their ships into position. Two of the Swedish ships became grounded in tricky shoals and were forced to evacuate under fire.

In 1702 elements of the newly formed Russian fleet under Czar Peter in disguise and Lt. Alexander Menshikov scored victories against difficult odds and captured Lake Ladoga and fortresses at Oreshek and Kanzi as well as several Swedish fighting ships. Peter then proceeded to relocate his new "Western" capital to St. Petersburg in 1703. The Russian navy, being constructed near the mouth of the Neva River, continued to be mostly successful against the superior Swedish navy throughout the war. Narva was retaken by the Russians in 1704, and Swedish attempts to take St. Petersburg from the sea were repelled.

Charles was focusing on an assault through the Ukraine and into Moscow (1708/1709) to depose of Czar Peter. The Swedish king had allied himself with Cossacks but feigned retreats deep into the steppes and burned fields left the Swedish army to face the crushing wrath of the Russian winter. Charles was forced to turn southward where they lost a decisive battle at Poltava on June 27, 1709. Peter's engineers had prepared the battlefield for weeks in advance to force the Swedish army into smaller units and crush them. The wounded Swedish king had no alternative except to escape to Turkey.

Unwisely, Peter followed up his southern Ukraine victory with an assault upon the Ottomans in 1711. That confrontation led to a Russian defeat and forced the return of Black Sea ports that had been seized in 1697. The Ottoman Sultan did not take further advantage and refused to be aligned with Charles XII as requested. The Swedish king was soon expelled from the Ottoman Empire in 1714, but he was not finished.

The czar's northern armies recaptured much of northern Latvia and southern Estonia and actually pushed the Swedes back to Finland. Still, the Swedish king would not surrender. It was not until a battle in 1718 and the king's death that a peace agreement could be initiated. By 1721 the Treaty of Nystad ended the Great Northern War and restored much of the Baltic coast to Russia.

The czar preserved his new capital, opened seaports and feudal Russian minds to the West and in late 1721 was granted the title of Emperor. By 1724 his second wife, Catherine, once a Livonian peasant-girl, was crowned as Empress. At Czar Peter's death, or possible murder in 1725, of "an intestinal disorder," Catherine succeeded him as Czarina Catherine I of Russia and lived for only two more years. As a result of Peter the Great's determined efforts, an impoverished, feudal conglomeration of regions was transformed into a European power of depth and substance.

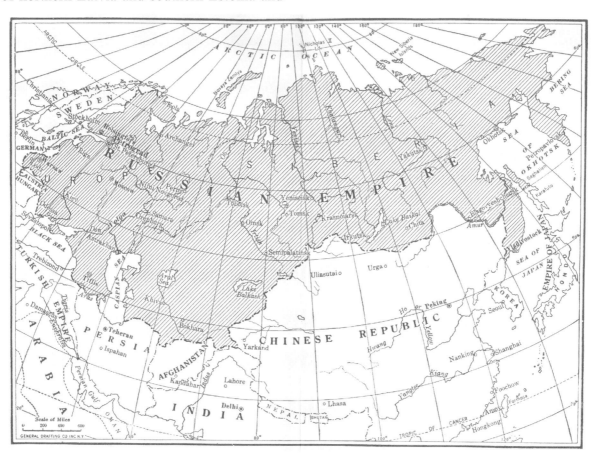

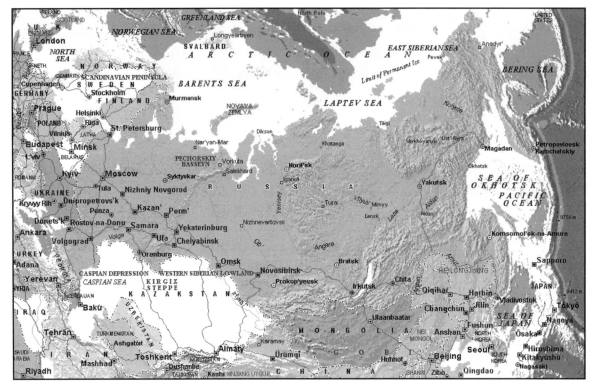

Russia

Capital: Moscow (Russian Federation, 1991)

Population: Almost 145 million

Area: Approximately 6.6 million square miles

Religion: Russian Orthodox, Muslim, Jewish, Protestant, Roman Catholic, other

Climate: Typically very cold continental weather that ranges from some of the lowest temperatures in the world to warm summers in the lowland area toward the south.

Topography: Russia is by far the world's largest country and varies greatly from to vast steppes and plains suitable for short season agriculture and extensive mountain ranges

Surrounded by Finland, Arctic Ocean, Bering Sea, Sea of Okhotsk, Sea of Japan, China, Mongolia, Kazakhstan, Caspian Sea, Azerbaijan, Black Sea, Ukraine, Belarus, Latvia, Estonia, Gulf of Finland, and Finland.

Summary: The former Soviet Union was approximately 8.7 million square miles in area or roughly one-third larger than the present Russian Federation. The population figures are reduced by close to one-half. The biggest single difference is that the intimidation of the Cold War mentality that followed World War II is mostly dissipated. As early as 862 C.E. the Viking Rus tribe gained control of large areas of northern Russia. The Eurasian city of Moscow was originally founded in 1147 and became a capital of the region about 1340. The relatively isolated Russian people began to expand into Siberia about 1604 and had established settlements on the coast of Siberia by 1637 and later into the territory of Alaska. Following the violent overthrow of Czar Nicholas II the Bolshevik Revolution of 1917, the Russians, led by Vladimir Lenin, withdrew from the Europe's Great War in 1918. By 1922 the U.S.S.R. was formed and a series of absolute dictatorships moved that huge nation into a closed and militaristic society. The financial collapse that was projected by President Reagan's Star Wars defense in the mid 1980's finally ended the impossible arms race that threatened to destroy the earth many times over. In many respects the Russian Federation is now an open society that encourages tourism, a shared space station, and competition more often seen in the Olympic sports arena.

22
The Battle of Yorktown, August-October, 1781

In the fall of 1781, American colonial forces were facing bankruptcy and defeat at all levels. Few victories had been attained, and resounding losses to the British at Savannah and Charleston in the southern colonies were further evidence that a push by General Cornwallis in the south and commanding General Clinton in the north would soon put an end to the colonial rebellion. The British, of course, were counting on the assistance of the British navy. Cornwallis and his 8,000 British regulars allowed themselves to become trapped near Yorktown when they lost the support of British naval forces. The surprise surrender was a truly incredible moment and a decisive factor in bringing about the end of the American Revolution.

The victory at Yorktown was an allied effort that owes much of its success to naval and army land assistance given by France at critical moments. Substantial amounts of credit can also be given to the strength of character and tenacity of the commanding general from the beginning, George Washington. He was tough-minded and persistent and he served the cause of independence for many years before taking a leave of absence. At 6'3" he was distinctly "larger than life" in many respects. He was a great horseman, a hero of the French and Indian Wars, and a very wealthy man of honor. General George Washington consistently inspired trust and dedication in holding together an often ragtag fighting force. His "militia" was made up mostly of colonial citizens with mixed loyalties, shifting obligations, and little financial support. Prior to his crossing of the Delaware his army was typically on the defensive and suffered many losses. Washington utilized great instincts for survival and exploited the vastness of the American colonies against a far more rigid, professional army that was accustomed to huge-scale battles in very confined areas of European battlefields.

By 1781 the British were holding all of New Jersey, New York City, and key cities in the South such as Savannah, Georgia and Charlestown, North Carolina. The British had also contracted with a total of almost 17,000 mercenary Hessian soldiers from small provinces in Germany to assist in suppressing the rebellion. The colony of Virginia was almost defenseless under such outside pressure. British General Cornwallis sought to take the offensive initiative after his victories in the South by relocating his forces along the York River between the small towns of York and Gloucester on August 1 and 2, 1781. He intended to break the stalemate in the rural areas of the Carolinas. Little notice, however, was taken of the defensive weaknesses of the Yorktown area because Cornwallis fully expected to be backed up by British naval forces who controlled all of the Chesapeake Bay and the York River at that time. The weaknesses of the site first became apparent with the arrival of French Admiral de Grasse's fleet of 28 warships at the mouth of Chesapeake Bay. The elements of an impending siege were rapidly becoming apparent to the British commander of the southern forces. A dispatch from Cornwallis to Clinton acknowledging the arrival of the French fleet did not get to the senior commander for at least five days. The quickest communication at the time was by horseback with a dedicated rider.

General Washington and his French ally, General Rochambeau, had advance knowledge of the French fleet's intended movements and eagerly awaited confirmation that the fleet was in position to block Cornwallis' forces and the British fleet. By September 2, 1781, Washington's forces marched through Philadelphia and increased their numbers along the way by roughly 700 men for a total of about 2,000 troops. On the same date, Saint-Simon landed troops that had been brought from the West Indies by Admiral de Grasse. French troops marched through Philadelphia on September 3 and 4 to join up with the American troops. By September 5, Washington received confirmation that de Grasse was at the Chesapeake with 28 French warships. Unknown to Washington, on the same date, the British fleet under Admiral Thomas Graves arrived at the mouth of the Chesapeake with 19 warships. de Grasse set out to sea and engaged Graves' fleet (known as the Second Battle of the Capes). The naval maneuvers with Graves became a stalemate and de Grasse returned to the Chesapeake. It would be September 12 before de Grasse again put out to sea to engage the British fleet.

By September 14 the armies of Washington and Rochambeau reached Williamsburg, Virginia, and joined with Lafayette's forces. On that date the allied forces learned of de Grasse's naval successes and that the British fleet had withdrawn and was no longer a factor in providing Cornwallis with support. de Grasse was thus able to use smaller ships to assist in transporting French and American troops from Annapolis to the Williamsburg area (14 miles west of Yorktown). By September 22 the noose around Cornwallis' forces of approximately 8,000 troops was clearly tightening.

A British attempt to break out from the French blockade failed. A total force of approximately 16,000 French and American troops were concentrated in the Williamsburg area by September 26. By September 30 the allied forces against the British were firmly in siege positions and outnumbering "the defenders" by at least two to one. British attempts to break out at Gloucester on October 3 failed. Artillery bombardments from the French Grand Battery and American artillery pieces began on October 9. Trench works were moved to within 300 yards of British defenses by October 12. Two days later British earthen defenses (redoubts #9 and #10) were assaulted and seized. On October 16 the British launched a morning attack and temporarily seized two French bat-

teries. Cornwallis' desperate attempt to ferry his troops across the York River to Gloucester Point was severely disrupted by a sudden storm. The following day British drummers tapped out the request for a parley. On October 19, 1781, Cornwallis surrendered.

It would be September 3, 1783, before a final peace treaty was signed between the British and the Americans. The Paris Peace Treaty granted the American colonies their independence. At the moment of surrender, however, Cornwallis was so shattered to be defeated by a rabble army that he feigned illness and instructed his second in command, General O'Hara, to offer the sword of surrender to the allied forces. Washington, not to be outdone, stunned the British even further by instructing his second in command, General Benjamin Lincoln, to accept the sword of surrender. Eighteenth century codes of conduct, morality, and social stratification tended to be quite rigid for privileged Europeans and those who aspired to a life of privilege. Effete values as well as technological innovations were especially slow to change during that time. It was not uncommon for British soldiers to show their contempt for the surrender and the apparent lack of protocol with the American victors.

The victory at Yorktown was one of the most critical battles of America's long fight for independence. Total casualties were miniscule compared to the American Civil War that would follow in three generations. The British soon entered into trade agreements with the United States and benefited from exchanges without the cost of supporting such a large and antagonistic colony. The American victory was very much due to the direct intervention of the French military. Ironically for the French monarchy, the cost of financial and military assistance that made the American victory possible was a major contributory factor for the French Revolution beginning in 1789.

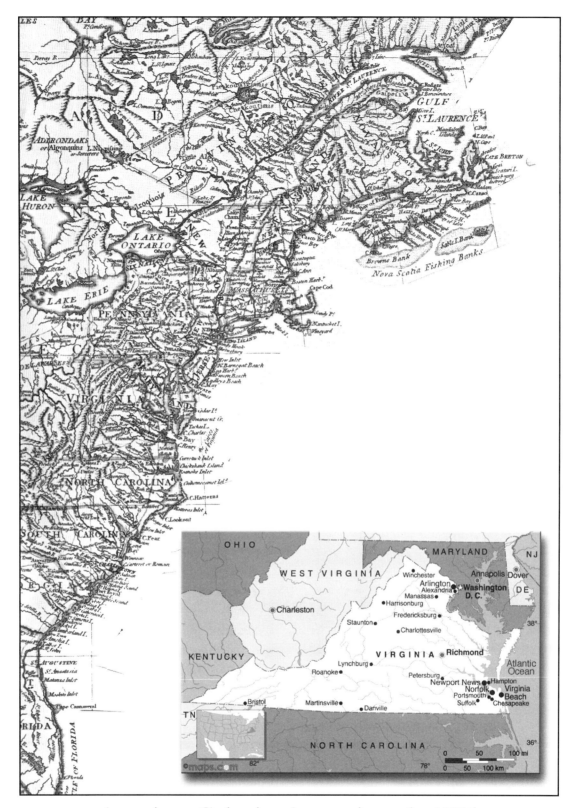

American Colonies Approximately 1776

23
Storming the Bastille, July 14, 1789

For people who earnestly believe in the value of representative government and respect for the individual, it is difficult to overestimate the significance of the fall of the Bastille. It was steeped in symbolism as a despised dumping ground for all who opposed the absolute authority of a debauched French monarchy. The attack on the Bastille was a definitive statement that tolerance had been grossly exceeded. It was a symbolic act and also a source of critically needed armaments that were essential to the smoldering rebellion.

The Bastille was located on the east side of the City of Paris. As a former fortress it had multiple towers over 90 feet high, 10 feet thick masonry walls, and was heavily armed with cannon, royalist guards, and other armaments of the period. It was used as a totally secure prison for political dissenters as well as criminals. The authority of the French monarchy was such that anyone could conceivably be imprisoned at the Bastille, or like places, for any reason.

When the political boiling point for huge numbers of French citizens at all levels was exceeded on July 14, 1789, there were only seven prisoners at the Bastille. Only three of those might be described as political prisoners at that moment. Previously, such well-known dissenters as Francois Arouet Voltaire (1694-1778) had been imprisoned at the Bastille. The Marquis de Sade, infamous for other reasons, was being held as the Bastille came under attack. Earlier, he had wildly shouted out of a window that prisoners inside were being killed.

Under the sustained pressures of the times, rumors circulated that the fortresses' cannons had been aimed at the Parisian populace. Large crowds of people formed outside the Bastille to demand that the cannon not be aimed at French citizens. There was some communication with the prison director, Marquis Bernard-Rene de Launay, when several men broke into a guardhouse and were able to lower a drawbridge. Additional efforts to rush the fortress for the next four hours were repelled by musket fire. In a twist of irony, the small number of guards began to reposition the cannons at the mob out of fear for their own lives. The guards pleaded with Marquis de Launay to surrender. Perhaps fearing his own execution with either outcome, de Launay made claims that he would blow up the fortress rather than turn it over to a mob. The guards took it upon themselves to raise a white flag and quickly negotiate a surrender on condition that their own lives would be spared. In the rush that followed, however, several guards were killed and de Launay was executed.

The capture of the Bastille was an open act of rebellion and an irreversible affront against the "divine" monarchy of France. For the somewhat spontaneous revolutionaries the immediate gains included fifteen cannons, hundreds of musket rifles, and up to twenty thousand pounds of gunpowder. The dissenters, facing execution for treason against the state, became revolutionaries. All French citizens, whether inspired by the American Revolution against the British monarchy or for other reasons, had to take a position.

Among the factors leading to the storming of the Bastille was the American Revolution at many different levels. For the French intellectuals (bourgeoisie) it was alternate forms of government plus the rights and dignity of the individual. For the wage-earners and poorest working classes, it was knowledge that "the common people" of America had rejected the authority of the British king, oppressive taxes, and survived. For the absolute monarchy,

King Louis XVI and Queen Marie Antoinette, the cost of supporting the American Revolution, getting back at the British, and of making the American Revolution successful further bankrupted the vastly overextended economy of France. The French monarchy was embittered with the archrival British following their defeat by the British in the Seven Years War. That war, twenty-five years earlier, and horrid fiscal management since the war, in addition to the wildly extravagant excesses of the French monarchy, had produced tremendous debt.

Louis XVI of France

Louis XVI was intelligent and reared in the style of the utter self-indulgence of his father and grandfather. In 1774 he reluctantly ascended to the throne of France at the age of twenty. The young king was timid, awkward, and distinctly uncomfortable with the bankrupt position and social conflicts that he had inherited. As a result, he was all too willing to accept the advice of his insensitive queen and the endless courtiers who simply wanted the ship of state to sail on as it had. Early in his rein, Louis XVI appointed Finance Minister Turgot and some improvement in the debt cri-

sis was made. Self-serving advisors to the king did not like making sacrifices and soon forced Turgot's dismissal. The debt situation deteriorated even more rapidly. Numerous efforts to tax the least able to pay only increased tensions. Efforts to tax 80,000 noble families and ranking members of the clergy simply failed. With the appointment of Finance Minister Calonne in 1783, futile efforts were made to solve the chronic financial crisis through borrowing. In 1785, upon demand of all bankers involved, additional money was loaned to the government strictly on the condition that Jacques Necker would be appointed finance minister. The king appointed Necker but was openly humiliated because Necker was both a Protestant and a commoner. The nobles and the church hierarchy became increasingly sensitive to the potential for being taxed. Too late, the king allowed the election of an Estates-General type of legislature of the people. It was the first such legislature in France since 1614.

There can be little doubt that the American Revolution had a tremendous impact on the French Revolution less than one decade later The same can be said for the European Enlightenment philosopher's and writer's impact preceding the American Revolution. However, without Admiral Comte de Grasse's fleet to blockade British General Cornwallis in the Yorktown, Virginia, area, and General Rochambeau's forces to assist General Washington's forces in completing the entrapment of Cornwallis, the Americans probably would have failed. A huge impact and transfer of revolutionary new ideals was conveyed by Benjamin Franklin, American Minister to France from 1778 to 1785. Thomas Jefferson, the Marquis de Lafayette, and French Foreign Minister Comte de Vergennes likewise were indispensable in building the intellectual foundation for massive change in France. One of the key goals for France's support of the American Revolution was to secure needed trade agreements between the two countries.

Writers such as Francois Voltaire, Saint-Simon, Diderot, Condorcet, d'Alembert, Jean Jacques Roussau, Montesquieu, Thomas Paine, Benjamin Franklin, and others did much to spread the word of enlightenment. A new concept of hope quickly spread to grossly oppressed people being forced to live under appalling, feudalistic conditions. A different, but necessary, message went out to a decadent monarchy and a privileged hierarchy of the clergy and nobility. The message was: "liberty, equality, and fraternity." The final spark that ignited a revolution was the storming of the Bastille. That date, July 14, is now celebrated as the French Independence Day, and continues to be a model for representative government for oppressed people throughout the world.

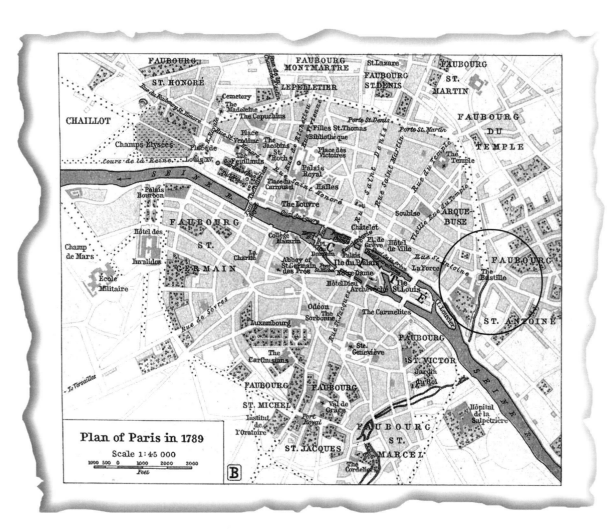

The Bastille (circled)

24
Tecumseh: Sunset of the Eastern Tribes, 1812

Tecumseh, a Shawnee chief in the early 1800's, led an extraordinary and yet doomed effort to limit the encroachment of American settlements on all Native American lands. After roughly two centuries of contact and cultural clash with European immigrants and their offspring born in the New World, it was indelibly obvious that huge numbers of the newly arrived people intended to take all of the land

Chief Tecumseh

rived people intended to take all of the land and its resources for themselves. The Native American's options were few. They could be aggressively pushed off of their traditional lands. They could be killed in armed conflicts, or, more likely, they could die en mass from European and Asian diseases for which there was little immunity.

It was disease in particular that decimated so many of the tribal peoples in the Western Hemisphere. Typically the losses were so pervasive and sudden that entire languages, cultures, oral histories, and acquired belief systems died with them. Tecumseh asked, "Where are the Pequot? Where [are] the Narraganset,

the Mohican, the Pokanoket and many other once powerful tribes of our people? They have vanished before the avarice and oppression of the white man, as snow before a summer sun…."

Tecumseh was a six-foot tall, charismatic and well-educated man for his time. As he matured into manhood his personal experiences and the tragedies he observed compelled him to take action in defense of all native woodland people. It was apparent to any who would see that individual tribal groups were vanishing and, in isolation, no match for the technologically and numerically superior Americans. As the value in mutual reciprocity of trade diminished, it was increasingly clear that the more powerful newcomers lost faith in a peaceful coexistence in part due to near hysteria about being brutally killed, raped, or abducted by the culturally inferior "savages." The implied message was that a "non-savage" should abandon all Native American ways and become devout Christian farmers something like the rural Amish communities.

Tecumseh was one of the most articulate and forceful leaders to recognize that most eastern tribes would not survive if they did not unite against the pressures of the totally invasive American settlers who consumed and controlled the land and all of its resources with minimal or little apparent regard for its original occupants. A great union of tribes had to be formed quickly before it was too late. Individual tribes, with their distinctive personalities and unique histories, no longer had the strength to resist the overwhelming numbers of Americans moving into their traditional territories. Age old differences, sometimes bitter hostilities, and even petty squabbles between tribal groups had to be resolved. The alternative was to face extinction.

Past tribal histories of feuds, grievances and periodic intertribal wars had been exploited by American colonists from the beginning. It was commonplace in early colonial America's history to pit one tribal group against another to make the most of ancient hostilities. The sentiment of early colonists was often reflected in the written materials and "common wisdom" of small, white communities that tribal natives were not to be trusted. Fears were often exaggerated and perpetuated that "savage" un-Christian behavior might simply occur spontaneously or with little or no provocation. Prior to James Fennimore Cooper's concept of the "noble savage" in *The Last of the Mohicans*, public references to Native Americans were typically negative. Obvious cultural conflicts and competition for much of the same resources continued to grow more intense with time and population growth. The newly formed United States had in excess of 2,000,000 citizens and sought "room to grow" in what appeared to be boundless and rich territories. Brutal incidents by a few on either side of the cultural divides were likely to be exaggerated and used as a justification for more brutality. Virtual Stone Age cultures quickly had to adapt to confrontations with musketry, cannon, unintentional diseases, and simply overwhelming numbers of alien intruders.

Because of the long histories of intertribal conflicts, few Native Americans had ever been known to reach across major territorial divides to unite tribes with vast differences among themselves against a common foe. The implied, Euro-American strategy toward Native Americans throughout the land was that they could simply adapt to the new, dominant culture, speak English, dress in the Euro-American style, accept Christianity and become virtually invisible farmers, ranchers and unskilled laborers. Native Americans were not encouraged to become doctors, lawyers, or high-ranking politicians.

Tecumseh was born in 1768 in the area near present day Dayton, Ohio. His people had been pushed westward and certainly felt the pressure on other tribal allies and enemies alike during that period. By the early 1800's the Shawnees had been pushed into the Indiana region and Tecumseh began to speak out against the encroachment of the Americans. Also, around the year 1800 he befriended a blonde, blue-eyed daughter of a local farmer. She was unusually well educated for the time and did much to introduce Tecumseh to the basics of the English language, Christianity, world history, Shakespeare and U.S. History from the American point of view. The question of marriage fell apart, however, when she made it conditional upon his abandoning all Native American ways and physically leaving his people. He refused and they parted.

By 1805 Tecumseh had traveled from one area to another effectively making claims that no tribe had the right to sell lands to Americans without the consent of all of the tribes who used that land. He was soon joined by his brother, Lalawethika, who had converted from a self-destructive life of alcoholism and depression to that of a compelling prophet for Native American people. Like Wovoka, a Paiute prophet in the 1880's and founder of the "Ghost Dance," Lalawethika's strong words about the need for tribes to unite was being acknowledged by many tribes east of the Mississippi and as far north as the central plains of Canada. Typically, there was a favorable response among younger generations and far less, if any, from older, annuity-dependent, or embittered tribal leaders.

By 1808 the two, charismatic brothers had helped to forge a union of several tribes in a village that would eventually become known as Prophetstown. Among the tribal members included were the Wyandot, Delaware, Ojibwa, Ottawa and Kickapoo tribes. Encouraged by the strength of that experience, Tecumseh took his message on the road as far as the Northwest Territories (i.e., Minnesota, Michigan, Wisconsin, etc.) and then into the South. The reaction was mixed but many began to take up his cause.

Back in Indiana, a very ambitious territorial governor, General William Henry Harrison, used cunning and alcohol to swindle a number of old chiefs into "selling" roughly three million acres of Native American lands for a few thousand dollars and without the common consent of area tribes. By the War of 1812, Tecumseh's efforts to rescind what should have been an illegal sale failed. Ultimately,

General William Henry Harrison

Tecumseh and his followers aligned themselves with the British because they appeared to be a far less intrusive force to Native American interests than the Americans. His value to the British was such that he was promoted to the rank of brigadier general and was instrumental in forcing the surrender of Fort Detroit although their forces outnumbered the British

and Native American allies by at least two to one.

Tecumseh's arch rival, General Harrison, later used an incident involving horse thefts to engage this dynamic leader and his followers in a battle near Tippecanoe Creek that would result in Tecumseh's battlefield death, the breakdown of the unification movement, and form a memorable bit of propaganda (Tippecanoe and Tyler Too!) that would contribute to Harrison's election as U.S. president 30 years later.

By mid-1811 several Potawatamis killed several settlers in Illinois. Indiana territory governor, General William Henry Harrison, used that incident to justify a confrontation in force against Tecumseh's growing, tribal unifications. From July through November tensions continued to build as Tecumseh continued his crusade in the South. In the fall of that year stories began to spread that some Indians had stolen some horses from an army dispatch rider. Harrison used that vaguely confirmed incident to launch an armed assault on Prophetstown during Tecumseh's absence. His force of over 1,000 men camped for the night just a few miles from the mouth of the Tippecanoe River. Tenskwatawa, Tecumseh's brother, saw an opportunity despite his older brother's specific orders to avoid armed conflicts. Tenskwatawa, like Wovoka 70 years latter, had also become a prophet of a new spirit-religion that would protect them from soldier's bullets. A major nighttime skirmish resulted and the magic protection failed. Tecumseh was enraged with his brother when he returned and learned of the destruction of Prophetstown.

Lacking sufficient military strength in his efforts to unify widely diverse tribes, Tecumseh reluctantly allied his shifting forces with the British. The U.S. had declared war on the British on June 18, 1812. A major confrontation between the Americans and the British with their Native American allies occurred near Detroit. The Lake Michigan fort at Detroit was commanded by an overly cautious and

General Hull surrendering to the British

perhaps senile man by the name of General William Hull. The old general was ordered to seize territory north of him into Canada. However, he quickly withdrew his force of about 2,200 men following only light harassment by Tecumseh's forces. Hull scurried back to Detroit where he would be besieged by the combined forces of Tecumseh and British General Isaac Brock. Tecumseh used the ploy of marching his force of perhaps 600 men past

Fort Detroit

the fort at a safe distance and at least three times to give the impression of a superior force. To the chagrin of the Americans, frightened, old General Hull surrendered without a fight and to a British/Indian force that was less than half the size of his own.

By October 1813, General Harrison set out with eleven hundred men to recapture Fort Detroit. Militarily, much had changed by that time. Highly competent General Brock had been shot and killed in the field. His replacement, Colonel Henry Proctor, was as excessively cautious as General Hull and contemptuous of all Native Americans as well. Major errors on the part of Col. Proctor allowed General Harrison time to build a decisive force of 4,500 men. On October 5, 1813, Harrison prevailed in a battle that exhibited great Native American valor and heroism, British incompetence, and the battlefield death of the man who did the most by far to unite and preserve exceedingly diverse, Native American tribes against a common foe.

General Harrison wrote of Tecumseh, "…one of those uncommon geniuses which spring up occasionally to produce revolutions and overturn the established order of things. If it were not for the vicinity of the United States, he would perhaps be the founder of an empire that would rival in glory Mexico or Peru." William H. Harrison, "a simple frontier Indian fighter," was the ninth president of the United States. He died of pneumonia on April 4, 1841, one month after taking office.

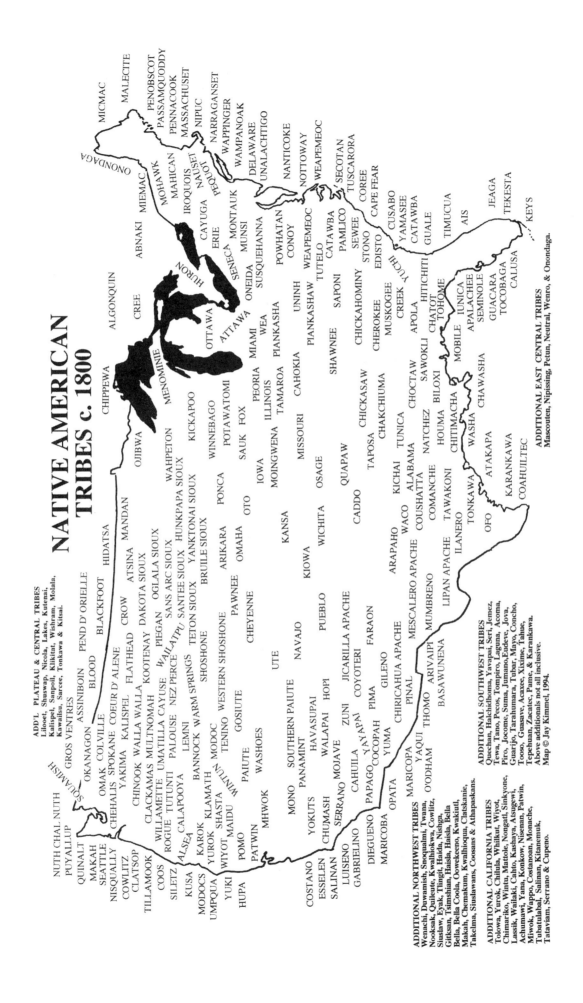

NATIVE AMERICAN TRIBES c. 1800

ADD'L PLATEAU & CENTRAL TRIBES
Liloeet, Shuswap, Nicola, Lakes, Kutenai, Kalispel, Sanpoil, Klikitat, Wishram, Molala, Kawaiisu, Sarcee, Tonkawa & Kitsai.

ADDITIONAL NORTHWEST TRIBES
Wenachi, Duwamish, Snoqualmi, Twana, Nooksak, Quileute, Kwalhiokwa, Cowlitz, Siuslaw, Eyak, Tlingit, Haida, Nishga, Gitksan, Tsimshian, Haisla, Haisla, Bella Bella, Bella Coola, Oowekeeno, Kwakiutl, Makah, Chemakum, Kwalhioqua, Clatskanie, Takelma, Siuslawans, Coosans & Athapaskans.

ADDITIONAL CALIFORNIA TRIBES
Tolowa, Yurok, Chilula, Whilkut, Wiyot, Chimariko, Wintu, Mattole, Nongatl, Sinkyone, Lassik, Wailaki, Cahto, Kashaya, Aisugewi, Achumawi, Yana, Konkow, Nisenan, Patwin, Miwok, Wappo, Costanoan, Monache, Tubatulabal, Salinan, Kitanemuk, Tataviam, Serrano & Cupeno.

ADDITIONAL SOUTHWEST TRIBES
Quechan, Halchidhoma, Yavapai, Seri, Jemez, Tewa, Tano, Pecos, Tompiro, Laguna, Acoma, Piro, Jocome, Suma, Jumano,Eudeve, Acoma, Guarijo, Tarahumara, Tubar, Mayo, Concho, Tooso, Guasave, Acaxee, Xixime, Tahue, Tepehuan, Zacatec, Pame, & Karankawa. Above additionals not all inclusive.
Map © Jay Kimmel, 1994.

ADDITIONAL EAST CENTRAL TRIBES
Mascouten, Nipissing, Petun, Neutral, Wenro, & Onondaga.

Federally Recognized Indian Tribes

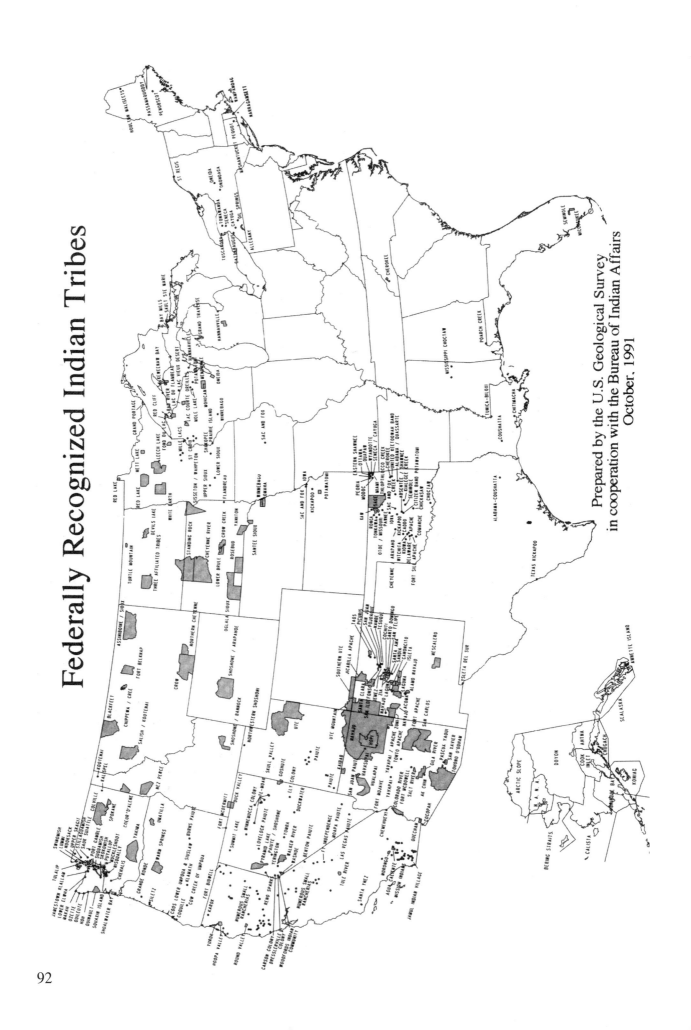

Prepared by the U.S. Geological Survey
in cooperation with the Bureau of Indian Affairs
October, 1991

25
Napoleon's Battle for Moscow, 1812

In the same year that the United States was entrenched in a war with the British, the Russian people used every means possible to extricate themselves from a very deadly land invasion by Napoleon's Grand Army. The combined death toll was in the millions.

Napoleon (1769-1821) invaded Russia with his Grand Army of 450,000 in 1812. It was the largest military force ever seen at the time

Napoleon Bonaparte

and size alone inspired great optimism of their invincibility. They were led by the most innovative and charismatic commander of the time. Morale was at a euphoric peak. The thought of grinding failure and defeat was unthinkable.

As Napoleon's disciplined and hardened army of infantry, cavalry, and artillery crossed the Niemen River in Western Russia, there was great optimism that the enemy would soon be engaged and that victory would be a certainty.

The army carried enough food, water, and supplies for at least four weeks in advance and fully expected to forage for any additional needs. Great personal honor and glory for France was all but certain. However, in the vastness of the Russian plains, the enemy faded further and further eastward without engaging the French any more than was necessary to slow their pace. Soon, weeks began to pass without any potential for a decisive battle. Food and supplies were consumed on a daily basis as the "journey into darkness" continued. In the heat of summer, food soon became scarce, disease rampant, and desertion became progressively more of a problem as winter approached.

By September, 1812, Napoleon's forces, which had declined from 450,000 to little more than 100,000, were able to reach Moscow. The residents put the city to the torch rather than willingly give aid to the invaders. Still, there was little confrontation that could destroy the Russian forces. Weather conditions were especially severe in that year. By October 19 Napoleon and the remnants of his once truly grand army started its westward return. The hostile distance was 500 miles from Moscow to the western frontier.

Napoleon's army was very much of an international force. Archeological recoveries of uniform buttons have established at least 54 different regiments. Often, these regiments contained large numbers of adolescents down to about age 15. Small numbers of women, some with infants or small children, also accompanied the now very beleaguered troops. In fact, the exposure to the elements and scarcity of food on the march to Moscow had been so severe it was decided to take an alternate route back to Western Europe.

South of Moscow there was a major confrontation in the area of Maloyavoslavets. Each side tended to bring several hundred cannon to the field. The degree and severity of injuries sustained by cannon fire, musket fire, and other weapons of the period added incredible burdens on the individual foot soldiers in particular. Over time, and with continued harassment by hit-and-run tactics of mounted Cossacks, Napoleon's Grand Army was further reduced to little more than the walking wounded. Extreme exhaustion was exacerbated by starvation, extreme cold weather and the increasing vulnerability to disease, infection and plummeting morale. Total losses for both sides at that battle were estimated to be over 70,000. The severity of the tragic battle was such that a decision was made to abandon the new route and return to the roads on which they had come in. All efforts would thus be made to reach Borodino with its bridge. Cossack warriors continued to endlessly harass this now doomed army.

The Battle of Borodino on September 7, 1812, had been very different. Previous to that date the Russians had conducted a very deadly cat and mouse tactic throughout the vastness of that often unforgiving country. At Borodino (just 75 miles from Moscow) General Mikhail Kutusov was prepared for battle. He saw to the preparation of the defenses to best use his 600-plus cannons and his more than 100,000 troops.

Napoleon's army of just over 130,000 men, and a comparable number of cannons, launched into a very deadly frontal assault. There was not a decisive outcome by either side. Both armies were completely exhausted by the end of the day and it was the Russian army that withdrew first. The Russians had experienced over 44,000 casualties and the French over 33,000 casualties. The battle was later described by Napoleon as the one he regretted most, but it did open the way for the capture of the burned-out Russian capital of Moscow.

It was the winter retreat from Moscow and the second attempt to cross the bridge at Borodino on October 28, 1812, that emphasized the failures and depleted nature of Napoleon's once Grand Army. The reason for again passing through such hostile territory was that the bridge was by far the preferred way to cross the freezing Niemen River. As the broken-down remnants of the Grand Army passed through that area they viewed the 30,000 French bodies still unattended on the surrounding hills. As the horrendous retreat continued on foot virtually the entire French army was either killed, died of injuries or disease, or deserted, or were captured.

The straggling army of 100,000 was reduced to perhaps 40,000 as they approached Smolonsk. It soon became mentally crushing to realize that a 40 day march lay ahead to return to the relative safety of the west. By December of 1812 extreme, subfreezing temperatures continued to tear at whatever starvation, injuries, and extreme exhaustion had not already consumed. No major battle was fought there, but in the Lithuanian city of Vilnius, a mass gravesite of approximately 3,000 was discovered in 2002. It was the mostly male bodies of Napoleon's retreating army that had succumbed mostly to the extreme cold conditions compounded by their severely weakened condition. Forensics showed great wear and tear on bone structures and partial, often crude, healing of a multitude of injuries, even among the youngest troops. The combination of extreme cold weather and extreme distances to critical food and supplies were huge factors in bringing Napoleon's Grand Army to its knees. One hundred and twenty-nine years later, and with Hitler's apparent disregard of the lessons learned, the Nazi Wehrmacht experienced a similar defeat outside the gates of Moscow and again at Stalingrad (1942-1944).

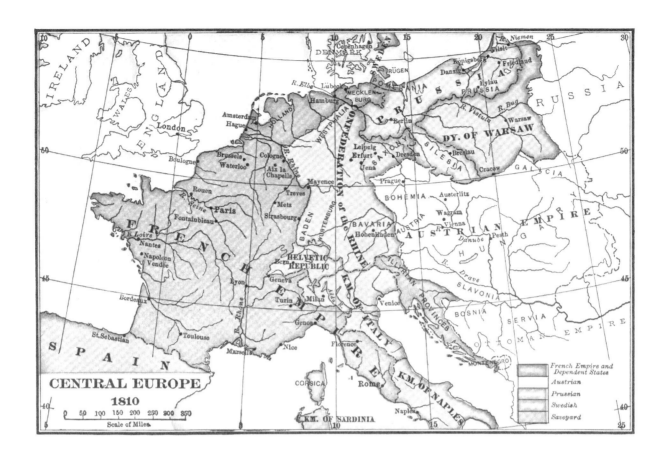

CENTRAL EUROPE
1810

French Empires and Dependent States
Austrian
Prussian
Swedish
Savoyard

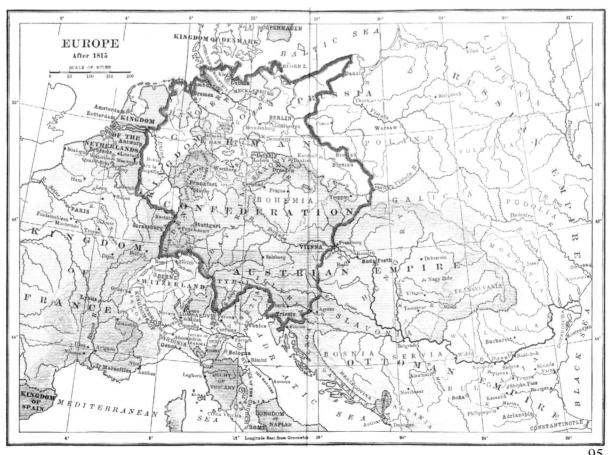

EUROPE
After 1815

26
USS Monitor vs. *CSS Virginia*, March 9, 1862

The first battle of ironclad warships in naval history occurred during the American Civil War near the mouth of the James River, Virginia. It was a pitched, three and one-half hour fuselage of cannon fire that has been described by many as "a draw." The unprecedented combatants, *USS Monitor* and *CSS Virginia* (aka: *USS Merrimac*), did very little to impact the outcome of the civil war. What did happen on March 9, 1862, was a battle to make thousands of years of naval combat in wooden ships obsolete.

Civil war ships were not the first ironclads. That distinction appears to reside with an allied, French and English effort during the Crimean War (1854-1856). Iron plating was added to wooden ships for protection from incendiary, "hot shot" cannon fire. Soon, a decision was made that the next class of French warships would have metal armor. The wooden keel of *La Gloire* was laid in April, 1858, at Toulon, France. The masted and steam powered warship was first constructed of wood and then plated with roughly four and one-half inch thick plates of iron. Upon her completion in, August, 1860, she was by far superior defensively to all wooden warships

that preceded her. *La Gloire* and her sister ships, *Normandie* and *Invincible* were never used in actual combat. The inherent flaw of each ship was inferior workmanship and there was even some rotten wood that caused their early deactivation.

The British, always sensitive to having their Royal Navy upstaged, laid the keel for the first iron hull warship, *HMS Warrior,* in June, 1859. Actually, the Royal Navy had experimented with poor grades of iron plating in the 1840's and discovered that it didn't hold up well against cannon fire. The first British, all-iron warship was fifty percent larger than the *La Gloire.* It was also notable for having the first watertight compartments and being the longest and largest warship ever built to that date. With combined sail and steam engines, she could reach 14.5 knots on the open seas. She was also, in part, armed with breech-loading cannons. Her service record missed the limelight, however, because she sailed in relatively peaceful waters during the "Pax Britannica" period.

The *USS Monitor* was a radically different, iron warship. In response to a Union newspa-

per ad asking for submissions of ironclad warship designs, John Ericsson, a Swedish inventor, made a proposal that was accepted by President Abraham Lincoln. Otherwise, both the radical concept and the man behind it would have been flatly rejected by Union naval authorities of the time. In a word, Mr. Ericsson was considered a "screwball." His cannon design demonstration in 1844 exploded and killed both the Secretary of the Navy, Thomas Gilmer, and Secretary of State, Abel P. Ushur. It was only by chance that the explosion did not kill President Tyler of the United States. Therefore, the navy accepted Ericsson's pillbox design only on the condition that the government received delivery in 100 days. The navy certainly did not think he could deliver, but they had underestimated both Mr. Ericsson and the Brooklyn navy yard. Ericsson made delivery in 101 days. The 172 foot long vessel was nearly submerged in roughly 10 feet of water and had many elements of later submarine design. The unprecedented, rotating turret had two 11 inch, smoothbore cannons. Designs included over 40 original patents, including the Ericsson screw propeller. Except for rough water, the warship proved to be well ahead of its time in many respects.

The *CSS Virginia* had a radically different history. As it became apparent that the Norfolk navy shipyard in Virginia would be controlled by the newly declared Confederacy, efforts were made to move Union ships out of port. The *USS Merrimac* happened to be one of the first screw-propelled warships in the U.S. Navy. She was a wooden ship that had been commissioned in 1855 but was in the harbor for boiler repairs as the Civil War broke out. Boiler tenders were able to start her engines but blockades in the channel prevented her escape. She was therefore torched and scuttled to prevent use by the Confederacy.

With every ship being important to the new Confederacy, the *USS Merrimac* was raised,

refitted with armor plating and a ramming device on her bow. The "superstructure" above the waterline was made of thick walls slanted at roughly 35 degrees and with four cannon ports on each side and one cannon each at the rounded stern and aft. The massively increased weight made her awkward to handle and limited her top speed to about four knots. The weight and new configuration made it improbable that she would handle well in rough seas. Her deep draft (22 feet) made it impossible to navigate in shallow waters—a failing that severely limited her military usefulness.

The *CSS Virginia* was primarily intended to be a blockade buster. On February 24, 1862, Capt. Franklin Buchanan assumed command and, though still needing work, got the ship under way on March 8 down the Elizabeth River and toward Hampton Roads. As she neared the Yorktown Peninsula that had been made famous in George Washington's time, she encountered five Union ships forming a blockade to the Atlantic. The first wooden ship to feel the full impact of the *Virginia's* firepower and ramming device was the *USS Cumberland.* A total of 121 sailors died aboard that ship but she kept firing up to the point of actually sinking. The *CSS Virginia* then turned upon a much larger, wooden warship, the *USS Congress.* In a panic that ship had become grounded and could only fire two of 44 guns at the *Virginia.* Within a short time the Union ship was on fire from incendiary shells and exploded later that night. The remaining Union vessels were by then making all the speed they could away and in the direction of Newport News, Virginia. The sister ship of the *Merrimack,* the *USS Minnesota*, went aground in all of the confusion and came under fire from the *Virginia.* Shallow water prevented the Confederate blockade-buster from closing and finishing off that warship as well.

The *USS Monitor,* which had been built in Brooklyn, New York, was released for battle by the U.S. Navy on February 25, 1862. She steamed into the mouth of the James River (near Hampton, Virginia) on March 9, 1862, and permanently changed the course of naval warfare. In virtual slow motion compared to later warships, the *USS Monitor* confronted the very slow and cumbersome *CSS Virginia* in an area that allowed little room for maneuver. Cannons aboard the *CSS Virginia* were placed in fixed positions. Aiming their cannon required repositioning of the ship.

Confederate sailors viewed the new contraption with little more than open contempt. One sailor reportedly described his new adversary as a "cheesebox on a raft." The first very important distinction not recognized by that sailor was the flexibility and effectiveness of the rotating, 11 inch pair of cannons in that "cheesebox." After firing, the turret rotated as needed to avoid direct fire that might damage either cannon. The rounded surface of the heavy turret made a direct hit almost impossible. Like the angled defenses above the low deck of the *CSS Virginia,* cannon fire was mostly repelled.

The broadside cannon dual continued for three and one-half hours without either ship showing lethal damage. The battle broke off just after noon when Lieutenant John L. Worden ordered the *Monitor* into water too shallow for the *Virginia* to follow. The battle ended without a clear victor on either side.

The *Virginia* withdrew to dock facilities at Norfolk for roughly 30 days of repairs. On April 11, 1862,

she escorted the *CSS Raleigh* and *CSS Jamestown* on an assignment to capture several troop transports that were intended to support General George McClellan's campaign to assault historic Yorktown. There were no further confrontations between the two iron warships. The *USS Monitor* had demonstrated its ability to protect the blockading warships of the Union navy.

The *CSS Virginia* eventually became grounded, and fearing capture by Union forces, she was set on fire on May 11, 1862. She exploded as the fire reached the ammunition stored on board. The *USS Monitor* was ordered south along the eastern seaboard. On December 30, 1862, she was swamped by high seas and sank off Cape Hatteras, North Carolina. In 1974 the wreckage of the *USS Monitor* was discovered and has since been designated as the United States' first marine sanctuary.

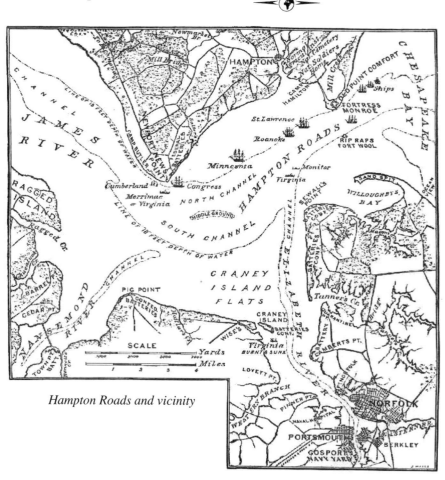

Hampton Roads and vicinity

27
Gettysburg: Little Round Top, July 2, 1863

A small, boulder-strewn area in Gettysburg, Pennsylvania, was known as Little Round Top. It also represented the Union's extreme, left flank at the quickly improvised, Battle of Gettysburg (July 1-3, 1863). Holding that left flank was essential to victory on those three scorching days in July.

Little Round Top

By chance, or perhaps because of a major blunder, the critical left flank position had been abandoned by General Daniel E. Sickles' (1819-1914) move forward to confront General James Longstreet's (1821-1904) forces. It was being held by just a few Union soldiers. The rocky hillside, that had been partially logged just a few years earlier, remained unoccupied until late in the afternoon of July 2. General Gouverneur K. Warren (1830-1882) was dispatched by General George G. Meade (1815-1872) to verify conditions at the Union's left flank. Meade, incidentally, had just been appointed to command of the Army of the Potomac just three days before Gettysburg. With a cursory inspection, General Warren recognized the defensive importance of the rocky, lightly wooded area. He clearly sensed that Confederates under General John B. Hood (1831-1879) might seize the unoccupied left flank. General Warren quickly transferred a

brigade of Union troops to the craggy hill below the more heavily wooded, Big Round Top. Orders were given to Colonel Joshua Chamberlain (1828-1914) and his Twentieth Maine Infantry Regiment that the area was to be held at all costs.

The Twentieth Maine was barely in position when it was assaulted by veteran forces of Colonel William C. Oates' (1833-1910) Fifteenth Alabama Infantry. The Alabamans started out on the morning of July 2 and had marched all day to cover the 18 mile distance to Little Round Top. Orders to assault the hill arrived so quickly there was no chance to rest from the heat of the summer's hard march, or to fill empty canteens. There was no choice except to advance against artillery fire and sharpshooters entrenched in good, defensive positions. The Confederates had to cross over open fields and into the thick woods of Big Round Top. Colonel Oates again sought the opportunity to rest his men near the summit of Big Round Top, but a message was almost immediately received to push northward toward the rocky area known as Little Round Top and to engage Union forces there.

The Fifteenth Alabama did as instructed and soon was engaged in a major exchange of gunfire. Several waves of assaults were made from the base of Little Round Top up its rocky and wooded slopes. The intensity of the fighting made it one of the most intense fire-fights of the war. Colonel Oates courageously pushed his men to advance further to the west to get around the Union force. The Union forces held their defensive positions behind large boulders and trees that were far less exposed than the advancing rebels. The casualty rate was appalling. Still, the Confederates were able to drive the Twentieth Maine from its strong, defensive position several times. Each time, the Union forces rallied and gained back their position. Often the fighting became so close that it was hand-to-hand conflict.

Colonel Oates recognized the futility of taking more losses without tangible gains and he ordered a retreat. At virtually the same moment, Colonel Chamberlain ordered a bayo-

---

"Stand firm, ye boys from Maine, for not once in a century are men permitted to bear such responsibility for freedom and justice, for God and humanity as are now placed upon you"
Theodore Gerrish (20th Maine)

---

net charge. His men were virtually, if not actually, out of ammunition and on the border of panic themselves. The bayonet charge down the hill was to be in a swinging motion like a hinged gate. The moment for desperation for both sides favored the Union defenders over the far more exhausted and dehydrated Confederate forces. Large numbers of Confederates surrendered in the confusion or were run through with bayonets or rifle butts as close-in fighting intensified. Colonel Oates, who survived by running back to the cover of Big Round Top, later wrote, "There never were harder fighters than the Twentieth Maine men and their gallant Colonel. His skill and persistency and the great bravery of his men saved Little Round Top and the Army of the Potomac from defeat."

After the war, Col. Oates, who wrote extensively about the Battle of Gettysburg, acknowledged that if one more Confederate regiment had stormed the weaknesses on the Union's left flank, "We would have completely turned the flank and have won Little Round Top, which would have forced Meade's whole wing to retire."

The Battles of Gettysburg and Vicksburg in the same month were huge turning points for the previously successful Confederate cause. The South's superiority of leadership on the battlefield had been evident until that midsummer month. General Robert E. Lee (1807-1870) had taken on a huge, calculated risk that a Southern victory deep in Union territory would turn the extremely discontented North toward a peace settlement. General Lee's genius for overcoming impossible odds failed him at the unplanned Battle of Gettysburg. He disregarded General Longstreet's reservations about assaulting a superior, defensive position. He lacked the "eyes" of the army without JEB Stuart's cavalry report (tied up by Custer's Wolverines and other details). His artillery routinely overshot the defensive ridges and he lacked logistical support. General Pickett's open field assault was a waste of dedicated manpower that he was in no position to lose. The failure of General Meade's horribly beat-up forces to hound Lee's forces all the way to Richmond perhaps added another one to two years to America's most costly war. A total of 7,158 soldiers were killed on both sides at Gettysburg. A total of 51,112 soldiers were wounded or missing. By war's end an estimated 620,000 Americans were killed.

For his steadfast bravery under intense fire, Colonel Chamberlain received the Medal of Honor years after the conflict ended (1893). Before entering the service, he was a college professor with a fluency in seven different languages. After the war, he served four terms as the governor of Maine (1866-70) and later as president of Bowdoin College (1870-83). The courageous defense of the Twentieth Maine at Little Round Top protected the Union's left flank and prevented what may have become a Confederate victory at Gettysburg and a suit for peace as two separate nations. Following the major Confederate defeats at Gettysburg and Vicksburg, the South remained on the defensive for the remainder of the war.

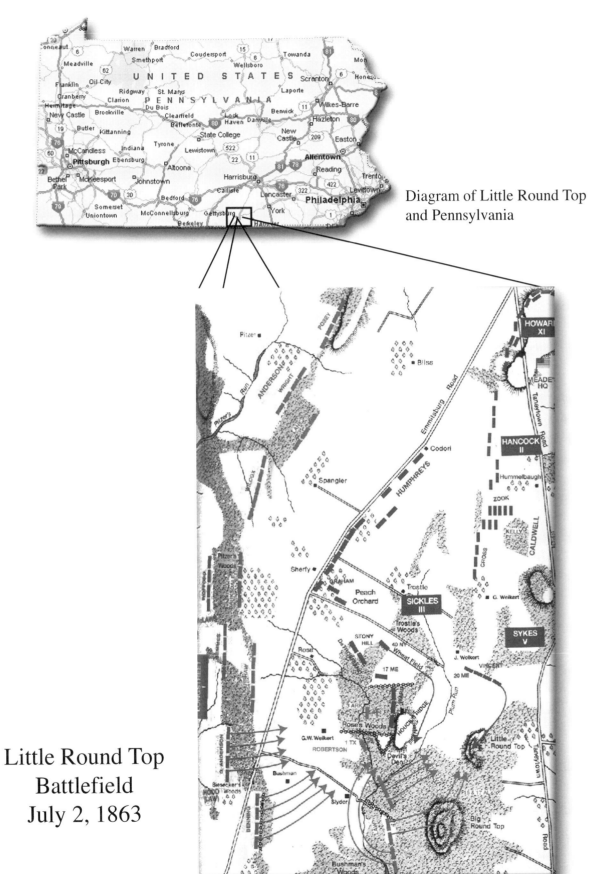

Diagram of Little Round Top and Pennsylvania

Little Round Top Battlefield July 2, 1863

28
Vicksburg: Key to the Mississippi

Strategically, the heights of Vicksburg, just 210 miles north of New Orleans, and 180 feet above sea level, were in a position to control much of the river traffic both north and south. Effective cannon fire could be rained down upon shipping in either direction. The mighty Mississippi to this date continues to be one of the country's most important highways for commerce. It was especially true during the Civil War since there were few good roads and the lack of bridges made non-water transport slow and difficult. Both Abraham Lincoln and Jefferson Davis knew that taking that position from the Confederacy would be a critical factor in the outcome of the America's most divisive war.

The defense of Vicksburg was entrusted to Lt. General John C. Pemberton, a Pennsylvania-born West Pointer, who demonstrated great tenacity and courage in two, protracted siege campaigns. His wife was born in Virginia and he had many years of service in the South before the civil war. He was appointed to the Department of Mississippi and East Louisiana by Confederate president, Jefferson Davis, in October, 1862. Within six months his forces and residents of Vicksburg would come under the siege of Major General Ulysses S. Grant (1822-1885).

From May 1 to July 3, 1863, the publication, *Official Records,* reported the following losses of Vicksburg defenders: 1,260 killed, 3,572 wounded and 4,227 either captured or missing. On July 4 approximately 20,000 Confederate troops, near total exhaustion, surrendered. More than half were either too weak or too ill to continue fighting. Numerically superior, Grant's army of approximately 71,000 succeeded in maintaining a most tortuous siege that was sufficiently strong to keep General Joseph E. Johnston from coming to the aid of Vicksburg.

Effective October 16, 1862, upon his appointment as commander of the Department of the Tennessee, Union Major General Ulysses S. Grant initiated immediate plans for a campaign to move southward to take control of Vicksburg, Mississippi. By November 8, 1862, Grant positioned his troops around LaGrange, Tennessee, just north of the Mississippi state line. The plan was to follow the rail lines southward toward Vicksburg. General Pemberton could spare few troops to oppose the federals. Grant's progress southward received steady resistance, especially from Brigadier General Nathan B. Forrest's cavalry attacks on supply lines, but Grant could not be stopped. By November 24, 1862, General Joseph E. Johnston was assigned to aid in the defense of Vicksburg, but like General Braxton Bragg, could provide little, if any, support. Still, Grant's multiple attempts to take Vicksburg failed. The outcome of major losses of federal supplies was for Grant to recognize the futility of trying to maintain supply and communication lines along rail lines in territory subject to continued enemy raids. The first Vicksburg campaign ended with Grant's resolution to sustain pressure on the strategic port town by other means. He would launch the first of many waterborne siege plans through the backwater swamps of the Mississippi.

The period of April 1 to July 4, 1863, marked Grant's second campaign to take Vicksburg by traversing swamps and crossing from the west bank of the Mississippi River to a point south of Vicksburg and thus drive against the city from the south and the less defensible east. Naval support was to come from Rear Admiral David D. Porter's fleet north of Vicksburg.

Porter was to push southward past Confederate batteries and then ferry Federal troops to the east bank. There, infantry would face Pemberton's defenders at Vicksburg and General Joe Johnston's forces nearer to Jackson, Mississippi. Grant's field commanders, including Generals John McClernand, William T. Sherman, Stephen Hurlbut, James B. McPherson, and Nathaniel P. Banks, each had diversionary assignments to thin Pemberton's defenses. The Federals won an engagement near Jackson, Mississippi, that was effective in isolating General Joe Johnston from the remainder of the excruciating Vicksburg campaign. Two failed attempts to scale the heights of Vicksburg's defenses convinced Grant that only a protracted siege would succeed. That intensely grinding siege with progressively less

Union Major General Ulysses S. Grant

food, ammunition and medical supplies for the Confederates would last from May 22, 1863 until the surrender on July 4, 1863.

Grant was reluctant to offer surrender terms when first requested on July 3. Once the garrison at Vicksburg surrendered on the following day, Grant quickly paroled most of Pemberton's surviving force. The federal victory at Vicksburg was exactly what President Lincoln was seeking to put new life in the Union's goal to hold the nation together. Upon the surrender of Vicksburg, John Pemberton resigned his commission and continued to serve as a lieutenant colonel of artillery for the remainder of the war. Thus, he erased any doubt of his loyalty to the South.

The "news of victory" was obscured to a major extent by the monumental events that were unfolding at the same time at the battle of Gettysburg. Lincoln sought a division between east and west supply lines for the Confederacy. In part, what he found was a tenacious, cigar-smoking general who could give him victories. Grant was rewarded with promotion to major general in the regular army effectively backdated to July 4, 1863, by President Lincoln.

By the election of 1868, Grant was elected as President of the United States and was in office from 1869 to 1877. Ironically, the Grant family lived in virtual poverty after he retired from the Presidency. There were no pensions for ex-presidents at that time and he had a business failure that left him with debts and was diagnosed with throat cancer. The solution proposed by Samuel Clemens (aka: Mark Twain, 1835-1910) was that he would purchase the rights to Grant's autobiography. Soon after the former president finished writing the last page he died. The proceeds of his biography provided for the support of Mrs. Grant for the remainder of her life.

The Mississippi River is the world's third longest river after the Nile and the Amazon. The Confederacy, prior to the siege of Vicksburg, did not have true control of the Mississippi River but the loss of Vicksburg, combined with the losses at Gettysburg the day before, placed the Confederacy on the defensive for the remainder of the war.

29
The Battle of the Little Big Horn

June 25, 1876, resonates as the date of Custer's Last Stand. The date barely preceded the planned celebration of America's first centennial on July 4, 1876. The incident, however, was not reported instantaneously as it would be today. News of the "massacre" of one of the Union's most famous Civil War generals by "savage Indians" was first distributed by horseback, and then by telegraph to the much-less-than-objective newspapers of the time. Shocking stories were printed almost at the exact moment that most Americans prepared to celebrate one hundred years of democratic independence and achievements since the end of the Revolutionary War. The news that Custer and over 200 cavalry troopers had been killed to the last man came as a profound shock to most Americans at that time.

The U.S. centennial was already somewhat lackluster because tragedies of the Civil War had touched virtually every family. There had been periods of severe economic depression, repeated scandals in Grant's White House, and greedy exploitations by industrialists in railroading, mining, steelmaking, and banking. The guarded mood of the country soon turned to anger and desire for vengeance rather than a full understanding of what actually happened on several dusty hills in southeastern Montana. The situation was ripe for misinformation and the creation of myth and legend based upon skimpy facts, rumors, and exploitative storytelling.

Lieutenant Colonel George Armstrong Custer (Brevet Major General) nearly missed the Battle of the Little Big Horn. "Auty," as he was known to friends and his wife, Elizabeth (Libby), incurred the extreme wrath of President Ulysses Grant when he testified before Congress about severe abuses by greedy Indian agents, such as the president's brother,

Orville. It was only due to the intervention of Custer's great friend in Washington, General Phil Sheridan, that he was allowed to join the expedition under the command of General Alfred Terry. Upon departing for the Little Big Horn, Custer darkly prophesied to Libby that he would either find glory or death.

The Grant administration's plan was to use force to compel the remnants of the nomadic Northern Plains tribes to live on government reservations. The government's plan was also to open up vast territories for settlement, railroads, gold mining, logging, and general expansion of U.S. domain. It mattered little to Washington decision makers that the 1868 Treaty of Laramie was openly being violated because Plains tribes had consistently refused to sell their land at any price. Custer's illegal expedition-in-force into the Black Hills of South Dakota in 1874 broadcast to the nation that clumps of gold could be found in the roots of grass sod. The stampeding gold rush that followed made the Treaty of Laramie impossible for the U.S. Army to enforce.

The U.S. government's self-serving strategy was to issue "published notices" that Northern Plains tribes living off the reservations were to return to reservations by January 31, 1876, or face military confrontation and be forcibly moved onto a reservation. There was little expectation by anyone that the ultimatums would even be noticed, and certainly not respected. It is doubtful that any of the nomadic tribal groups even received the notice.

The military plan for the following summer was to use overwhelming force in a three-pronged assault that would locate the renegade "hostiles" and do whatever necessary to force them onto government reservations. The likely "unofficial" plan was to scatter any encampments, burn their housing and supplies, kill anyone who resisted, and starve the remainder into submission. The example had been well established by the government's exploitation of Kit Carson's scouting skills to brutally starve the Navaho at Canyon de Chelley in 1863.

Three columns were lead by General George Crook, General Alfred Terry, and Terry's subordinate, Colonel John Gibbon. Lt. Colonel George Custer was assigned command of the cavalry unit of John Gibbon's infantry column. On the strength of Custer's reputation as an Indian fighter on the Plains, he was given virtual *carte blanche* authority to seek out and engage the non-reservation "hostiles." Gen-

eral Crook's column was confronted by a comparable number of Sioux warriors led by Crazy Horse and others along the Rosebud River. Crook's people took such a mauling that they withdrew from the pursuit without notifying the other two columns.

Custer, being an aggressive self-promoter, forged ahead with the help of trusted Native American scouts, such as "half-breed" Mitch Bouyer, to find the encampments that were described by the U.S. government as "hostile." Custer disobeyed orders to scout further south and instead followed a trail left by 8,000 to 10,000 tribal members. With all of their possessions and animals, the trail looked like a quarter-mile-wide plowed field. Knowledgeable scouts warned

Sitting Bull

Lt. Col. G.A. Custer

Approximate Battlefield location

Custer that there were far more aggressive Sioux, Northern Cheyenne, and Arapahoe than his small force could handle.

Custer's first sighting of the Indian encampment confirmed that it was far larger than anything ever seen on the Northern Plains. The numbers, however, did not deter Custer. He soon dismissed most of his scouts due to their pessimism in saying they would surely die. Fearing all chance of surprise may have been lost, Custer ordered Major Reno to take three companies of men and to begin a hard-charg-

Reno's face, it was every man for himself in a race to get across the river and to reach more defensive high ground.

From the ridges above Custer could see that Reno was stopped and in complete disarray. He moved further north to open a new assault from the east. Custer's cavalry companies, however, were heavily made up of immigrants seeking to learn English and basic skills that would allow them to remain as U.S. citizens. Panicked orders were given to Joe Martin (Italian immigrant Giovanni Martini) to carry a

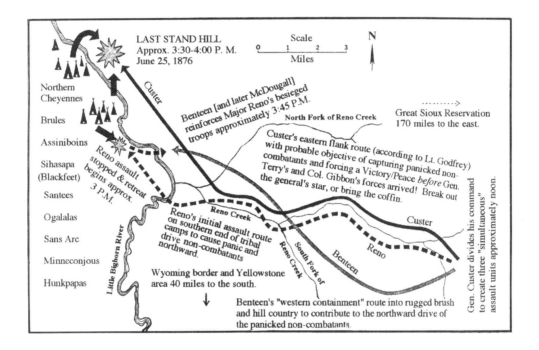

ing assault upon the southern end of the village. Captain Benteen was assigned to take his men and the supply pack train in a broad western containment movement. Custer took his five companies of men and galloped quickly northward along the eastern ridges above the village and east of the Little Big Horn River. Reno's assault was met with such a wall of rifle fire that his force was halted. He dismounted and attempted to form a skirmish line. The defensive counterattack from the village was so intense that Reno gave a number of confusing orders. Finally, after Bloddy Knife's brains were splattered into

note back to Captain Benteen (Brevet Colonel) to bring up the [ammunition] packs quickly! It didn't happen. Benteen later rejoined Reno's defensive position and remained until the village of almost 10,000 men, women, and children voluntarily moved out rather than use up ammunition needed for the coming winter hunting season. Sitting Bull, who would not sell even one handful of land, had urged his people to not take the possessions of the whites as it would only make them more dependent and less free.

Courtesy National Archives

Custer, leading his troops and dressed in buckskins (like a detested scout) is believed to have sought a crossing of the Little Big Horn to provoke panic and a stampede of the village. Flight from an assaulted village had always occurred in the past. This assault was different. Also, chances are excellent that the defenders, with large numbers of repeating rifles and warlike hunting skills, fatally wounded Custer before, or as, he crossed the Little Big Horn River. As a result, and in apparent disorientation, a member of Custer's family, or whoever was close to him, probably secured his body to a horse and retreated to more defensible higher ground. That site later became known as "Last Stand Hill."

Native American accounts, which rarely were given any credence until at least 50 years after the fact, say Custer's troops were all killed within approximately 30 minutes. The "oil-painted image" of Custer standing and fighting valiantly as the last heroic figure to die is purely the stuff of myth and legend. In fact, Edward S. Curtis (1868-1952) did a very ambitious, 20 volume study that included the Little Big Horn Battle. He learned that Native American participants had an entirely different interpretation of what occurred. When Mr. Curtis shared the written description with President Theodore Roosevelt, the president wrote back and basically said that we should not demean our American heroes. President Theodore Roosevelt did write a forward for the 20 volume study. In deference to the president, the entire story of the Little Big Horn was omitted.

Additional reasons for the Sioux, Northern Cheyenne, and Arapahoe departure included knowledge that Terry's column was approaching with fresh troops. Those troops would arrive by the following day.

There were also vast differences in the concepts of warfare and honor in the afterlife between

Custer battlefield cemetery

the Native American cultures and that of professional soldiers of the U.S. Army. Wars of extreme high attrition and virtual annihilation of the enemy such as in the Civil War were both foreign and contemptible to the far more ritual-bound native tribes. Their departure to Canada soon ended in starvation and forced return to impoverished reservations because buffalo herds on the plains had been virtually annihilated. North American buffalo were systematically killed for decades to permit ranch and farming settlements; plus construction of roads, rail lines, and small towns. Buffalo that once numbered 50 to 100 million animals on the plains of North America, were at one point reduced to about 200 scrawny animals that had been chased so hard they looked more like emaciated cows. The implied message to Native Americans was that they were to emulate the lower rungs of Euro-American civilization. They should speak English only, follow all U.S. laws, observe most customs and choose "elective" religious beliefs, not paganism, or simply fade away and die. That unofficial sentiment was made more official with the Dawes Act of February 8, 1887.

Curtis, Edward S., *The North American Indian (1890-1930)*, 20 volumes

Writer's opinion: Custer could have waited one more day, but the risk was in having to share "the glory" of a great victory. A victory that would get him promoted to full general.

"Custer's Last Stand" Courtesy National Archives

30
"Remember the *Maine*," February 15, 1898

When the *USS Maine* was first commissioned on September 17, 1895, it was the first modern all-steel, American battleship. It was technically rated as a second-class battleship and painted white because it was a time of peace in American waters. The 310 foot long vessel carried 290 sailors, 24 naval officers, and a complement of 40 marines at the moment that President William McKinley (1843-1901) dispatched her to the harbor of Havana, Cuba. The *USS Maine* arrived at Havana on January 25, 1898. It was to be a friendly visit with implied pressure for Spain to moderate control of the Caribbean island.

Cuba had a long history of disputes with faraway Spain that produced tensions, but were far from open rebellion. Evidence of unrest by the locals in Cuba at the time was directed at Spanish officials, but was in no way comparable to the American and French Revolutions more than a century earlier. The American newspapers of that time often used great creative license to provoke "juicy stories" that might improve circulation. William Randolph Hearst's *New York Journal,* for example, dispatched famed American artist, Frederick Remington, to Havana as the colonial crisis began to catch the public's interest. Remington requested that he be reassigned because there was so little to report. Hearst sent back a cable saying, "Please remain. You furnish the pictures, I'll furnish the war." The cabled prophecy was absolutely correct.

Rival newspapers in New York City, in particular, kept up entirely fabricated stories which had pressured President McKinley to respond in the first place. Actually, the president had served the Union at one of the bloodiest battle of the Civil War—Antietam. He reportedly told a visitor to the White House, "I have been through one war; I have seen the dead piled up; and I do not want to see another." From that comment alone, it could have been implied that the U.S. government did not have colonial aspirations in mind at Havana, Cuba. McKinley's understood goal was to calm tensions, not to create them. In fact, Spanish officials and military at Havana welcomed the very visual presence of the *USS Maine* in a cautious way. There were extremely polite exchanges among the various officers and dignitaries. The biggest concern for the sailors was in fighting boredom. The American battleship had been at anchor in the harbor for three weeks without incident. About 9:40 on the evening of February 15, 1898, there was a tremendous explosion. It was immediately apparent to Capt. Charles D. Sigsbee (1845-1923) what had occurred and almost as quickly he realized the ship was sinking. There were 254 seamen killed and 59 wounded. Of the wounded, eight more died a short time later. Crews from nearby ships, especially the Spanish *Alfonso XII,* did everything possible to rescue the surviving seamen of the *USS Maine.* A navy investigation of the incident was conducted but responsibility for the explosion was never disclosed.

Major American newspapers, of course, had no difficulty in assessing the blame. It was representatives of the Spanish government. The papers, noted for their "yellow journalism," whipped the few skimpy details into a frenzy of recriminations against Spain. One of the most gripping headlines was the phrase, "Remember the *Maine*, To Hell with Spain." The first part of that derogatory headline manufactured a demand for revenge among America's citizenry. The phrase was the catalyst for declaring the Spanish-American War. There would be no stopping the emotions that had been stirred up. Theodore Roosevelt, Assistant Secretary of the Navy (1897-1898), for example, resigned in May, 1898, to join the volunteer cavalry (Rough Riders).

President McKinley issued a report to both the public and the Senate on March 28, 1898. Both Congress and the public had come to the conclusion that Spain was responsible. This "international act of treachery" made war inevitable. A declaration of war with Spain was signed by the president on April 25, 1898. A naval blockade of Cuba was quickly put into place.

The brief war that followed included the first naval battle between U.S. battleships and Spanish battleships off the coast of Santiago, Cuba. Just ten days after the explosion, Teddy Roosevelt, Assistant Secretary of the Navy, wired Commodore George Dewey, commander of the U.S. Pacific fleet in Hong Kong. "Keep in full coal, in the event of declaration of war with Spain, your duty will be to see that the Spanish squadron does not leave the Asiatic coast and then offensive operations in the Philippine Islands."

In San Francisco, the newly completed battleship, *USS Oregon* (McKinley's Bulldog) was just completing trials and final fittings when it was dispatched to Havana, Cuba. That battle-

USS Oregon

ship arrived in Havana in record time and was clearly the fastest and best armed warship for its time. The Spanish warships were no match and escaped to Spain.

President McKinley's report disputed Spain's claim that the explosion was due to an inter-

nal combustion. By insisting that the explosion was due to external forces, the public's demand for war reached feverish levels. On March 27, 1898, McKinley issued his final terms to Spain:

- Declare an armistice
- End the reconcentration policy in Cuba initiated by General Weyler
- Begin the process of granting Cuba independence

On the same day that war was declared by Congress on April 25, 1898, and backdated to April 21, 1898, American warships soon bombarded Spanish forces at Matanzaras, Cuba. Land assaults, including the Rough Riders with Teddy Roosevelt, were begun. Fighting was intense but ended when Spain signed the Treaty of Paris on Oct. 1, 1898.

Half a world away, the U.S. Pacific fleet under Commodore George Dewey was prepared to implement orders he had received in the form of a cable from Assistant Secretary of the Navy, Theodore Roosevelt. Spain's claim to the Philippines had been in place since the islands "discovery" by Ferdinand Magellan in 1521. That claim was likewise challenged by battleship diplomacy. The Spanish-American war was concluded with America's first venture into colonialism, and in spite of the resistance of the Philippine Insurrection. On September 6, 1901, Theodore Roosevelt became the 26th President of the United States following the assassination of William McKinley. By 1909 "TR" retired from the presidency and died in 1919.

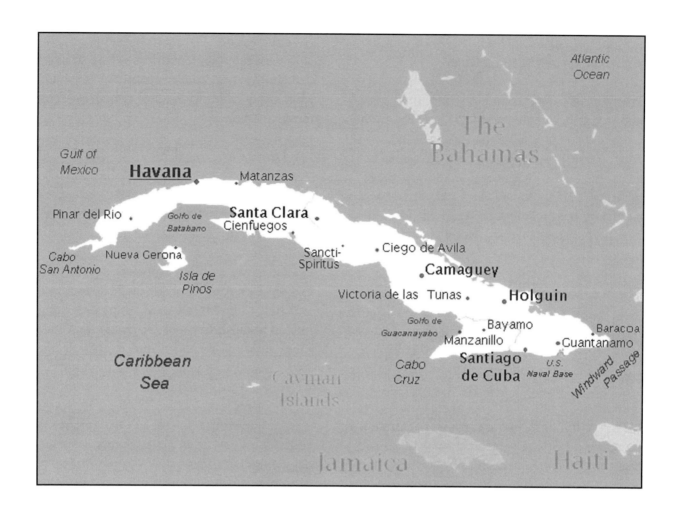

Cuba

Capital: Havana

Population: Almost 12 million

Area: Just under 69,000 square miles

Religion: About half Roman Catholic, half nonreligious, or other

Climate: Subtropical, subject to periodic hurricanes

Topography: Mostly not over 600 feet above sea level. Some hills to 3,000 feet

Surrounded by Atlantic Ocean, Gulf of Mexico and Caribbean Sea. Cuba is approximately ninety miles south of the southern tip of Florida and north of both the Cayman Islands and Island of Jamaica.

Summary: Prior to Fidel Castro the island of Cuba was controlled by a strongman dictator named Fulgencio Batista. Castro and his socialist/communist followers forcefully assumed power in 1959. There have been hostile relations between Cuba and the United States since that time and almost a fifty year ban on travel to Cuba by U.S. citizens. Castro nationalized all American interests in Cuba and imposed a repressive dictatorship that has kept the small island nation in a state of continued recession for many decades. Cuba had been a colony of Spain from the earliest Spanish explorations until the Spanish-American War of 1898. The island's primary industries are tourism (non U.S.), sugar, nickel, and cigars.

The Philippines

Capital: Manila

Population: Over 77 million

Area: Approximately 116,000 square miles

Religion: Mostly Roman Catholic, Muslim in some southern islands

Climate: Warm and humid all year. Rainy season is from June to October

Topography: Mountainous tropical islands with extensive coastal regions and valleys Located in the Pacific Ocean east of Southeast Asia and north of Indonesia

Summary: Composed of over 7,100 islands (about 1,000 uninhabited). The islands are subject to earthquakes and volcanoes. An area of many different ethnic minorities, the archipelago was "discovered" by Ferdinand Magellan and his crews in 1521. Spain claimed the region as a Spanish colony from that time until the Spanish-American War of 1898-1901. The islands were invaded by Japan on December 8, 1941. The intent was to invade the Philippines simultaneously with Pearl Harbor, Guam, Wake, Indochina, and Formosa (Taiwan) on December 7, but was postponed one day due to fog. Following great resistance to the Japanese occupation the islands were liberated by the United States as part of the defeat of Japan on September 2, 1945. One of the greatest strengths of the Philippine Islands is their rising agricultural productivity and one of Asia's strongest economies.

31
Churchill's Folly: Gallipoli, Turkey, 1915

The Gallipoli Peninsula, just southwest of present-day Istanbul, is an area of steep hills that guard the entry to the Dardanelles. The seagoing route is a narrow channel connecting the Aegean Sea and the Sea of Marmara. Istanbul (Constantinople until 1915) guards the Straights of Dardanelles, the "gateway to the Black Sea" and the southwest access to Russia.

As the complicated alliances of the Great War (WWI) began to weave their wicked intrigues among nations, the Mideast nation of Turkey aligned with Germany and the Central European powers and blockaded the Bosporus. The closure of that sea route frustrated allied efforts to keep Russia in the war on the eastern front. The impoverished and technologically deficient Russians were in desperate need of all possible supplies.

Turkey, in coordination with Germany, attacked southern Russia in the Caucasus mountains just after the Russians had experienced a devastating loss of over 200,000 casualties at the hands of German forces at the Battle of Tannenberg (August, 1914). Russia, under Czar Nicholas II, pleaded with the allies to open a new front to relieve pressure on their southern flank. Instead, by October, 1917, the Bolsheviks and other political parties forced Russia to withdraw from the Great War.

Winston Churchill, Britain's First Lord of the Admiralty, was singularly intent upon intervening on this southeastern front. The expectation was that the stalemate on the horrific western front could somehow be broken. With the backing of Lord Kitchener, Minister of War, Churchill pushed through a paper plan to reopen the passage through the Dardanelles. Most of the general staff thought it was too risky. It was known in advance that any hope

for success of the plan would require flawless execution.

The British, who were losing hundreds of thousands of their finest young men, could ill afford to lose the Russian front. Churchill's plan was to rely almost entirely upon a naval assault. It was unrealistic to anticipate use of aircraft or support from hard-pressed Russia. Commanding the fleet was Admiral Sir Sackville Carden (1857-1930) who possessed a far less than overwhelming force. The very cautious admiral was hampered by Turkish mines and his restricted positioning resulted in a negligible effect for the shore bombardment. Under heavy assault himself, Admiral Carden actually withdrew his forces during March, 1915, and was replaced by his second in command, Admiral John de Robeck (1862-1928). Robeck managed to lose four battleships to Turkish mines. The only remaining option was to send in the infantry.

British Army General Sir Ian Hamilton (1853-1947) was selected to lead a force of approximately 320,000 British, Australian, New Zealander and French forces (ANZACS). His forces, however, were fewer in number than the Turkish defenders who held the clearly superior, high ground. The results would once again be catastrophic. There were 200,000 casualties and 113,000 troops that were finally evacuated. There would be no element of surprise and no brilliant strategy or tactics. The plan of the high command was apparently to hammer out breakthroughs under the worst possible conditions for the allies.

The Turkish defenders, in contrast, were further assisted by General Liman von Sanders. A brilliant, senior officer on loan from Kaiser Wilhelm's army, his task was to assist in planning the defense of Gallipoli. Most fortuitously, von Sanders was allowed a full month to set up a flexible defensive plan because of allied bungling in getting into position. The defender's rocky elevations, up to 200 feet, were at the core of that defensive plan. The proud Turkish defenders were also smoldering at the condescending and dehumanizing publicity that kept appearing in the British press.

The British and Anzac landings, late as they were, were not seriously opposed. Once in position, however, they received hailstorms of rifle and automatic weapon fire at every attempt to assault the steep bluffs. Before the Allied troops were evacuated there were the following casualties: Britain (120,000), France (27,000), Australia (26,111), New Zealand (7,571), India (1,350) and Canada/Newfoundland (49).

Colonel Mustafa Kemal (1881-1938), who would later be known as "the father of modern Turkey," effectively coordinated the Turkish defenses. It was his forces that had one victory after another until the Anzac, British forces were evacuated. Kemal, who was later known as Ataturk, or "father of the Turks," later founded the Turkish Republic and was its first president. His defensive campaign at Gallipoli was one of great intensity and close proximities that at times became hand-to-hand combat in trenches. It was still not the type of battle that the allies intended to break the stalemate on the western front.

The extreme and futile loss of life at Gallipoli was also a personal and political disaster for Winston Churchill. He was quickly demoted to an obscure, government position. He soon left that to head an infantry battalion on the western front of France. For the remainder of his career of public service, many British voters remembered this tragic waste of lives as he clawed his way to the wartime position of prime minister.

In little more than six months the allies would have almost 200,000 casualties, four lost battleships and extremely little to show for their effort. By the end of July, 1915, many of the troops had died due to illness. Sanitary conditions had deteriorated so much that both dysentery and infections were major problems. Morale of the troops, under a succession of poor commanders and a poorly executed plan, could have hardly been worse. When General Ian Hamilton was relieved by General Charles Munro (1860-1929) on October 16, 1915, there was little to recommend except evacuation. That was exactly what he did. When hearing about the decision, an enraged Winston Churchill described Munro as follows: "He came, he saw, he capitulated."

Had success at Gallipoli been possible, there was the distinct possibility that Constantinople would have been taken in a short time and that Turkey would have likely withdrawn from the Great War. Open supply lines to southern Russia may have kept that impoverished giant in the war and prevented the 1917 Russian Revolution.

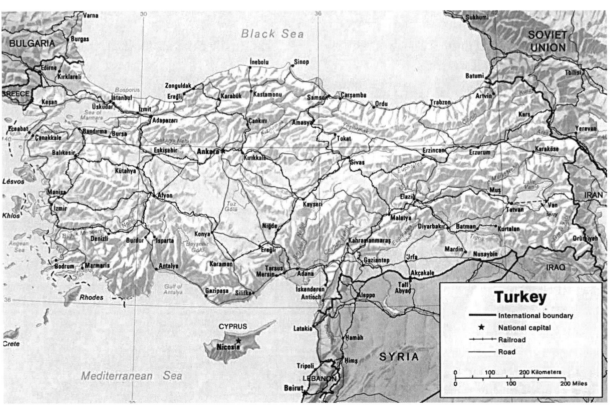

116

32
The Battle of the Somme, July-Nov., 1916

One of military histories' worst conceived and executed plans of all times occurred on gently rolling hills of northwestern France north of Paris and along the Somme River. In opposing trenches and dugouts stretching over twenty miles was a stalemated "No Man's Land" that threatened to become another, protracted killing field such as Verdun, which it was intended to relieve. A "breakthrough plan" was actually intended to relieve pressure on Verdun, to pin down Germans and their allies on the "Western Front," and keep the fragile "Eastern Front" in the war. In reality, the grossly unimaginative and anachronistic assault plan failed in a far more dismal manner than words can express. The commander, a man of striking good appearance and credentials, was in reality an inept and insensitive old cavalryman whose efforts to prove a good cavalry charge wasn't dead, (it was), made decisions that contributed to 600,000 British and French casualties. A personal favorite of King George V (who ruled from 1910 to 1936), his name was General Sir Douglas Haig (1861-1928).

Originally this diversionary assault was conceived in reaction to the mass slaughters on western and eastern fronts and at Gallipoli. The madness that was the Battle of the Somme produced well over one million combined casualties and ended basically where it began. The 55 year old cavalryman in charge, when confronted with the casualty lists, whimsically said, "The nation must be prepared to see heavy casualty lists."

In case of any doubt that the western world has not produced a worse commander, Haig wrote the following in his 1926 book *Dispatches*, "I believe that the value of the horse and the opportunity for the horse in the future are likely to be as great as ever. Aeroplanes and tanks are only accessories to the men and the horse, and I feel sure that as time goes on you will find just as much use for the horse—the well-bred horse as you have ever done in the past." Such boneheaded sentiment represents a great love of horses and is a great tribute to the likes of Ghengis Khan who did not face barbed wire, massive trenches, and concrete hardened bunkers with artillery and machine gun defenses. In 1936 David Lloyd George's *War Memoirs,* he referred to him as, "Brilliant to the top of his army boots." Another description by William Manchester in *American Caesar; Douglas MacArthur 1880-1964* was as follows: "In World War I, Douglas Haig butchered the flower of British youth in the Somme and Flanders without winning a single victory." Also, E.K.G. Sixsmith in, *British Generalship in the Twentieth Century,* wrote, "Haig failed perhaps to see that a dead man cannot advance, and that to replace him is only to provide another corpse."

The diversionary assault near the Somme River was conceived as a joint British and French operation. French Commander-in-Chief, Joseph Joffre was credited with the plan. It was the British Expeditionary Force (BEF) commander, General Sir Douglas Haig, who totally accepted the plan without ever seeing its weaknesses and over the objections of many other generals. The essence of the plan was to pour in up to 100,000 artillery shells per day for five days before launching a massive, 66,000 man infantry to "mop up" any remnants of an enemy army that could possibly survive such an attack. Obviously, earlier artillery experience in the war had not demonstrated to General Haig how dug-in troops survive monotonous bombardments. Barbed wire entanglements are merely raised up into the air and then settle into even more intense entanglements. The record, however, suggests that General Haig never became intimately involved with the actual battlefield either before, during, or after that horrendous event. Haig's plan was to use the force of numbers. He pitted up to 750,000 British and French allies against roughly 450,000 German and allied forces.

The broader plan was to squeeze the Kaiser's coalition of German-Austrian-Hungarian forces on three sides with the British Expeditionary Forces pushing them into the Italians and Russians. Tremendous pressure was on the British to come up with a military solution. Every day thousands of lives were being lost on all sides. The essence of Haig's ill-conceived plan was an extremely unimaginative push along the entire front to find any weaknesses and to exploit that weakness with mounted cavalry charges. It was a swashbuckling plan that must have had its roots back in the last crusades.

The British infantry (Tommies) filled the switchback trenches stretching over an 18 mile area. The French held comparable trenches between the Tommies and the Somme River. The open, leafless area stretching before them was known as "No Man's Land." The German Axis occupied the well dug-in high ground. Surprise was not an element of the attack as German General Fritz von Below was well aware of the BEF buildup opposite his forces.

Without confirmation of the effectiveness of the artillery bombardment, General Sir Henry Rawlinson (1864-1925) scheduled his infantry to assault on June 29. The assault was to follow five days of very intense artillery bombardment. It was the biggest artillery bombardment since the war began. So confident of success was General Rawlinson that the enemy would be pulverized that he ordered his troops to march smartly toward the German lines. Successive waves went forward after they had completed their breakfast, starting in broad daylight at 7:30 AM.

The massive bombardment was pelted with an almost equal number of days of rain. Conditions became a muddy bog with standing water in the trenches. The weather forced postponements, greatly increased tensions, and a slowed down the rate of artillery fire to avoid running out of ammunition. The thunderous shelling continued for a period of seven days. Smoke, fire, dust and a trembling of the earth was apparent everywhere. The night was lit up with eerie colors and the extreme noises where overwhelming. "Even the rats were terrified," reported one German soldier who lived to describe that nightmare.

Therefore, on July 1, not June 29 whistles blew directing waves of attackers of the original 66,000 man force to march cautiously into No Man's Land as if it were some kind of parade. A German machine gunner, after the war, described the scene as follows: "The officers were in the front. I noticed one of them walking calmly and carrying a walking stick. When we started firing, we just had to load and reload. They went down in the hundreds. You didn't have to aim, we just fired into them." That day, July 1, 1916, became the bloodiest day in British military history.

The dug-in Germans had radically thinned their lines during the obligatory barrage. Once it predictably ended they repositioned themselves along trenches and machine gun posts as if nothing had occurred. They poured devastating fire into the now fully exposed BEF troops as wave after wave came toward them. A single machine gun nest could take out an entire battalion of men with little cost to themselves.

Frontline British troops, carrying too much gear to be agile or fast, were pressured by the mass numbers of forces coming up from behind them. Huge numbers of mostly raw troops fell with little or no ability to defend themselves. Advancement in most instances was all but impossible. Soon, the BEF found themselves well behind schedule. Without creating or finding gaps in the defensive lines, there was no point in directing the mounted cavalry reserves into the line. The entire assault line was virtually frozen with respect to forward movement. Jammed up numbers of troops often found themselves in very poor, open positions. Gunfire was literally murderous. Few successes were apparent anywhere along the front. Nearly half of the assaulting force had become casualties within the first hour of the continuous assault. Like the inexcusable waves of assaults at Fredericksburg, Virginia, by American's worst civil war general (Ambrose Burnside), Haig ordered Rawlinson to continue pouring in more and more forces in the blind hope of creating a breakthrough. The tactic was like the exact opposite of blitzkrieg to be used in the following war where overwhelming, coordinated force was used to punch through a defensive line and to pour overwhelming pressure on the enemy's newly exposed flanks and rear.

By afternoon of the same day a brief lull in the carnage was followed by renewed ferocity of the same order. Some progress was being made on the BEF and French right flank. The British forces, however, stopped the advance when the day's objective was fulfilled, rather than exploit a possible breakthrough as wanted by the French troops. General Rawlinson refused to exploit the apparent weakness on his right by exposing his mounted cavalry. The "prepared" cavalry that had been held in reserve was actually retired from the field.

By the end of the first day of fighting a gross underestimate of the actual casualties was reported to top command. To anyone on the battlefield, it was readily apparent that all evacuation and medical services were completely overwhelmed. Both the dead and the dying were typically left on the sun-scorched battlefield day after day. Actual casualties for the first day of murderous fighting were over 57,000 men. Almost 20,000 of that number were fatalities.

The Germans, who expended their own troops at a less comparable rate, mostly held their ground. Pressure was on the German troops to hold their position at all costs. General Haig, intent upon victory at any cost, showed he was committed to sustained assaults well into the fall, but not in the disastrous manner of July 1, 1916. Incidentally, Adolph Hitler was one of the soldiers wounded at the Battle of the Somme. He was wounded in the leg and spent at least two months in a field hospital.

By September the British tank was introduced. Early successes were good but were not sufficient to alter the direction of the war. Too many problems quickly set in. It was especially true as the weather turned worse. By November 19 of the same year, the offense was abandoned mostly due to the poor weather. Zero progress had been made except for the ludicrous claim that the Axis forces had been effectively "pinned down." The total casualties for the four and one-half month campaign were estimated at 600,000 British and French troops. A similar, but much lower number was estimated for the German casualties. General Haig, who should have been court-martialed for mass murder, claimed a "victory" in relieving the battle of Verdun, and for pinning down and wearing down German forces who would otherwise had been moved to the Russian or Italian fronts.

British presses of the time–*Daily Mail and Daily Mirror*– reported grossly optimistic propaganda as if writing for a naïve, German audience. On July 3, 1916, *The Daily Chronicle* reported, "At about 7:30 o'clock this morning a vigorous attack was launched by the British Army. The front extends over some 20 miles north of the Somme. The assault was preceded by a terrific bombardment, lasting about an hour and a half. It is too early to as yet give anything but the barest particulars, as the fighting is developing in intensity, but the British troops have already occupied the German front line. Many prisoners have already fallen into our hands, and as far as can be ascertained our casualties have not been too heavy." A similar statement released by the British army on July 3, 1916, said, "The first day of the offensive is very satisfactory. The success is not a thunderbolt, as happened earlier in similar operations, but it is important above all because it is rich in promises. It is no longer a question here of attempts to pierce as with a knife. It is rather a slow, continuous, and methodical push, sparing in lives, until the day when the enemy's resistance, incessantly hammered at, will crumple up at some point. From today, the first results of the new tactics permit one to await developments with confidence."

On the day before the Battle of the Somme, General Haig made a statement as follows: "The nation must be taught to bear losses. No amount of skill on the part of the higher commanders, no training, however good, on the part of the officers and men, no superiority of arms and ammunition, however great, will enable victories to be won without the sacrifice of men's lives. The nation must be prepared to see heavy casualty lists."

Nearly twenty million people died as a result of the war of 1914 to 1918. The cause was said to be triggered by the assassination of the Hapsburg heir, Archduke Ferdinand. The consequence was that huge numbers of the first generation to mature into the beginning of the twentieth century in Europe, North America, and the Middle East were either killed or seriously injured. The senseless carnage was so great it spawned a huge anti-war sentiment among millions of people, and opened the way for more senseless carnage for others in the following world war.

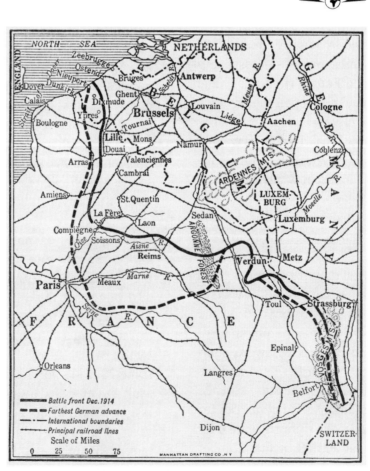

The Western Front in 1914; Binnis, F. Lee, *Europe Since 1914*

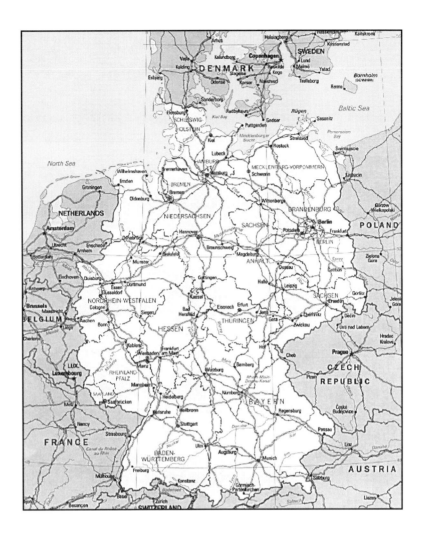

Germany

Capital: Berlin

Population: 82 million

Area: About 138,000 square miles

Religion: Equally divided among Roman Catholic, Protestant, and other

Climate: Cooler continental climate; especially in mountains, warm summers

Topography: Mostly pastoral hills, valleys and mountain areas Bavarian Alps, Black Forest and Harz Mountains. Germany has numerous navigable rivers and northern seaports

Surrounded by North Sea, Baltic Sea, Poland, Czech Republic, Austria, Switzerland, France, Belgium, Luxembourg, and the Netherlands

Summary: Long inhabited by Celts, Saxons, and Teutonic tribal groups since the last Ice Age this has been a hardy region because of the cooler temperatures and shorter growing seasons. The German principalities and small (feudal) kingdoms were relatively isolated for many centuries. Early conflicts with the Roman Empire to the south increased as the Roman Empire began its slow demise. The Teutoburg Massacre of the year 9 C.E. resulted in a loss of up to 25,000 Roman Legionnaires. The Goths who sacked Rome in 410 C.E. may have been in part Teutonic and Swedish in origin. The rapidly growing German city-states and agricultural regions were united in 1871 as Otto von Bismarck and German forces defeated France. Rapid industrialization were big factors in Germany's entry into both world wars and in one of the world's most dramatic recoveries since that time.

33
The Battle of Britain

The spring of 1940 was a particularly ominous time for Western Europe. Northern France was about to fall to Nazi control. Almost 240,000 British Expeditionary Force soldiers barely escaped the shores of Dunkirk without facing certain capture or death. The aggressive German war machine, Wehrmacht, appeared to be unstoppable. Field Marshall Hermann Goring stood on that abandoned and forlorn beach and was advised by key staff members that no time could be lost in launching massive air invasions of the British islands that began just 20 miles across the English Channel. Reluctant at first, Goring showed great enthusiasm for plans to concentrate his Luftwaffe and destroy both the Royal Air Force and the Royal Navy from the air.

British Spitfires in formation

Invasion of Britain at this extremely vulnerable moment was stopped literally by one man—Adolph Hitler. It was Hitler's naive assumption that Britain would recognize the certainty of defeat and would seek a peace settlement. The reality of Britain's gritty resistance to defeat was contained in Winston Churchill's remarks before Parliament, "We shall fight on the beaches, we shall fight on the landing-grounds, we shall fight in the fields and in the streets, we shall fight in the hills; we shall never surrender." Every hour of every day after the evacuation of Dunkirk was precious in building the island defenses. One of Britain's preeminent defenses was the early development of radar so they could allocate their limited defenses with the greatest effectiveness. Another was that they gained progressively greater access to German military code after capturing one

or more of the enigma code machines that were considered throughout World War Two to be nondecipherable.

It was not until mid-July, 1941, before Hitler authorized plans to invade England (code named Sea Lion). His crucially delayed, yet grandiose, plan was to land 250,000 German soldiers in sea barges throughout the southern shores of England, including Pevensey, which had been the landing site of William the Conqueror's successful Norman invasion in 1066. First, Germany had to obtain complete air superiority to protect an ill-conceived amphibious invasion rather than air transport landings.

Much has been written about the successes of the outnumbered Royal Air Force (RAF) against Germany's Luftwaffe. Additional acknowledgment has been given to Britain's early development of radar to provide advance warning systems and allow the best allocation of limited, defensive resources. Discovering and misguiding the German's radio-beam navigational system to targets was another important factor. But the majority of credit goes to the courage and stamina of individual pilots who fought against staggering odds with little training and little assurance of their ultimate survival as an effective fighting force.

It was the Luftwaffe's mission to destroy the RAF bases at all costs and a near certainty that they would do so. Ironically, a Luftwaffe bomber on its return mission with a partial bomb load obtained permission to release those bombs over London. This occurred in September, 1940. As news reached Hitler he was reportedly convinced that such attacks would break the fighting spirit of the English people and ordered an intensified continuation. The result, known as the Blitz, was both devastating and had the exact opposite effect on Britain's will to resist. The shift in focus was a major reprieve for the hard-pressed RAF with its limited number of pilots and need to scavenge for parts to keep aircraft in the air. The RAF's ability to continue fighting back can be largely credited to the tragic yet counterproductive shift to bombing of civilian targets.

Winston Churchill would ultimately say, "Never in the field of human conflict has so much been owed by so many to so few." The reference, of course, was to Britain's Royal Air Force (RAF) that had defeated Hitler's plan to gain air superiority over British skies before launching his weakly designed amphibious assault upon the British Isles. Notice was received that 500 German aircraft were on their way. They were intercepted by 300 RAF fighters. By end of the day the RAF claimed 185 kills (later revised to 60). Still it was a very close battle, but one that proved Britain's ability to resist. Two days later Hitler abandoned his invasion plans code named "Sea Lion." The British spirit was lifted by the successes of the Spitfire. German ace, Heinz Gudarian, was later asked what it would take to defeat the RAF. His response was "Give me Spitfires."

Hitler acknowledged his lack of confidence in naval matters. He described himself as a hero on land and a coward at sea. Therefore, rather than trust Admiral Dönitz and secretly construct a huge fleet of U-boats, much of the naval budget was squandered on vulnerable surface ships such as the *Bismarck, Tirpitz,* and *Scharnhorst.* Large stealthy U-boats could have also served as troop transports. One significant factor in the failed coordination of U-boats and the Luftwaffe was the extreme contempt Dönitz and Goring had for each other.

German Stuka Divebomber

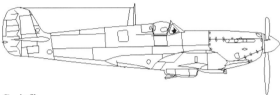

Spitfire

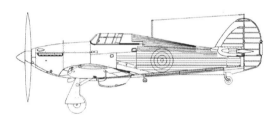

Hurricane

Casualties of the Battle of Britain, Summer, 1940

Pilots	Origin	KIA
1822	Royal Air Force	339
56	Fleet Air Arm	9
21	Australians	14
73	New Zealanders	11
88	Canadians	20
21	South African	9
2	So. Rhodesian	0
6	Irish	0
7	American	1
141	Polish	29
86	Czech	8
26	Belgian	6
13	Free French	0
1	Israeli	0

German Losses: Bomber Crews: 1,176, Stuka Pilots: 85, Fighter Bombers: 212, Fighter Pilots: 171, and Missing Crews: 1,445 (assumed killed). Chart reprinted by permission of MGM/UA.

England

Capital: London
(United Kingdom of Great Britain)
Population: Over 60 million
Area: Almost 95,000 square miles
Religion: Anglican, Other Protestant, Roman Catholic, and Other
Climate: Rainy, damp, and down wind from North Atlantic. Warm summers
Topography: Predominantly lower rolling hills with scattered highlands up to 3,500 feet
Surrounded by Atlantic Ocean, Scotland, North Sea, English Channel, Celtic Sea, Irish Sea and Wales, Just 20 miles across English Channel to France at nearest point.
Summary: A major part of the United Kingdom. England was a land of Celts (builders of Stonehenge) before the Romans, Anglo-Saxons, and Normans. Julius Caesar's forces invaded the British Isles in 55 B.C.E. The Romans also founded the town of London (Londinium) in 43 C.E. By 425 C.E. the Angles, Saxons, and Jutes invaded Britain from Western Europe. The French Normans ("settled Vikings) invaded southern England

in 1066 following the failed efforts of Norwegian Viking King Harald Hardrada to invade northern England just one month earlier. The Bubonic Plague also descended upon Britain in 1318. By 1387 Geoffrey Chaucer authored *The Canterbury Tales.* In the early 1600's, William Shakespeare described his island nation as "This royal throne of kings...the fortress built by nature...this blessed plot...." With the encouragement of Queen Elizabeth I, in particular, England moved on to become the British Empire "where the sun never set." Very frequent wars with other European nations before and after the American Revolution, financially devastated the British Empire. Colonial rebellions and the Great War of 1914-1918 were traumatic to the British in every way. The stamina of the British to withstand the Nazi onslaught of the next generation was especially reliant upon their development of radar, code-breaking, the RAF, and the Nazi's inability to launch a major amphibious assault without first gaining control of the skies.

34
Pearl Harbor
History's Most Costly Hit-and-Run

The meticulous planning and "successful" execution of the surprise attack on U.S. naval and army forces at Pearl Harbor on December 7, 1941, produced the worst, or one of the worst, consequences in the military history of the world. Millions of people, both military and civilian, either died or were permanently injured as a result of the war in the Pacific

The reluctant principal designer of the attack upon America's Central Pacific forces, Admiral Isoroku Yamamoto, expressed his own great reservations when he said, "I fear all we have done is to awaken a sleeping giant and fill him with a terrible resolve." The admiral had been an exchange student at Harvard University as a language officer from 1919-1921. He was keenly aware of the industrial capacity of U.S. companies, such as Ford Motor Company. He was also aware of the potential resources of the United States. Yamamoto clearly did not underestimate the Depression-era military of the U.S. that was ranked behind the nation of Portugal. Nor was he fooled by anti-war pacifists who literally dominated the politics of the post-World War decades. Admiral Yamamoto was one of the few to recognize that the American will to fight back with an overwhelming vengeance would follow the day that would become known as the "...a day that will live in infamy." As a senior military officer, he did what his country ordered him to do.

Major provocative elements motivated the militant new government of Imperial Japan to expand by conquest. The "imperialist strategy" brewed intently along with Japan's technological advances, their critical need for raw materials, and aggression toward Manchuria, China, and by July, 1941, the conquest of Indochina. Hostilities intensified toward "ABCD Encirclement" (i.e., American, British, Chinese, and Dutch strangleholds on the Pacific). Expansionist plans were also fueled by the lust to become a great colonial power like their ABCD counterparts. The militant new government of Japan, aligned with Axis Germany (Tripartite Pact, September, 1940), was quick to interpret U.S. embargos of oil and scrap metal as "acts of war." Well before December 7, 1941, Japan informed the U.S. that such embargos would be considered acts of war. Tremendous pressure was also placed on Japan's militant government by the ultra-nationalist, secret, Black Dragon Society of Japan. It was the specific fear of that ruthless group that lead FDR to set up Japanese internment camps after the attack on Pearl Harbor for all persons of Japanese descent living near the West Coast of the United States.

The "Bushido Code," which traces its origins to the warrior code of the Samurai, directly contributed to the desire to challenge the weakened ABCD nations with a "fight to the death" confrontation for regional supremacy. Western European nations with colonies throughout the Western Pacific (Britain, France, and the Netherlands) faced domination by Japan's military ally, Nazi Germany. China was weakened by centuries of poverty and constant warlord strife. The Chinese lacked an effective military force to resist Japan's aggressiveness. The United States, the remaining opposition, likewise had a ridiculously small military force (except for aircraft carriers and B-17's), an image of "softness and unwillingness to fight," and little more than an antiquated naval force concentrated at Pearl Harbor.

Battleship technology was fast becoming obsolete by the end of the World War in 1918. On July 21, 1921, Brigadier General Billy Mitchell had proved that a plane can bomb and sink any ship from the air in minutes. General Mitchell, in fact, testified before a Congressional House subcommittee in February, 1921. He stated that, "… 1,000 bomber aircraft could be built and operated for the cost of one dreadnaught…." It was obvious to all who would listen that aircraft bombs, submarine torpedoes, or mines could sink a ship for pennies compared to the horrendous cost of a battleship. The proof was not well received by navy traditionalists, but was an established fact decades before the assault on Pearl Harbor. The exception tends to be the aircraft carrier. America's three carriers in the Pacific (*Lexington, Saratoga* and *Enterprise*) were outnumbered and protected by aircraft that were inferior to Japan's Mitsubishi fighter aircraft and experienced pilots.

One of America's best long-range weapons at the time, B-17 bombers, were attempting a landing in the midst of the Pearl Harbor attack. All were unarmed and either damaged or destroyed. The B-17's on the ground *on the following day* at U.S. bases in the Philippines experienced the same fate. Foggy weather conditions south of Formosa (Taiwan) prevented a simultaneous assault on American bases in the Philippines. On December 7, 1941, Japan attacked multiple Oahu targets, Guam, Wake Island, Midway Island, Hong Kong, Malaya, and assorted islands in the Pacific.

Failure to respond to "appropriate war warnings" fell exclusively on the two commanders at Pearl Harbor, not General Douglas MacArthur, or to those higher up the chain of command. In this writer's opinion, however, President Roosevelt was morally obligated to maneuver and to interpret "world incidents" in a manner that contributed to the preservation of western civilization in war-torn Europe. The president's motives can be imputed to be noble, far-reaching, and intended to preserve democracy, not fascism and slavery for much of the world. Every U.S. president has had to

make decisions that could result in the loss of some lives. Pearl Harbor was one of those crushing decisions. No one, apparently, had any idea just how hard Japan could hit. In FDR's "Infamy" speech he stated, "…the attack was deliberately planned many days or even weeks ago." Obviously, as a former Undersecretary of the Navy, FDR was fully aware that the most far-reaching attack in world history was not planned and executed in merely a couple of days or even a couple of weeks. Above all, FDR could not be held personally accountable and function as the president.

The U.S. political environment following the disastrous and pointless loss of life in the Great War or World War of 1914-1918 dictated that no politician would drag young American men and women into another dirty war of attrition on European soil. Therefore, an "incident" had to be extremely provocative to alter the prevailing antiwar mindset. At the presidential level, something very significant had to be done before the British Isles were lost to Nazi Germany. Sinking the U.S. river gunboat, *Panay,* in the Yangtze River of China was insufficient. Sinking of American merchant marine ships in the Atlantic was insufficient. Nazi atrocities against all persons of Jewish descent were insufficient. Atrocities against Gypsies, homosexuals, mentally retarded, mentally ill, physically imperfect, or even those opposing National Socialism were insufficient. The rape of Nanking, China, was insufficient. The impending loss of the British Isles was insufficient. America needed an incident of great national humiliation and tragedy that each American could feel in their gut to change the anti-war stance. The vicious ferocity of the Japanese attack and reported lack of provocation on a Sunday morning, and the disastrous sinking of the *USS Arizona* was sufficient.

The severity of the strike upon Pearl Harbor was an extreme shock to the American people.

The U.S. administration was likewise shocked but probably for different reasons such as:

1. The declared neutrality of the U.S. should have reduced the potential for being attacked across many fronts. News journalists didn't ask if FDR was provoking the Japanese. The record showed that he was.

2. A formal declaration of war was anticipated but not yet fully received in the form of the intercepted 14 point message to the Japanese embassy in Washington, D.C. FDR feared that British-American code breakthroughs would be exposed and therefore lost.

3. U.S. military intelligence was incredibly unsophisticated and grossly underestimated the Japanese war machine because they were bogged down in an Asian land war. China lacked an effective army, navy, or air force and still avoided being completely overrun by the Japanese military.

4. There were strong prejudicial factors against "technologically backward" Japanese people who exported "junk toys," were small in stature, were "yellow" in complexion, and possibly could not see well due to "slanted eyes." Administrations as well as the populous can get caught up in such war-provoking bigotry, but reactions to incidents can be very difficult to predict.

5. The president knew most pre-war Americans were caught up in a decade-old, economic depression, and that few Americans knew where Pearl Harbor was located, or even that their president for more than two terms was mostly confined to a wheelchair. FDR must have known that neither he, nor top members of his administration, could be held personally accountable for 2,403 lives lost at Pearl Harbor.

6. There was the shock of not knowing exactly where the Japanese would strike. The expectation was that the Philippines would be the most likely, sacrificial target. Multiple targets deeply shocked the Roosevelt Administration.

7. The president, being a former undersecretary of the navy, was acutely aware of most naval matters. FDR literally fired Admiral Richardson over a dispute about keeping the fleet *in* Pearl Harbor and replaced him with Adm. Kimmel when Adm. Nimitz declined. A scandal over motive could have resulted.

8. FDR was aware that one of Japan's major carrier task forces was at sea in November, 1941, but he did not alert Commander-in-Chief of the Pacific Forces, Admiral Husband E. Kimmel [not an immediate relative of this writer]. A leak to the press might have forced FDR's "blind eye" strategy into the open, or expose Oahu's MSI-5 unit.

9. FDR also shared enigma code transmissions with Winston Churchill's government that assaults upon American *and* British interests in the Pacific were imminent, but did not share that information with the base commanders at Pearl Harbor. That FDR missed both the scale and severity of Japan's assaults must have been a great shock. The U.S. was truly unprepared for a world war on two fronts. Realization of such vulnerabilities would be shocking to any U.S. administration.

10. New radar systems in Hawaii, under mysterious control of Lt. Tyler, were given a low priority, but might have tipped off the Pearl Harbor commanders. It may have been a distinct shock to FDR if American radar sources had exposed Japan's plot before it happened. A weak attack on Pearl Harbor might have meant a non-U.S. entry into Europe's war. Another "failed" incident.

11. A skilled commander-in-chief relies upon intelligence to protect his aircraft carriers, not "luck." What if the press asked endless questions about the carriers, or FDR's responsibilities?

12. On hearing the news of the assault upon Pearl Harbor, Winston Churchill reported that for the first time in a very long time

he had "slept like a baby." FDR might have been truly shocked if only British targets were assaulted. The biggest shock at that time would have been credible exposure that FDR did have advance knowledge of Japan's planned attacks in the Pacific.

There has been a long-standing debate since 7:55 AM on Sunday, December 7, 1941, about FDR's advance notice of Japan's intent to attack Pearl Harbor. Did he know almost everything in advance? Was the president completely naïve, uninformed, blind-sided and completely ignorant of events in the Far East? Many books have addressed such questions under headings such as "Pearl Harbor conspiracy theory." The answers over the years have varied depending on the political or military orientation of the writers. It's far too dismissive, however, to ignore good answers based on the notion that "hindsight vision is 20/20," or that Japan didn't formally announce their multiple surprise attacks in advance.

There is no debate that Japan's diplomatic code was being intercepted on the morning of December 7, 1941. A 14 point virtual "declaration of war" was being transmitted to the Japanese Embassy in Washington, D.C., as the attack was launched. Details of the intercepts were not shared with the base commanders at Pearl Harbor until long after the attack. The infamous telegram of a war warning was sent by the lowest possible priority, commercial means and could only be interpreted as routine "correspondence." The key officials in Washington, D.C., understood FDR's directive to let the Japanese "make the first strike."

Completely neutralizing a Japanese attack could have left the U.S. fully entrenched in an anti-war stance within less than two years after the fall of France, Belgium, Netherlands, Norway, Denmark, Poland, Czechoslovakia, North Africa, and Indochina. In 1941 there was little reason to believe the British Isles could hold out against the Nazi onslaught. U-

boats and bombers were crushing the life out of England. Ecstatic with the attack on Pearl Harbor, Hitler publicly declared war on the United States on December 10, 1941. British interests in the Pacific, including Australia and New Zealand, were soon to be threatened by the fall of once-impregnable Singapore on the tip of the Malay Peninsula on February 15, 1942. The plan to control most of the world together with Japan, code-named "Orient," was hatched by geopolitician, Karl Haushofer and Adolph Hitler as they served time in a Munich prison, and was totally on track with the fall of Singapore.

The actual carrier-based air assault on the army and naval bases of the island of Oahu disproved the untested assumption that aerial torpedoes cannot be effectively delivered from the air and detonated in shallow waters of approximately 30' or less. The destruction of the French fleet in Oran, North Africa (July, 1940), and the Italian fleet in Taranto, Italy (Nov., 1940) by aerial assault kept those vessels from being used by German naval forces.

The concentration of mostly outdated U.S. warships at Pearl Harbor was both a forward line of defense in the Pacific and comparable to provocation that Japan could not resist. U.S. warships, pushed as far west as possible, were clearly intimidating to Japan's expansionist plans. Oddly, it has generally been described as "luck" that the three aircraft carriers based at Pearl (vs. Japan's eight carriers) were well away from the assault on December 7, 1941. These carriers were the true naval fleet defenses that FDR, as commander-in-chief of all U.S. military forces, could not afford to lose.

The failure of the Japanese to occupy all of the Hawaiian Islands sealed their ultimate doom. In not taking full advantage of their powerful "sucker punch," the Japanese failed to control the U.S. submarine bases, millions of barrels of fuel oil, repair facilities, and military bases that would soon have a catastrophic consequence for the Japanese at the Battle of Midway just seven months later when four Japanese carriers were sunk (June 4-7, 1942), and one U.S. carrier lost.

With the main exceptions of the *USS Arizona, USS Utah* target ship, and *USS Cassin* and *USS Downes* (destroyers), most of the Pearl Harbor fleet was refloated and effectively fought against the Japanese in the Pacific. Admiral Chester W. Nimitz, a top submariner, assumed command of the Pacific fleet aboard the submarine *USS Grayling* on December 31, 1941, at Pearl Harbor. The hit-and-run tactic of the Japanese both shocked and infuriated Americans who considered themselves to be at peace, non-provocative, and considered the Pearl Harbor attack to be "a dirty sneak attack." It mattered little to young American enlistees that Imperial navy officers wore white gloves and adhered to an ancient, chivalric code of conduct in launching a surprise attack. Millions of people either lost their lives or were permanently injured as a direct result of Japan's surprise attack on military bases on the Hawaiian Islands. The horrible consequences made the attack on Pearl Harbor the most costly hit-and-run in history.

For one of the best, detailed descriptions of the Pearl Harbor hit and run debacle, see John Costello's *Days if Infamy*, Published by Pocket Books, 1994.

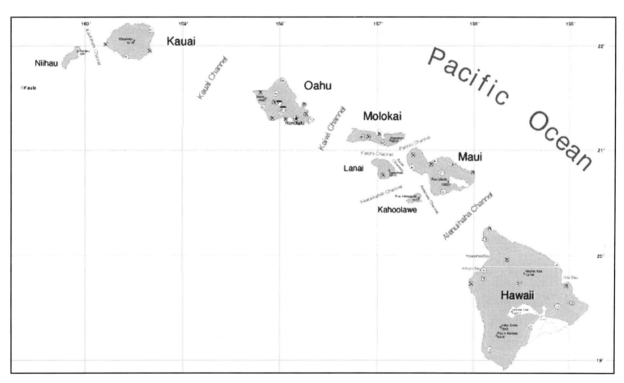

Hawaiian Islands

Pearl Harbor on December 7, 1941

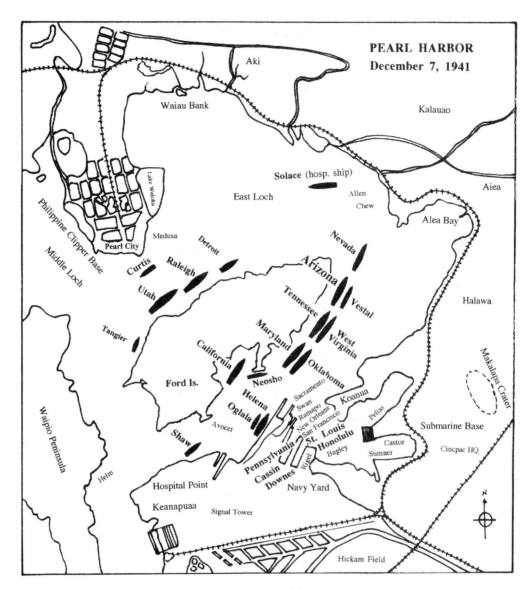

PEARL HARBOR
December 7, 1941

Hawaii

Capital: Honolulu, Island of Oahu

Population: Almost 1.25 million

Area: 8 Major islands: Hawaii, Maui, Molokai, Lanai, Kahoolawe, Oahu, Kauai & Niihau

Climate: Subtropical except at higher elevations. Typically there is a dry side and wet side of each island due to trade winds and ocean currents.

Location: An archipelago in the Central Pacific about 2,500 miles southwest of Southern California and roughly 3,900 miles southeast of Japan

Summary: The original inhabitants (Polynesians) from the Marquises Islands arrived by outrigger canoes between 300 to 600 C.E. Their distinctive culture was discovered by Captain James Cook and his English crews in 1778. The strategic location in the Central Pacific made the harbor facilities at Pearl Harbor one of the very few locations in the vast Pacific to construct and maintain a naval base. Hawaii was admitted as a state of the United States of America in 1959. The Pacific Fleet continues to be anchored at Pearl Harbor.

Japan

Capital: Tokyo
Population: Over 127 million
Area: Almost 146,000 square miles
Religion: Shinto, Buddhist, Christian
Climate: Warmer than mainland Asia due to ocean currents, hot, humid summers
Topography: Four main islands and up to 5,000 smaller ones. Typically mountainous with most residents living in coastal areas or valleys.
Surrounded by Sea of Japan, Pacific Ocean due east of Korea and south of Siberia
Summary: One of the last major civilizations to become actively involved with the remainder of the world. Japan was very protective of it isolation and cultural identity without suc-cumbing to the control of external forces. Major attempts by Kublai Khan to invade Japan with numerically superior Mongol forces failed in both 1274 and 1281. The strong sense of never being defeated contributed to the ultranationalism of the 1930's that led to expansion into Manchuria, China and ultimately assaults throughout the Western Pacific including Pearl Harbor, the Philippines, and Southeast Asia. The overly ambitious plan to become a colonial power like Western European nations led to extremely tragic results and then a reemergence as one of the world's great industrial powers without having world-class armies and navies.

35

Battle for Moscow: Stopping the Wehrmacht Juggernaut

Stymied by the Battle of Britain and with unresolved issues on the western front, Hitler took it upon himself to launch Operation Barbarosa. Rather than entrench for a defensive replay of World War One, the aggressively-minded führer launched a wildly optimistic second front to the east. Timing dictated that major elements of the plan be completed before Christmas, 1941. There was no realistic contingency plan. The ex-corporal-turned-military genius openly expressed raw contempt for the communist nation with 185,000,000 people ("untermenschen") with remarks such as, "Kick the door in and the whole rotten structure will fall." The reasoning appears to be based upon the USSR's primitive industrialization compared to Germany's, and extreme purges of the Red Army officer corps due to Stalin's paranoia. Ironically, Hitler's jail-mate and the philosophical architect of geopolitical world domination, Karl Haushofer, knew the invasion of the USSR would quickly result in Germany's doom.

Unlike the precision coordination of the piston-like "blitzkrieg" unleashed on Poland two years before with Panzer Divisions, infantry, artillery, and assault aircraft in overwhelming force, the Soviet Union was relying upon its natural defenses of vast distances, the weather, the spirit of its vast population, and the best tank of WWII, the T-34. By July, 1942, the first T-34's were ordered into action.

Hitler's best assault weapon, his Panzer Divisions, had crushed French defenses within a matter of weeks despite the numerical superiority of French tanks. Early in the Barbarosa assault, the Wehrmacht was again virtually unstoppable in punching holes in the Soviet defenses. Gaps were exploited with concentrations of assault forces (armor, infantry and air) that could maximize mobility and firepower to devastate everything in its wake. The supreme arrogance of this no longer secret tactic is that extreme distances required constant supplies of fuel, ammunition, food, water, medicine, and even warm clothing. Soviet dirt roads became impassable rivers of mud. Replacements of every kind could not keep up with the advances. Troop reinforcements were likewise impeded. The best hope was for frosty conditions to firm up the muddy ground. Temperatures, however, soon dropped to minus 20-40 degrees. Most of the armored vehicles could not be started. The grease in weapons froze and made them inoperable. The Wehrmacht's nearest advance was approximately 17 miles from Moscow's Kremlin. Advancing troops could actually view Moscow church spires on the horizon.

Joseph Stalin, who initially discounted reports of the intended invasion, was close to abandoning Moscow as cold weather further halted the assault. He received credible intelligence that Japan would not attack his eastern flank. This information allowed him to release 25 divisions of Siberian infantry who were both prepared and skilled at winter combat. A counter-offensive with these winter troops was launched with great success. The stunned Germans retreated but were finally able to hold a defensive line. At that point the Germans could no longer progress further into Moscow. By July, 1942, the Soviets introduced the T-34 tank, arguably the best tank of World War Two. The Napoleonic experience, as anticipated by the Soviets, had become a simple *déjà vu*. Many veterans of "The Great Patriotic War," as WWII was known in the USSR, say they never imagined at the time that they would lose the war. The war on Germany's eastern front has been aptly described as a tank war.

Hitler had previously warned against the dangers of again being drawn into two military fronts. It should have been painfully apparent to him that the British Isles represented an unsinkable aircraft carrier poised against the Wehrmacht. A southern front from North Africa and the Mediterranean was becoming a reality. Instead of a defensive posture, Hitler gambled everything by ordering an assault upon the oil rich region of Stalingrad. He committed the German Sixth Army under Field Marshall Freidrich Paulus to expand the eastern front. That objective was to quickly become another stalemate with phenomenal loss of lives on both sides. By January 31, 1943, the German Sixth Army was cut off, surrounded, and forced to surrender with approximately 91,000 remaining troops, including 22 German generals and Paulus himself. The myth of German invincibility was shattered at Stalingrad. Fewer than 5,000 of the 6th Army captives returned to Germany.

From the earliest confrontations in July, 1942, the Germans were shocked by the fire power and defensive qualities of the T-34 Soviet tank.

Soviet T-34 tank

Russian T-40 tanks

The 2" of armor plating and sloped design made it very resistant to German attempts to stop it. Toward the end of the war roughly 2,000 T-34's were being produced each month. A total of over 50,000 T-34's were eventually produced. As the Battle of Kursk approached, the largest tank battle of the war, the Soviets knew the German plans in advance. The Soviets were able to prepare massively destructive ambushes and defensive positions. From the end of that battle the momentum was with the Red Army. The Soviets outnumbered the Nazi's by at least 3:1 and picked up speed as they pushed westward and viewed the scorched earth devastation that the retreating Nazi's were leaving behind them. By January, 1945, Red Army forces were moving across Poland. Within six weeks they had reached the German border and launched a spring assault along a 100 mile front. By April 16, 1945, the assault upon Berlin was met by bitter resistance by home guard defenders, mostly old men and young boys—folkstrum—

Boggy conditions made progress very difficult even for tanks.

who made the "invaders" pay dearly. The T-34's lost much of their offensive and defensive capability in the crowded cities and a great many were lost. Overall, roughly 400,000 Russians became casualties in the assault upon Berlin. As a direct result of the war, it was estimated that twenty-seven million Russians were killed.

A successor to the 56 ton Tiger tank, the 70 ton King Tiger tank, was introduced to counter the T-34 tank. This monstrous new tank may have been superior, but no more that 1,300 were ever produced. The extreme weight required special bridges. Marshy conditions could also be problematic. The American Sherman tank and even the Sherman Firefly with a larger gun were of little threat to diesel-powered German tanks, except for the vastly superior numbers being produced. The T-34 was also diesel-powered, fast, and agile and

German King Tiger tank

had virtually the same firepower as the German counterparts. Designed by Mikkel Koshkin, who was once held in a gulag, the T-34 was mechanically challenging to operate, but contributed directly to ending the Nazi war machine in the east. The major factor was the commitment and sacrifices of the Soviet Union's military and civilian population. It has been estimated that 20 million Soviet lives were lost. Fascism was stopped.

134

36
Singapore: Gibraltar of the East

On December 9, 1941, Japanese planes attacked Royal Air Force bases in Singapore. Nearly all of the antiquated, RAF planes were lost on the ground. The day before battleships HMS *Prince of Wales* and HMS *Repulse* put out to sea from the Royal Navy base in Singapore. Both ships, pride of the royal fleet, were sunk off the coast of Malay by Japanese torpedo bombers on December 10 due to lack of air cover. The severity of the losses to the British people was very comparable to the shock felt by most Americans upon hearing about the losses at Pearl Harbor. The shocks kept coming. Almost simultaneously the Japanese invaded Hong Kong, the Malay Peninsula, Singapore, the Philippines, Guam, and Wake Islands. By December 10, 1941, both Germany and Italy declared war on the United States. The world was reeling and in shock.

The British colony of Singapore was known as the Gibraltar of the Far East for its superior defensive qualities. The strategically important base is actually an island located at the tip of the Malay Peninsula. The position is central to Southeast Asia, the East Indies and has direct access to India, China, Australia, and the South Pacific. The island is located about 120 miles south of the Portuguese, then Dutch, then British colony of Malacca—center of the famed "Spice Islands" and central to the most active trade routes of the Far East. Few doubted the power of the British Royal Navy to protect the island fortress from all sea lanes. The fortress itself had been reinforced in the midst of the difficult, world depression year, 1938. The island fortress was further defended by approximately 90,000 military personnel. Finally, there was the often touted notice to the world that Singapore was impregnable. The defensive image was so strong that the English apparently down-played intercepted code details of the actual Japanese invasion. Winston Churchill, Britain's Prime Minister at the time and Franklin D. Roosevelt, U.S. President and Commander-in-Chief of all U.S. military personnel shared critical military and political information in great detail. Both men had previously served as heads of their respective navies. Both men, however, underestimated the ferocity and skill of the Japanese army. The major cause was the apparent floundering in the land war against impoverished and virtually defenseless China. The technological advances of the Japanese military were grossly underestimated. By the first month of 1942, there were good indications that Britain would fall to Nazi Germany and lose its colonies as France had done when it lost Indochina. The Americans, with a military force that ranked behind the tiny nation of Portugal, appeared too weak to make any difference in the early going. The militant government of Imperial Japan wanted a far bigger "Asian sphere of influence" to gain needed resources, wealth and power on the international stage.

As the Japanese moved their conquests southward after the assault on Pearl Harbor, it was anticipated by the British in particular that Singapore would be a target. The military command at Singapore, however, remained confident that such an attack would fail completely. It was the British opinion that they were professional soldiers, not a weak force such as the defenders of China. In realty, the Japanese forces had become "hardened" by their incursions into the Asian mainland. Most of the 90,000 British defenders at Singapore were made up of British, Asian Indian and Australian troops with little or no combat experience. The British army at Singapore was led by Lieutenant General Arthur Percival. By war's end, he was flown to the Tokyo Bay surrender aboard the *USS Missouri* on September 2, 1945, following his release from captivity in Manchuria.

The Japanese force of 30,000 men was led by General Tomoyuki Yamashita. Most of the invading force had fought in the Chinese/Manchurian campaigns to the north. They rapidly moved southward, down the Malaysian Peninsula on foot or bicycle through terrain that had been considered impassable. Any prisoners taken along the way were executed rather than allowed to slow down the attack. The first encounter with the British at the Battle of Jitra (December 11-12, 1941) routed General Percival's men and pushed them into full retreat. The Japanese drive was as relentless as it was vicious. By January 11, 1942, the Malaysian capital of Kuala Lumpur was captured.

As the Japanese assault southward on the peninsula progressed, it was fully expected that the attack on the city of Singapore and its military fortress would come across the Johor Strait. By January 31, 1942, Percival's forces withdrew across the causeway that separated Malaysia from Singapore. Facing a final stand, Percival spread his defensive forces relatively evenly around the 70 mile perimeter of the island. The result could not have been more tragic for the defenders.

On February 8, 1942, the Japanese attacked across the Johor Strait as anticipated. Their smaller force was concentrated and far more aggressive. Lacking artillery the Japanese punched through the thinly defended lines. Percival's troops were often too far away to counter the Japanese, or held back for some defensive purpose. On February 15, 1942, the Japanese took approximately 100,000 prisoners in Singapore. There were widespread executions of the Chinese living in Singapore. The captured prisoners would serve out the remainder of the war under the harshest imaginable conditions. Most would die of starvation and disease compounded by abuse, accidents and executions. Approximately 9,000 men died as forced laborers in the construction of the Burma-Thailand railway.

The Americans and especially the British were profoundly stunned by the Japanese victory against superior numbers at Singapore. Military intelligence could not have been more mistaken. Japan was suddenly in a position to extend its "Asian Sphere" to Australia, New Zealand, the remainder of Southeast Asia, India, and Tibet. Operation "Orient" was well on track.

The British Singapore defenders were undersupplied, had only anti-ship ammunition, and couldn't turn their artillery toward the jungle roads. The 158 RAF aircraft available were mostly obsolete biplanes and were not sufficient to provide effective air cover for *HMS Prince of Wales* and *HMS Repulse.* Yamashita had only 30,000 troops compared to Percival's 88,000 troops, but he did have better equipment and aircraft plus some tanks. Mostly the Japanese used superior tactics of aggressively assaulting from the poorly defended rear. Without the Battle of the Coral Sea and the Battle of Midway the entire region would have been lost to Japan.

Japanese Soldiers & The British Prisoners-Of-War (POW) Give Last Salute To British Soldiers Who Had Died In Burma. From Singapore National Archives

Singapore

Capital: Singapore City

Population: Over 4 million (about 75% of the residents are Chinese)

Area: 239 square miles

Religion: Buddhist, Muslim, Christian, Hindu, Sikh, Taoist, Confucianist

Climate: Typically hot, humid, rainy area

Topography: An island roughly 25 miles across with many small offshore islands

Surrounded by the Strait of Singapore and Indonesia to the south and the Johore Strait and the Malaysian Peninsula immediately to the north.

Summary: Long a part of Malaysia, this very strategically located island has probably impacted saltwater trade routes in some manner for as long as there have been boats. Oddly, it was mostly uninhabited until Stamford Raffles of the British East India Company recognized the island's importance to ocean trade routes in the Far East and he established a trading settlement there in 1819. Considering Singapore's importance today as one of the most dynamic and recognizable commercial centers in all of the Far East, it is very odd that the value of its location was not recognized sooner. Singapore is roughly 120 miles south of the "Spice Island" city of Malacca (not an island) that was the final destination for Portuguese ships in the early 1500's who found certain spices more valuable than gold once returned to Europe. The fall of Singapore on Feb. 15, 1942, to Japanese invaders totally shocked the British who thought their fortress was impregnable.

37
The Battle of Midway, June 4-7, 1942

The essence of the Battle of Midway Island, 1,150 miles west of Hawaii, was the ability to use the enemies' most secret communications against them in a military way. With a guarded reliance upon the intercepted code transmissions, the United States was able to assault and sink four Japanese carriers. No nation is likely to recover from such an unanticipated disaster. The broad cultural distinctions between the two very different adversaries are reflected by that wholly disproportionate outcome.

The Japanese could be described as at the peak of their military expertise and the Americans were playing catch up with nominally inferior equipment and training. The top-down authoritarian Japanese followed orders and protocol even when it was not to their distinct advantage. The Americans, in contrast, showed great courage, sacrifice, and flexibility in adapting to the unique circumstances to accomplish their goal: find and sink enemy carriers. The Japanese commanders fretted over following original orders to take Midway and left themselves completely vulnerable in continuing to rig for bomb attacks, rather than torpedo attacks on what had to be American carriers. The distinction in military styles was such that Admiral Nimitz in Hawaii could have far more give-and-take with his admirals than Admiral Yamamoto could possibly have with his admirals even though his flagship, *Yamato*, (the super-battleship with 18.1" guns), accompanied the invasion fleet.

Except for Lieutenant Colonel Jimmy Dolittle's mostly symbolic bombing attack on Tokyo on April 18, 1942, and the Battle of the Coral Sea in early May, the Battle of Midway was the decisive factor in the outcome of the war in the Pacific. Up until that moment, the Japanese had unleashed a fearsome offensive throughout much of the Western Pacific and

Asian mainland. Pearl Harbor had been severely mauled and then abandoned for a possible later conquest (the military equivalent of hit-and-run). The Philippines, knowing for at least 12 hours that the U.S. was at war with Japan, shared much of the same fate and was unable to mount a major defense. At Midway all of that changed. It was the western-most island in the Pacific that still flew the American flag. Midway was probably the most dramatic and most lopsided victory in the history of naval warfare. Japan's losses were as follows: four carriers, one cruiser, 322 planes and 3,500 men including more than 100 first-line pilots. The American losses were as follows: one carrier, 150 planes and 307 men—mostly pilots plus the seamen aboard the destroyed *USS Yorktown*.

In failing to occupy Pearl Harbor the Japanese had failed miserably in their quest to neutralize American military forces in the Pacific. The Pearl Harbor facilities were very much a threat to Japanese naval forces because of their strategic position in the Central Pacific. The Japanese had failed to target the submarine pens, the repair facilities and the fuel tanks which contained over four million barrels of vital petroleum. Most of the ships damaged at Pearl Harbor were eventually refloated and used against Japan. It would not have been physically possible for the United States' small number of carriers to patrol the Pacific from West Coast bases without extreme risk of being destroyed by one or more of Japan's eight modern carriers and massive complement of support ships and aircraft. Finally, it was the cryptanalysts stationed at Pearl Harbor who deciphered Yamamoto's master plan to attack Midway that took all of the surprise away and in fact positioned them for the destruction of four carriers—*Akagi, Kaga, Soryu* and *Hiryu*. Most of the credit for accurately "reading" and decoding the master plan to assault Midway in great force goes to Lieutenant Commander Joseph J. Rochefort and his team of unconventional navy code-breakers.

Japan's understood intent was to make Midway an advance base to carryout the destruction of the U.S. Pacific Fleet. The seizure of Malaysia, Singapore, the Dutch East Indies, and the Philippines were effectively complete

Japanese Admiral Yamamoto

by March, 1942. The Battle of the Coral Sea (May 7-8, 1942) was something of a stalemate that resulted in two seriously crippled Japanese carriers that greatly hampered Admiral Yamamoto's plans. The rigid structure of the Japanese military command slowed repairs to such an extent that the decisive fifth and sixth carriers were not available for the Midway assault. Those two carriers and the carrier sent on the foolish diversion to the Aleutian Islands may have completely reversed the outcome at Midway Island. Admiral Yamamoto had again been compromised by military superiors who diluted an original plan that was sure to succeed.

The United States, in contrast, had four carriers and only three were in the Pacific. The

USS Yorktown had been severely damaged at the Battle of the Coral Sea but repairs began as she was under way and around-the-clock at Pearl Harbor. An estimated 60 day repair job was completed in the astonishing time of 72 hours. Success at the Battle of Midway would not have been possible without the major role played by the *USS Yorktown*. In an all-out gamble based on guarded confidence that the code data was real, and not a trap, three American carriers (*Yorktown, Enterprise & Hornet*) positioned themselves to destroy four Japanese carriers as they were diverted with a single-minded objective of seizing Midway by force.

Meeting that goal at the expense of 150 U.S. aircraft and ultimately the loss of the *USS Yorktown* carrier, was sufficient to break the back of the Japanese Imperial Navy (which was heavily modeled after the British Navy) and put them strictly on the defensive for the remainder of the war in the Pacific. Admiral Yamamoto alone had to confront his emperor, a living god, with the terrible news. Following that battle the Japanese Imperial Navy, probably the world's most powerful navy immediately before the Battle of Midway, went into an accelerating spiral of decline.

Admiral Chester Nimitz

Midway Islands

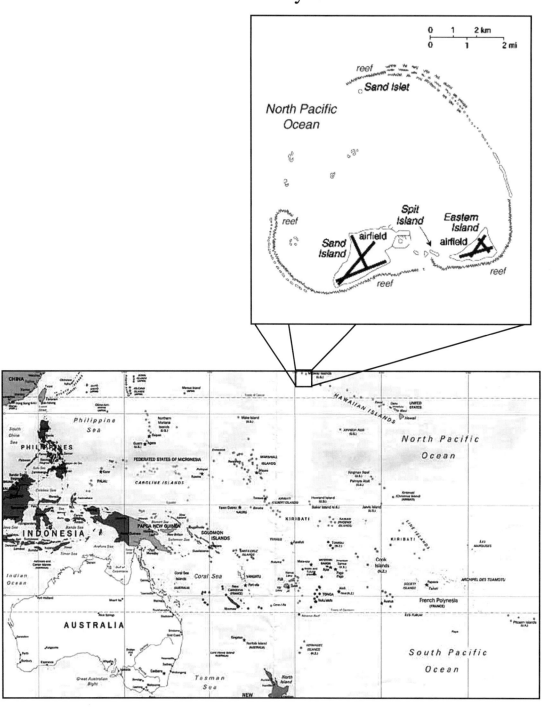

Vast Area of North and South Pacific Oceans

38
The Battle of El Alamein, 10-23 to 11-4, 1942

In conjunction with agreements forged with fascist ally Benito Mussolini, German forces backed up the muddled efforts of the Italians to extend their influence into Ethiopia and Libya. The master plan of the Germans, however, was to take all of North Africa, including Egypt and the vital Suez Canal. From that point the Germans expected to sweep through the oil-rich Middle East and link up with Japan somewhere in India. The plan was a segment of the Nazi plan for sharing world domination (excluding North America) with the Japanese. The German code name for the plan was Operation Orient.

Field Marshall Erwin Rommel's vaunted *Afrika Korps* attained a reputation for high mobility victories. Often outnumbered and under-supplied, especially of petroleum, he was able to outmaneuver his adversaries in stunning ways that earned him the reputation and legend as The Desert Fox. However, unknown to Field Marshall Rommel, the allies were intercepting German enigma (code) transmissions with great accuracy. The intercepts were near enough to real time to be able to often disrupt German supply lines across the Mediterranean and yet create the illusion that an overhead British aircraft had accidentally discovered the transport ships. By mid-1942 the code breakers at Bletchley Park, England, were able to greatly reduce the time needed to interpret German military transmissions from two weeks back, to one day back and, finally, real time. Code transmissions were sometimes being decoded in England quicker than they were being received and decoded by German commanders in the field. The mathematical sophistication of the ratcheting dials of the enigma machine produced such extreme numerical permutations that Nazi leadership was convinced their codes could never be broken in time to be useful to

an enemy. The simple secret was to capture a copy of the enigma machine without the knowledge of excessively authoritarian Adolph Hitler and to go from there.

Field Marshall Erwin Rommel

One of the most decorated soldiers of World War One, Field Marshall Erwin Rommel, was not one to lead by endearing himself to his subordinate officers and men. Much of his success was due to sheer quickness and decisiveness. His successes allowed some discretion in interpreting orders direct from Adolph Hitler that would have been suicidal for a lesser commander in the field. He often "outfoxed" his allied opposition.

Instead of implementing Operation Orient, as outlined above, the German and Italian forces were caught between the British under General Bernard Montgomery, the U.S. under General Dwight Eisenhower and the free-French under General Charles De Gaul. The German and Italian armies were soon forced to surrender. Hitler had emphatically forbid a German surrender and ordered Rommel fight to the last man. Such an antiquated and counterproductive order did not make good sense even in the trenches of World War One—Hitler's primary reference point. Rommel was among the few who challenged Hitler and survived. The North Africa Army did not survive, but Field Marshall Erwin Rommel did. He served as the commanding officer assigned to reinforce the Atlantic seawall of Hitler's Fortress Europe. He did so through the Normandy Invasion but was later implicated in one of the ongoing plots to assassinate Hitler and was pressured to end his own life with poison less than one year from the end of World War Two.

Before the end in North Africa, Hitler had instructed, "Hold fast, and don't give up a millimeter of ground. It's victory or death." It was the same pattern for somehow turning defeat into a victory that Hitler mandated at the Battle of Moscow, the Battle of Stalingrad, the Normandy Battle, and following the Battle of the Bulge. Hitler appeared to be strictly a predator with no faith in his ability to defend without envisioning the hopeless quagmire of World War One. His strokes of military genius were usually offset by his bone-headed rages and stubbornness. In Africa Hitler expected military miracles yet he didn't understand why fuel and supplies were mysteriously not getting to North Africa. One of his best tank commanders, Rommel, was provided with only 850 tanks. At least 600 of the tanks at his disposal in North Africa were inferior Italian tanks.

At the second battle of El Alamein six miles of British guns opened up. Rommel was in Germany at the time being treated for a sinus problem. The British, under General Bernard "Monty" Montgomery, insisted upon not confronting Rommel until he had overwhelming force. Monty had full code data at his disposal. He knew exactly where Rommel's troops would be positioned and their plan of attack. The British general therefore amassed three times the arsenal that Rommel was known to possess. He put up a wall of fire that simply overwhelmed the undersupplied German forces. An unconventional act of illusion was also put into place to insure the defeat of Rommel's forces at El Alamein. A British magician by the name of Jasper Masculin effectively disguised an entire convoy of tanks to look like a supply train and to create an artificial base at the southern end of El Alamein. The result was that Rommel's forces, perhaps

due to Rommel's absence, attacked the imaginary British forces in the south before coming under massive assault themselves.

The failure of the Germans to capture the Suez Canal, as well as the failed capture of Gibraltar, due to the intrigues of German Admiral Wilhelm Canaris (1887-1945), set in motion the future doom of German-Italian fascism and exposure of "the soft underbelly" of Europe to allied invasion. Winston Churchill said, "Before Alamein we never had a victory. After Alamein we never had a defeat." That first victory was heavily reliant upon detail received from cracking the German enigma code. General Montgomery had all of the details in advance and was able to position overwhelming force.

Adolf Hitler

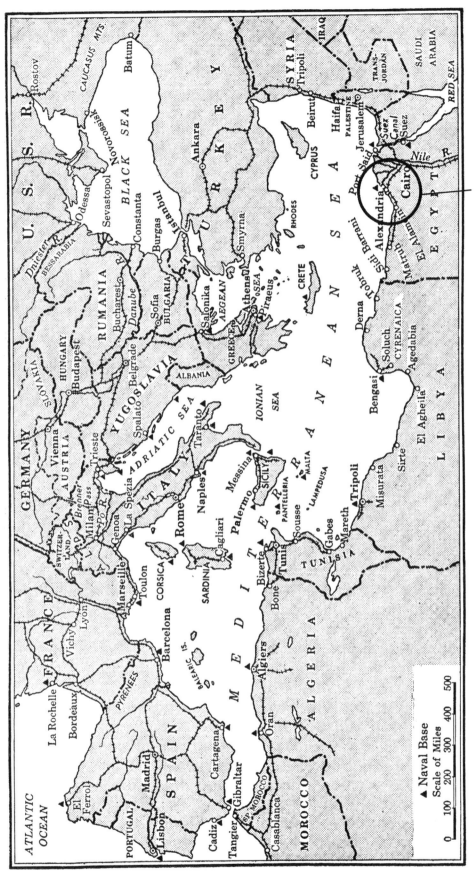

El Alamein

The Mediterranean area in the Second World War
Benns, F. Lee; Europe Since 1914

39
Admiral Dönitz' U-Boat Battle (1914-1945)

In 1901, Admiral Alfred von Tirpitz said, "Germany has no need of submarines." His apparent sentiment was typically shared by senior fleet officers of the world's navies. Tirpitz, however, later clarified his comment to mean he would not spend money on submarines *if they could cruise only in home waters*. Consistent with carved-in-stone naval traditions of the times, few senior naval officers could relate to a cramped mini ship that looked and behaved like a predatory fish. Oddly, the Tirpitz message seemed to contain the awareness that it was the stealthiness of submarines that freed them from home ports or virtually any undersea boundary. A young submariner in 1914, Karl Dönitz, certainly did not feel limited to his home port.

*Grand Admiral Karl Dönitz
(1891-1980)*

The first U-boat (Unterseeboot) was commissioned for German naval service in December, 1906. This first somewhat crude effort trailed the rival navies of Britain, France, United States and Russia. A major distinction was the German penchant for excellence in machine trade technologies that did much to move U-boat design well ahead of their rivals. With no chance of numerical parity with the British Royal Navy, there was real potential for German superiority under the sea.

As the War to End All Wars (1914-1918) began, Germany possessed only 20 combat ready submarines to Britain's 74. The real distinction at that time was one of focus. The British ideal for submarine use was for defense and

Above, two German submarines surface off the Mediterranean coast in 1915.

in strict compliance with maritime laws dating back, in some cases, to the 1600's. For Germany, the industrialized nation in need of catching up to other superpowers, submarines could be one of their best offensive tools. Given that basically different mind-set, the German's first undersea mission was no less than to attack the British Grand Fleet. The encounter was a disaster for Germany, but much was learned. Soon, the focus was to sink merchant shipping to cut off fuel, food,

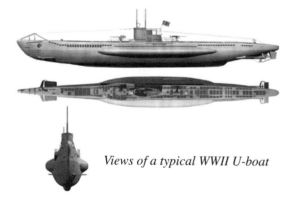

Views of a typical WWII U-boat

and munitions destined for the British Isles. As the war progressed notice went out that any ship in designated war zones might be sunk without warning. It mattered little that one gentleman would never treat another gentleman that way. Total war was different. What had been unthinkable brutality on the open seas would soon be a U-boat tactic to "win the war." Lost shipping tonnage increased at a geometric rate. By WWII's end, 743 U-boats were lost and roughly 30,000 submariners were killed. U.S. Merchant Marines, not counting those of all other nationalities, lost approximately 9,500 seamen. Millions of tons of merchant shipping were lost during WWII. In 1941, 454 ships went down. In 1942, 1,094 ships were sunk. During the month of May, 1943, 42 U-boats were sunk. The trend for U-boats from that time onward was very negative.

As the all-but-inevitable Second World War began just one generation later, Adolph Hitler had acquired almost complete control of the German political and military apparatus. Similar to his fanatical, yet intellectual, mentor, Karl Haushofer, Hitler had his dogmatic opinions that were very resistant to change. Parkinson's disease may have been a distinct contributing factor to his mental rigidity as his dictatorship came under more and more pressure. This new chancellor of Germany since 1932 had acknowledged that he was uncomfortable with saltwater warfare. His particular "genius" was in the area of land battles. As a result, he dismissed Admiral Karl Dönitz'

A U-boat in high seas

strenuous recommendations that Germany possess a fleet of at least 300 U-boats prior to a declaration of war and ignored his advice. Like the previous war, the undersea division of the navy was relegated to a supportive role with grossly insufficient vessels, but very dedicated volunteer crews. Such men were known as the cream of the Kriegsmarine.

Top naval brass invested in status-oriented mega-battleships such as the *Bismarck, Tirpitz, Scharnhorst* and related surface vessels that would always be numerically inferior to the British navy. Ships without air cover had about as much chance as the *HMS Hood* and *HMS Prince of Wales* that were both sunk off the Malay Peninsula by Japanese air attacks at the beginning of the war. The cost of the *Bismarck* was great enough to have produced huge numbers of U-boats that would have gone mostly unnoticed and would have been far more productive to the early Nazi war effort.

Larger submarines capable of carrying assault troops and supplies could have doubled as the landing craft that Chancellor Adolph lacked to make his planned invasion of England. That is, once he was convinced that the "British Bulldog" could not be bluffed into capitulation based on an imperfect siege and the near loss of the British Expeditionary Forces at Dunkirk. The English Channel is little more than 20 miles wide in some places but had not been invaded by rowboats since the Viking raids between the years of 793 to 1066 C.E. Karl Dönitz, in other words, had to scrape and beg for every U-boat not because of their ineffectiveness but due to conflicting priorities "up the line." The delays due to bullheaded Nazi priori-

A German band welcomes a Type VIIC U-boat, the mainstay of the German World War II submarine fleet, returning from a war patrol.

ties allowed the Allies to greatly improve anti-submarine defenses. As the assault weapon that Winston Churchill feared most, there was great effort put into convoys, asdic, radar, sonar, depth charges, mines, aerial

Seaman from H.M.C.S. Chilliwack boarding a badly damaged German U744 U-Boat.
ID #20946 Credit: National Archives of Canada

attack, reconnaissance from blimps, wire nets, shore watches, etc. The moment to capture the United Kingdom's "unsinkable carrier" was lost in that first year or two of the war. In both world wars the U-boat came close to forcing the capitulation of the British Isles.

In contrast, the Axis partner, Japan, had the best torpedo of the war in the early years. They demonstrated the effectiveness of their aerial torpedo design in a convincing, but costly, hit-and-run fashion at Pearl Harbor. One of the very last acts of the war in the Pacific was the torpedo sinking of the *USS Indianapolis*. Early in the war, the Japanese military elite, however, had a strong cultural bias against submarine warfare because it lacked the face-to-face honor of the military dual to the death. For them it was ironically the military equivalent of the cowardly hit-and-run. The disrespect for the submarine as an Imperial Navy weapon of war was so great that the submarine pens at Pearl Harbor were not even targeted. To their later chagrin, the new commander at Pearl Harbor, Admiral Chester Nimitz, was a subma-

riner and accepted the transfer of command aboard the submarine, *USS Grayling.*

Sufficiently large wolf packs of U-boats at the beginning of World War Two would have stopped all, or virtually all, shipping to and from England. Surface craft were all extremely vulnerable to U-boat attack because of their stealthy nature and great firepower. Even aircraft carriers such as the *USS Yorktown* in the Pacific were sunk by aerial assault and submarine torpedoes. The ability to dive and evade an attacker could not be matched by any other weapon system at the time. Too late, and long after the *Bismarck* sat on the bottom of the Atlantic, the priority to build huge fleets of U-boats was put in place. Dönitz was expected to achieve the kind of results that were distinctly possible in 1940, but, due to huge increases in anti-sub technologies, were no longer possible in 1943, 1944, and 1945. Still, the U-boat forces, with the highest casualty rates of any German military force, produced with such success that Admiral Karl Dönitz was named to succeed Adolph Hitler. He helped to bring about the unconditional surrender of Germany. At the Nuremberg trials that followed, Grand Admiral Dönitz convinced the court that he was unaware of the mass murders of millions of people. He was sentenced to prison and was released on October 1, 1956. He died on December 24, 1980.

40
D-Day, June 6, 1944

The critical "western front" that Joseph Stalin had desperately sought since the early days of World War Two would become a reality on a military scale never before seen. The outcome of the war with the Axis Powers was uncertain for many years after the invasion of Poland on September 1, 1939. The U.S.S.R. was invaded far too late in the year for any hope of success on June 22, 1941. It was definitely not certain that the Soviet Union could survive. However, the failure of the Japanese to assault Siberia freed up 25 divisions of excellent winter troops to face the German invaders. By the wars end in the summer of 1945, the Soviets had lost up to 27,000,000 of their people. The pressure and destructiveness to every aspect of Soviet life was beyond measure.

 The "western front" had been anticipated in many different forms from the moment France and England declared war upon Germany following the invasion of Poland. The Battle of Dieppe on the French coast was a trial run for the largest amphibian assault ever planned in the history of armed conflict. It was a total disaster. Operation Tiger, a training maneuver on the west coast of England, became real when assaulted by U-boats and resulted in the

Quartermasters hit the beach
(Quartermaster Review Sept-Oct 1944)

highly classified loss of nearly 6,000 allied soldiers. In the air, it required 25 bomber missions over Europe to be sent home, yet the average survival rate for bomber runs was 14.

U.S. soldiers landing on D-Day

The Battle of Normandy was one of the best kept secrets of World War II. The outcome and the cost in lives was a grave uncertainty. It required a broad, international effort to provide credible disinformation. The objective was to prevent Hitler from effectively reinforcing his "Fortress Europe" in such a manner that the cost of overcoming those defenses would be too great to pay. Patton's illusionary army, for example, was positioned opposite the Pas de Calais and was one of the most successful decoy efforts to keep many of Hitler's Panzer Divisions away from the real objective. Additional ruses in Norway, the Balkans, and the south of France kept hundreds of thousands of Wehrmacht troops away from the real objective. "Garbo," a Spanish double agent with proven credibility in the Nazi hierarchy, was a major contributor in convincing the German high command that the Pas de Calais was the real target. Most important was the British cracking of Germany's "unbreakable" enigma code system. Code breakers stationed at Bletchley Park, north of

London, were able to eventually provide real time, or almost real time, access to nearly all of Germany's military and diplomatic transmissions.

Following Nazi failures outside of Moscow and Leningrad on the eastern front and at El Alamein in North Africa, the defense of "Fortress Europe" was assigned to Field Marshall Erwin Rommel, a consummate military professional and exalted figure in his own country. Refortifying thousands of miles of European coastline was an enormous task in the wake of such massive failures as the Maginot Line and the Siegfried Line. Obviously, if major mountains, oceans, rivers, and deserts can be overcome, the "fortified wall" of Fortress Europe can be overcome. General George S. Patton referred to such fortifications as "monuments to the stupidity of man."

Allied Supreme Commander, Dwight D. Eisenhower, had the ominous task of preparing a multinational assault on a scale never before attempted. Tensions can only be imagined. There was always the potential of the secret plans being revealed and becoming abject failures, such as the Dieppe tragedy, only on a scale thousands of times greater. General Eisenhower, in fact, was known to have precomposed a heartfelt apology to be aired to all allies in the event of total failure. Winston Churchill told his wife, Clementine, on retiring the night before D-Day that upon waking as many as 20,000 young men were estimated to be killed. Others estimated that the casualty rate could be many times higher. Still, the necessary invasion to free Europe was launched. The commitments and individual acts of courage required of each person on D-Day were enormous.

Once Eisenhower made the actual decision, "Okay, we'll go," there were 13,000 British and American paratroopers dropped behind the "wall" to disrupt German defenses in every way possible. Rough weather disrupted much of the 82nd Airborne Divisions drop. Decoy paratroopers were also dropped to add to the defender's confusion. Undersea demolition teams fought darkness, strong currents and tides in efforts to reduce shore obstacles where possible, usually unsuccessfully. French resistance fighters (partisans) intensified sabotage efforts, especially in rail yards and communication lines.

Aerial bombardments by 800 aircraft were set in motion. Again, bad weather conditions and poor visibility resulted in major misses of the shore defenses. Naval shelling bombardments from the English Channel were intended to "soften" the hardened, concrete bunkers and gun emplacements, but mostly overshot the targets. By dawn, up to 156,000 allied soldiers of many nations (mostly American, British and Canadian)) would hurl themselves against these mostly intact defenses. The majority invaded from the belly of plywood landing craft known as Higgins Boats. Literally thousands of marine craft were involved and air supremacy was in favor of the allies.

A crucial factor in favor of the allies, besides the break in the weather, was the absence of Field Marshall Erwin Rommel. Headquartered at Roche Guyon, a French estate on the Seine River, he returned to Germany to be with his wife on her 50th birthday. It was Rommel's conviction that the expected invasion would come during high tide because that would create the shortest distance of beach to cross. However, the allies chose to invade at low tide to expose the shore obstacles. Had Rommel been present there is a good chance that he may have been the only field commander to override Hitler's directive and mobilize the Panzer Divisions at Pas de Calais. Hitler, known to not be a morning person, had taken sleeping pills the night before and was unapproachable until well into the mid-morning of the actual D-Day. Without Hitler's direct order the Panzer Divisions at Pas de Calais were not used to crush the Normandy invasion.

At dawn on that first day the artillery fire from big guns and machine gun fire rained down on allied troops with unbelievable ferocity. In some instances every man in a 30-man Higgins boat was killed by enemy fire as the ramp came down. In many instances the churning, cold sea water was chest deep and caused many overloaded soldiers to either drown or to be perfect targets as they struggled to get onto the beach and up to the bluffs. It was as if the German bunkers had not been damaged at all. Many veterans of that historic day have said that one of the most real depictions of that early assault was in the film *Saving Private Ryan* by Steven Spielberg and Tom Hanks. Other depictions of that very significant day in world history can be viewed at Steven Ambrose's D-Day Museum in New Orleans, plus the many films, books, and articles since that date.

At least two Panzer Divisions were held back near Paris that might prevented the allies from obtaining critical footholds along a broad expanse of French coastline. There had been roughly 6000 tons of bombs dropped on Normandy that were often ineffective because of poor visibility. Against all odds, by the end of the first day, the allies were still in control along a 50 mile wide stretch of beach. And, as estimated by Winston Churchill, by the end of the first day there were at least 20,000 allied soldiers killed and a great many more injured. Operation Overlord, as it was code-named, was by most measures a very important success. The world-scale war was far from over but the end could be anticipated. The British and Canadians assaulted beaches code-named Gold, Juno, and Sword. The Americans assaulted beaches code-named Utah and Omaha. By the end of that very bloody day the allies were soon joined by 156,000 invasion forces. By establishing a firm beachhead on the first day, the allies proved they were unstoppable. The Third Reich that was to last 1,000 years existed for less than one year from D-Day, 1944

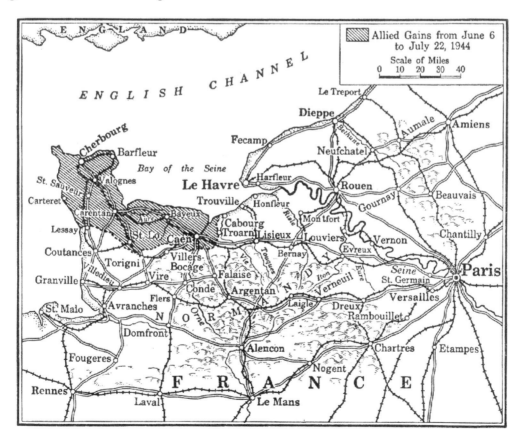

41
Okinawa: Last Major Battle of WWII

Okinawa is the major island in the archipelago chain known as the Ryukyu Islands with a total of roughly 480 square miles. Located about 400 miles south of the home islands of Japan, it was apparent to all concerned, especially the Japanese, that control of the Ryukyu Islands would be the final staging point for the invasion of Japan.

The Okinawan people at the beginning of World War Two numbered about 400,000 to 500,000. Their long and proud culture was distinctly different enough that the Japanese tended to think of Okinawans as a minority group and inferior to themselves. Early in the war in the Pacific, the people of the Ryukyu Islands were inducted into the Japanese war effort in part to create a defensive buffer. It has been estimated that by war's end as many as 100,000 to 150,000 Okinawans perished, Large numbers of original island residents, seeking shelter in caves and bunkers, died in the process of routing out the Japanese.

In many ways, the final major battle in the Pacific was unlike warfare that had preceded it. It was the largest amphibious assault in the Pacific war. Under the code name of Iceberg, approximately 1,600 U.S. ships of nearly every description were engaged. A total of 3,800 tons of naval ammunition was fired at Okinawa during the first twenty-four hours of the assault. Beginning on March 18, 1945, there was a greatly expanded use of kamikaze, i.e., suicide aircraft attacks against U.S. ships. A total of roughly 1,465 such flights were launched at the Americans from their home island of Kyushu. Also, suicide rocket bombs were launched at the Americans from the undercarriage of Japanese "Betty" bombers. The "fight to the death" mentality of the Japanese Bushido Code at this desperate time made Okinawa the deadliest campaign in the Pacific war.

The enviable commitment to fight to the death for the emperor in the defense of their homeland resulted in hugely disproportionate, Japanese losses. At the end of the battle it is estimated that 107,500 Japanese soldiers were killed. Extremely few surrendered (less than 11,000). Many took their own lives rather than betray the Bushido code of honor and pledge to their emperor.

Another distinction of the Okinawa battle was the Japanese decision to not defend the beaches but rather to move inland to fortified mountain defenses and cave defenses intended to make the price of taking the island extremely costly to the Americans. Drawing in the gargantuan American fleet was also intended to expose the combined fleets to the kamikaze attacks. These suicide air attacks were also known as "divine wind" in memory of the tornados that destroyed the Mongol fleets launched against Japan by Kublai Khan in 1274 and again in 1281. The reality was that 34 allied ships of all types were sunk. Another 368 ships of all types were damaged, plus 763 allied aircraft were lost. The total losses in lives was nearly 5,000 navy dead and close to 8,000 marine and army lives lost. A total of about 36,000 were injured.

Within the first hour of the April 1, 1945, landing, roughly 60,000 troops were able to get ashore with very little resistance. Included just off the invasion beaches were ten old American battleships, including several that had been recommissioned from Pearl Harbor (West Virginia, Maryland and Tennessee). In addition to the carriers there were at least nine cruisers, 23 destroyers and destroyer escorts and at least 115 rocket gunboats.

General Ushijima's 100,000 defenders included conscripted Okinawans who prepared themselves for a very protracted fight that would sap the will of the Americans to go onto the Japanese home islands without first suing for peace. Also, it could be argued that the Japanese defenders, knowing their limitations, wanted to minimize the Allies' almost unlimited air and sea power at that point in the war. Ironically, the Japanese throughout the Pacific had never learned to effectively counter sustained, allied assaults. Instead, there would be the gut-wrenching trade-offs of Japanese lives using mostly the same bolt-action technology and tactics they had used since going into Manchuria and China about seven to eight years earlier. The fighting spirit of the individual Japanese soldier was expected to overcome the superiority of allied weapons and tactics in every respect. That included the willingness to sacrifice lives in desperate assaults and absolute belief in death before surrender.

Taking the island of Okinawa was conducted in four phases. The initial phase was the deployment on the western beaches of Hagushi Island. Next, would be the clockwise rotation around the northern end of the island and the neutralizing of outlying islands to prevent possible rear guard assaults. Finally, the major

Okinawa was aided by propaganda leaflets, one of which (above) is being read by a prisoner awaiting transportation to the rear.

assault was to the southern end of the island with its entrenched defenses. The total, 82 day campaign bogged down to some of the most intensive ground combat of the war early on. Army and marine divisions assaulted one fa-

natic defensive position after another. Memorable battlefields of extreme carnage had innocuous sounding names such as Sugar Hill, Sugar Loaf, Chocolate Drop, Strawberry Hill, and the most ominous battlefield, Conical Hill. These highlands became especially horrendous to assault as the monsoon rainy season began in May and turned slopes into miserable, treacherous, mud slicks. Continued pressure on this "Shuri Line" convinced General Ushijima to withdraw his remaining forces to the final defensive position at the southern tip of the island on Kiyamu Peninsula. It would take another month of intense fighting before the battle ended.

Battle weary Allied soldiers fully anticipated being a part of a far more intense invasion of the Japanese homelands before the war would end. For many there would be little joy in the end of fighting in Europe. The cultural indoctrination to die fighting rather than surrender was expected to be a rigid part of the psyche of nearly every Japanese man, woman, and child in defense of their actual homeland. The nuclear bombing of Hiroshima on August 6 and of Nagasaki on August 9, 1945, did not end the war. It was the final bombing raid over Japan on August 14 and 15 with almost 1,000 aircraft involved and Japan's *total lack of fuel that ended the war*. Approximately 800 B-29 Super-fortresses (plus a fighter escort of 173 planes as far as Osaka) based in the Marianas Islands dropped over 5,900 tons of bombs on Japan's last oil refinery at Akita and other assigned targets. As much as any other single factor, it was the complete lack of fuel that brought the Japanese to the surrender table aboard the *USS Missouri* in Tokyo Harbor, September 2, 1945. The memorable change for the world was the horrific use of atomic bombs to end that war. The psychological horror of the Cold War was just beginning.

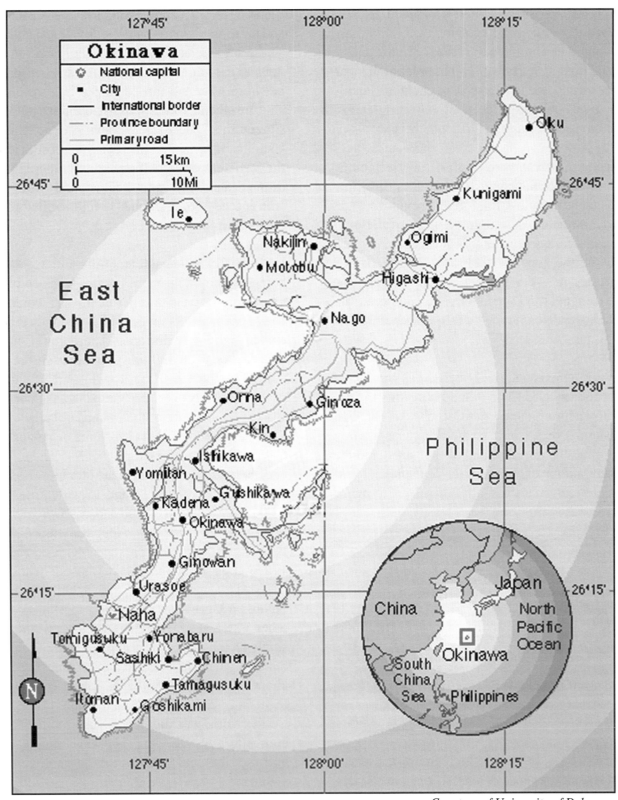

Courtesy of University of Delaware

42
Mao Zedong's Defeat of Chiang Kai Shek, 1949

The early history of China has been to never function as one, cohesive entity. Prior to Sun Yat Sen's Chinese Revolution starting in 1911, China had been largely made up of competing clans lead by local warlords. Abuses of the impoverished citizenry were epidemic. Dr. Sun Yat Sen's overthrow of the imperial government in 1911 began a process to bring China into the modern world. Sen's political party was known as the Nationalist Party (Kuomintang).

With unification of special interests in China a very long way off, Sun Yat Sen died in March, 1925. His position was assumed by a young general named Chiang Kai Shek. By

General Chiang Kai Shek

1926, almost half of China (mainly in the north) was coming under the influence of the Kuomintang (KMT). The failings of the KMT created many opportunities for growth of the Chinese Communist Party (CCP). Chiang Kai Shek hoped to stamp out such competition in 1927 with widespread massacres of communists. The killings forced Chiang to take more and more conservative positions politically and that lost him the support of the lowest income workers and peasants. The year 1927

thus became one of Mao Zedong's best years for recruitment to the CCP. Confrontations more and more took on the form of guerrilla warfare as the national forces continued to be overwhelmingly stronger.

There were at least five major attempts to kill off the communist guerrillas between 1930 and 1935. Mao escaped encirclement on the fifth try. A combined total of 100,000 communist troops and party members were forced onto a "Long March" of 6,000 miles. The hardships and the extreme high fatality rate along the way turned into the best recruitment campaign to date. Continuous battles with KMT forces and extreme hardships along the way resulted in losses of ninety percent of the original CCP forces.

Two years later the Japanese invaded China and terms were eventually reached between the KMT and CCP to drive back the common

Mao Zedong

enemy. However, from 1937-1945 Generalissimo Chiang Kai Shek vacillated between fighting the Japanese and the CCP. The Americans, not wanting another potential communist adversary, continued to funnel military hardware of all types to Chiang's people. Enormous amounts of supplies were shipped to support the anti-communist effort.

An inequity of another sort was Chiang's withholding of military hardware on a very big scale to use against his communist adversary after the war. Chiang's KMT was also riddled with continuous bribery and corruption schemes that further alienated the general population.

At the wars end in 1945, the U.S. also handed over most of the available war surplus to Chiang's forces. The CCP during the war had grown into a Red Army of roughly one million and a people's militia of at least two million. A full scale civil war soon broke out. Chiang's forces continued to be riddled with corruption and eroding support of the KMT. Mao's guerrilla forces—with war surplus assistance from the USSR—gradually reduced the effectiveness of the KMT. By 1949, Beijing fell to Mao's forces and Chiang's forces and followers escaped to Formosa (Taiwan) where possible.

Mao, the librarian-school principal-politician-poet, implemented his Marxist ideals with a passion. A total of three to five million "dissenters" were reportedly killed after the civil war ended. Extreme, radical changes imposed by Mao likewise had horrendous consequences. Over zealousness on the part of youthful party functionaries resulted in the deaths of millions more. The implementation of Mao's vision for approximately one-fifth of the world's people had fatal flaws that resulted in horrendous consequences. Yet China today, like Egypt, survives as one of the world's oldest cultures by adapting to changing circumstances.

A detailed article titled, "On the Role of Mao Zedong," *Monthly Review,* September, 2004, by William Hinton, disputes the "Mao-the-monster theme." His argument is that it is inappropriate to hold Mao Zedong personally responsible for all of the excesses of "the Great Leap Forward" and the ruthless reorganizations to bring feudal China into a modern, socialist world. Such radically imposed change, applied to one billion people, did not necessarily cause the famine that killed millions of people after Mao assumed government control. Mao's efforts to impose a "Cultural Revolution" to introduce socialism, land reform, and wealth redistribution inevitably provoked sustained political warfare between the peasantry, the landlords, the warlords, the intellectuals, and the foreign-based capitalists. A state of civil war among many competing elements produced conflicts and fatalities on a mammoth scale that cannot all be traced to Mao's policies. Simply breaking down the power of ancient feudal warlords throughout an impoverished nation produced huge numbers of fatalities. Military suppression of the basically ongoing civil war conflicts had its toll as well. It has been argued that it is far too simplistic to assign responsibility for millions of lost lives to the sometimes misguided leadership of Mao Zedong.

China

Capital: Beijing (People's Republic of China)

Population: Over one billion, 320 million

Area: Approximately 3,610,000 square miles

Religion: Taoism, Buddhism, Muslim and other

Climate: Wide variations without the extreme cold of Siberia or Mongolia except at high elevations. Southern China ranges from temperate to subtropical. East China contains much dry desert territory.

Surrounded by Kyrgyzstan, Kazakhstan, Russian Federation, Mongolia, Siberia (Russian Federation), North Korea, Yellow Sea, East China Sea, Taiwan Strait, South China Sea, Vietnam, Laos, Myanmar (Burma), former Tibet, India, Nepal, Pakistan, Afghanistan, and Tajikstan

Summary: Among the world's most ancient and highly developed cultures. Relative isolation and size allowed China to develop somewhat independently over thousands of years. External influences were typically absorbed into the dominant culture. Extreme disintegrations in the 19th and 20th centuries permitted far more foreign intervention and internal breakdown than the existing government could handle. Japanese army invasions began on July 7, 1937. Continued breakdowns during and after World War II made it possible for Mao Zedong's communist forces to overthrow the Kuomintang government of Chiang Kai Shek in 1949. An estimated 10 million lives were lost following the zealous changeover of governments, land reforms, and virtual civil wars that followed.. Market reforms since that time have allowed China to become one of the world's most industrialized and productive nations in the world. Tourism to China is also very much on the rise.

155

43
Inchon, September 15, 1950

It was one of the riskiest and most brilliant assaults behind enemy lines in the history of armed combat. The biggest risks were the conditions of the harbor itself. The Yellow Sea harbor of Inchon, Korea, has one of the severest daily changes in highs and lows of tide levels to be found anywhere. On average the variation from low to high tide is 33 feet. The potential for error with massive landing fleets in such turbulent and high current water is an open invitation for major disaster. Currents in the narrow access harbor often reached at least five knots. Also to be overcome were enemy mines, artillery covering the harbor from an island fortress, muddy beaches, and amphibious landings would be ideal only a few times each month. The delays from July to September, however, were due to the allies' gross lack of preparation for such a massive assault and the lack of the needed vessels. Meanwhile, Republic of Korea (ROK) troops and their allies at Pusan were nearly pushed off the Korean peninsula by North Koreans.

On June 25, 1950, North Korea invaded South Korea without warning and with overwhelming force. Defenders of the Republic of Korea (ROK) were being destroyed at a rapid rate. It was only through the intervention of the U.S., and then, eventually, of United Nations' forces, that the North Koreans (NK) were held short of "complete victory." U.S. and U.N. forces were still nearly pushed off of the peninsula. The outcome of the unexpected war was gravely in doubt. International support was not automatic and ROK forces were virtually neutralized in spite of dogged resistance.

Bitter fighting produced major losses in personnel and materiel. However, there was a two week cutback in the aggressiveness of the assault once the North Koreans (NK) recognized that the U.S. would be a significant deterrent to their plans. Both the U.S. and the U.N. were able to use that brief lull in the fighting to rebuild and reorganize. The North Koreans were finally stopped at the Pusan Perimeter. The outlook was grim.

The preparation for the invasion of Inchon was a Herculean task. General of the Armies, Douglas MacArthur, had to overcome great resistance from army, navy, and marines to sell his plan. Ships, aircraft carriers, and landing craft had to be brought in from a variety of sources. International coalitions under the United Nations had to be formed. The real aggressors, the Soviets' Joseph Stalin, and communist China's Mao Zadong, had to be held in check without escalating the "police action," as it was called by the U.N. Combat troops for a new kind of warfare had to be trained. A flap between President Truman and the USMC had cut combat-ready marines to an absurdly small number. Aircraft had to be positioned and refitted. B-29's would eventually be replaced with F-86 and F-86D jet fighters. Finally, intelligence had to be gathered.

A major breakthrough on intelligence gathering can be credited to Navy Lieutenant Eugene Clark, an "Old China hand." Along with two South Korean naval officers, and about four other specialists, he was able to make his way into Inchon Harbor several weeks before the actual invasion. They never were detected and were able to provide critical information about mines, mudflats, seawalls, tidal information and even data on the island fortress guarding the harbor, Wolmi-do.

Instrumental to MacArthur's plan was the need to knock out the heavy artillery guns that guarded the mouth of the harbor on the island fortress of Wolmi-do. To identify the enemy gun positions for aerial bombing, six destroyers of Squadron Nine moved up the narrow access of Flying Fish Channel. The plan was to spot and destroy mines and pour 5-inch gunfire into the fortress. Once the nearest destroyers could draw fire from the fortress, they moved out of range. Damage was light. The destroyers accomplished their mission and were able to exit the harbor under the fortresses ability to lower their fire. Several YAK aircraft fired on the exiting destroyers. One of the planes was shot down and then recovered in good enough condition to be an additional intelligence find. The guns of Wolmi-do were thus destroyed from the air.

The assault on the Harbor of Inchon was code-named Chromite and was a very aggressive plan for an amphibious landing of 70,000 well-armed troops hundreds of miles behind enemy lines. Another key element was to be behind their supply lines, to control the harbor, and nearby Kimpo airbase. Finally, there was the need to position themselves for a major assault on the South Korean capital of Seoul, just 25 miles from the invasion site. Part of the brilliance of the plan was also its ability to cut off nearly all rail, road and communication links needed by the North Korean People's Army.

On September 15, 1950, Joint Task Force Seven, with over 320 warships launched a counter-invasion with 70,000 combatants at least 100 miles behind NK lines in the harbor of Inchon. A major air assault and naval bombardment preceded the landing. By September 25, 1950, the ROK capital of Seoul was recaptured. Within two weeks of the counter-invasion, most of the North Korean troops "were on the ropes." Much of the credit for the success of Inchon rightfully goes to Far East Commander and U.S. Army General Douglas MacArthur. In his words, "We shall land at Inchon, and I shall crush them." It was a brilliant example of his "Hit 'em where they ain't" philosophy. Losses in the early going of the invasion were very light. However, by

April 11, 1951, the brilliant, controversial, remote, abrasive, theatrical, old man of the military was relieved (fired) by President Harry S. Truman because of his unwillingness to follow U.S. and U.N. policy, rather than formulate it himself and then announce it to the world.

The "old warrior" was born January 26, 1880 and died on April 5, 1964. He graduated from West Point in 1903 with highest honors and the direct assistance of his mother. His father, Lt. Gen. Arthur MacArthur, was a distinct hero of the American Civil War. He served during World War One in Europe and was superintendent of West Point from 1919 to 1922. By 1930 he was appointed as the military's Chief of Staff and as such was derided for harshly ending the World War veteran's protest in Washington, D.C. He sat or stood by for at least nine hours after the attack on Pearl Harbor and allowed his B-17 fleet to be destroyed on the ground. In 1942 he received the Medal of Honor. In 1952 he was involved in a misguided attempt to run for President of the United States. Among his many quoted remarks, he once said, "Upon the fields of friendly strife are sown the seeds that, upon other fields, on other days, will bear the fruits of victory."

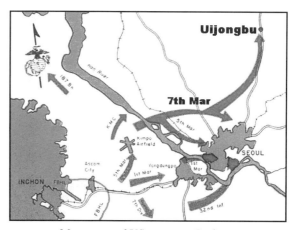

Movement of US troops at Inchon

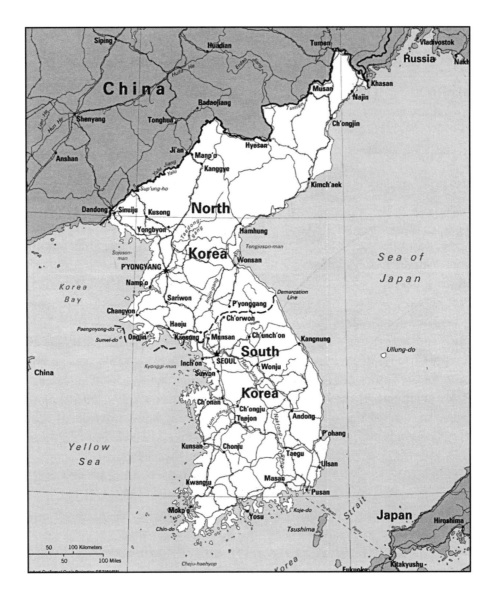

North Korea & South Korea

North Korean capital: Pyongyang
Population: Over 22 million
President for life: Kim Il Sung
Area: Almost 47,000 square miles
Religion: Reportedly non-religious up to 68%, others are Buddhist or Confucianist.

South Korean capital: Seoul
Population: 47 million
President: Kim Dae Jung
Area: About 38,000 square miles
Religion: Confucianist, Christian, Buddhist, Shamanist and Chodokyo

Summary: The Yi Dynasty ruled all of Korea from 1392-1910. It was a vassal state of China from 1644 until annexed by Japan in 1910. Korea was aggressively occupied by Japan during World War II and was finally divided at the 38th parallel in 1945. The Republic of South Korea was created in 1948. North Korea invaded the south in 1950 and used military force to impose a virtual civil war on its southern kin. A U.S.-led force of United Nations countries ultimately agreed to a stalemate at the 38th parallel in 1953. Tensions between North and South Korea have bordered on outright military confrontation since that time.

44
Dien Bien Phu, May 7, 1954

As the Japanese faced surrender in August and September, 1945, they also abandoned their occupancy of French Indochina. In their place was the new government of the Democratic Republic of Vietnam as announced by their new leader, Ho Chi Minh. The political forces that he represented since its formation in 1941 were known as Viet Minh. They had been the guerrilla fighters who did everything possible to evict the detested Japanese armies of occupation. The former colonial oppressors, the French had been themselves occupied by Nazi Germany (1940-1944). In 1945, however, the French refused to acknowledge the Democratic Republic of Vietnam. Ho Chi Minh even appealed to President Truman for assistance but Truman's loyalties and obligations were with the French. Little hope of independence remained without turning more and more to communist U.S.S.R., and, after 1949, Communist China for assistance of all kinds.

Supplies for the beleagured French garrison in Dien Bien Phu are parachuted in. The Vietnamese occupied the high ground.

In 1945 fighting began between the French and the Viet Minh. Early on, the Viet Minh under General Vo Nguyen Giap found their forces at marked disadvantages. The French troops in the early post-war years were typically better trained, better equipped, and had technological advantages not available to the much poorer "rebels." The situation improved little for the Viet Minh until 1949 when Mao Zedong and his Communist forces defeated General Chiang Kai-Shek's nationalist forces.

French planners began to recognize that their position would deteriorate unless something very dramatic was done. The French were confident that in an open, major battle they would win decisively as in the past. The challenge was to somehow draw the Viet Minh into such a large scale battle. The opinion of General Henri Navarre, commander of the French forces, was that such a battle would be a decisive victory for France. First, he would have to entice General Giap to commit his forces to a conventional military battle. Therefore, by December, 1953, Navarre ordered the construction of a "defensive" garrison at a site that appeared to have all of the right characteristics to hatch his overall plan of crushing the "rebellion." That site was a bowl-shaped valley surrounded by eight small mountains and near the borders of Laos and China in northwest "Vietnam."

The costly stalemates for both sides had contributed much to plans for a negotiated peace settlement in 1953. It was the French who wanted one big victory either to return to their old colonial position in Indochina, or to achieve peace terms more favorable to the future of France.

Planning for the Dien Bien Phu garrison moved ahead in place of genuine peace negotiations. The bowl-shaped valley was large enough to contain an airstrip. The surrounding eight hills were each given female names and were to contain strong firebases that would protect the valley. Supplies, ammunition, and reinforcements could be brought in by air as necessary. General Giap's lightly armed forces could be expected to waste themselves in making assaults upon this well-fortified garrison. Every contingency was anticipated. The target had to be attractive enough to lure in Giap's forces.

General Giap had been making plans of his own. First, his troops disassembled artillery pieces and antiaircraft weapons and literally muscled them up to high ground through terrain the French thought was impassable. He concentrated from 70,000 to 80,000 troops against the French force of approximately 15,000. Next, he poured in artillery fire that the French never believed was possible. Their roughly 200 heavy guns were so well entrenched that French efforts to knock them out were mostly futile. The French artillery commander was so severely depressed with his inability to knock out Giap's heavy guns that he quietly went into his dugout and committed suicide. The continued bombardment had the effect of closing the airstrip. Resupply became virtually impossible. Supply planes were forced to fly higher and higher because of effective, antiaircraft fire. The parachuted supplies were thus more and more unreliable in getting to their destination and often aided the Viet Minh.

Early on, two of the eight firebases were captured by the Viet Minh. Efforts to retake those sites proved very costly for the French. It was just a matter of time before the true, grinding effects of the siege set in. The monsoon season settled in to make the almost impossible conditions in the bowl-shaped valley even more miserable. Instead of putting his forces at risk with open assaults, Gen. Giap used what he later described as "a tactic of combined nibbling and full-scale attack." A metaphor used for the remainder of this particular siege was that it was like "slowly bleeding a dying elephant." The last replacements of 4,306 troops under General Marcel Bigeard were parachuted in between mid-March and mid-May and were not enough to replace those killed during that same period. A final, French assault to break out occurred on May 4, 1954, but was ineffective. Russian rocket artillery was introduced during the next few days. By May 7 the garrison surrendered as they were being overrun by a huge, frontal assault.

Over 2,200 of the close to 20,000 French troops were killed in action. Of the 80,000 to 100,000 Viet Minh forces an estimated 8,000 were killed and possibly 15,000 wounded. The ferocity of the battle could hardly be underestimated. The resourcefulness and tenacity of the Viet Minh certainly was underestimated. Far more grisly conditions and often death awaited the POW's. The 1954 Geneva Accords acknowledged the Viet Minh victory and partitioned Vietnam into a communist north and pro-Western south half that was to be reunited in 1956 through national elections. The elections did not happen because the southern government opposed the agreement. The south, under President Ngo Dinh Diem, had grave concerns that the more aggressive north, under Ho Chi Minh, would win such an election. The door was therefore left open for the United States, under President Dwight D. Eisenhower, to hold back the "red tide." Little was done by the U.S. and the "Southeast Asia problem" was passed on to the incoming President John F. Kennedy who took office in January, 1961. Aggressive at first, the plan to withdraw U.S. advisors from Vietnam in late 1963 and the appearance of going soft on communism may have been a major factor in the president's assassination. Instead, the U.S-led war in Southeast Asia mostly escalated until its conclusion on April 30, 1975.

160

Vietnam

Capital: Hanoi (Formed in 1976)
Population: Approximately 82 million
Area: Approximately 127,000 square miles
Religion: About 55% Buddhist, Confucianist, Taoist, and Roman Catholic
Climate: Tropical in the south and ranging to much cooler in north and mountains
Topography: Much of the country is little more than sea level. Over half of the country is dominated by heavily forested mountain ranges rising to almost 7,000 feet
Surrounded by China, Gulf of Tonkin, South China Sea, Cambodia and Laos
Summary: Occupying the eastern fringe of the Indochinese peninsula the fiercely independent Vietnamese have avoided domination from their far larger neighbor to the north for many centuries. Following the Franco-Chinese War of 1884-1885 the Southeast Asia colony of Indochina was formed by the French government in October, 1887. The region was aggressively occupied by the French from that time until the beginning of World War II. Indochina was then occupied by the Japanese during WW II. The Vietnamese people believed they could regain their independence after the war. The French, however, reasserted their claims and had to be ousted at the Battle of Dien Bien Phu in 1954. Subsequent civil war strife between north and south attracted U.S. intervention in the early 1960's to avoid a possible communist takeover of all of Southeast Asia. The north and south were reunited in 1976 following the withdrawal of U.S. forces and the fall of South Vietnam.

45
Israel's Six-Day War, 1967

The triggers for the Six-Day War had origins of conflict reaching back over many millennia. The key issue was Israel's right to exist. The opinion of much of the Arab world was that Israel should be "pushed into the sea." The conflicts of diverse groups centering around major crossroads of the Mideast have deep roots. Perhaps reflected as far back as the Code of Hammurabi, a perceived wrong tended to be addressed by the injured family, not simply turned over to the state. An "eye for an eye" related more to proportionality than to barbarity. Killing someone for putting out another's eye would have been disproportionate under the Code. Oversimplified, the early tribal cultures of the Mideast looked for justice in the form of balanced and proportionate revenge. Justice was therefore in the mind of the individual or small kin groups, not delegated to the governing authorities. The typical product of revenge-based justice, however, was irrational hatred. Denying the right of the Israeli people to exist is that kind of irrational hatred. With many such triggers in place, the Six-Day War began on June 5, 1967.

The strike was a pre-emptive one. The Israeli Air Force caught the Egyptian Air Force on the ground at 8:45 AM and destroyed 309 of their 340 fighter aircraft. Air supremacy was established in the equivalent of a few hours. The defeat was an enormous one yet the Egyptians did not seek peace, nor withdraw. Israeli intelligence had established that Egyptian forces, in coordination with Syria, Jordan, Palestinians, and Jordan were mobilizing against the nineteen-year-old nation to accomplish what they had failed to do in the 1948 war against Israel. By 11 AM on the first day, the Jordanian army (commanded by Egyptians) began shelling Israel. These artillery forces were quickly surrounded due to Israel's air superiority and were effectively neutralized.

The Syrians, however, were able to keep up artillery fire from the Golan Heights into Israeli territory. The situation had to be handled delicately to avoid bringing Syria's ally, the Soviet Union, into the mix. The Israelis represented two and a half million people compared to the Arab world's two hundred million people. A confrontation with the Soviet Union was the last thing Israel wanted.

At this delicate moment, Defense Minister Moshe Dayan made a unilateral end run and assaulted the Syrians. The result was very determined resistance on the part of the Syrian forces. In the south Egyptian forces were confronted as they attempted to make their way up the vast Sinai Peninsula without benefit of air cover. Soon, the Israeli forces were in control of the Sinai, the Gaza Strip, the Golan Heights, and the West Bank. Israel's territory was more than tripled within six days. The Israelis had done what they had to do to

survive as a nation. They were prepared at a far greater level of organization and of military equipment and training than was even imagined in the 1948 war. The total estimated losses for the Egyptians, Syrians, and Jordanians were almost 18,000 killed. No Palestinian losses were noted. The total number of Israelis killed was less than 700. Israel lost almost one quarter of its combat aircraft. Of necessity, Israel proved that it would not be "pushed into the sea."

Most wars have been launched, for a combination of reasons, with the expectation that they will end soon. Too often that is not the case. Here, great acrimony reaching back for countless generations and a stated goal of annihilation were foiled in less than one week. A fast and lopsided victory by the end of six days of intense fighting was an unmatched accomplishment. Arab hostilities had been gaining momentum since their defeat in the War of 1948. Suddenly, the aggressive Six-Day War started on June 5, 1967 and by June 10, 1967, a ceasefire had been ordered. Israel had proved beyond a doubt their determination and capability to survive as an independent nation. As a direct result of the Six-Day War, the strategic alliance of Israel with the United States was strengthened under the administration of President Lyndon B. Johnson. This U.S.-Israel relationship was fostered at least in part due to the strong alliances that both Syria and Egypt had with the Soviet Union at that time.

Gamal Abdel Nasser

Egyptian President Gamal Abdel Nasser (1918-1970) was a veteran of the Arab-Israeli War of 1948. He expelled the United Nations peacekeeping forces from the Gaza Strip and blockaded the Gulf of Aqaba. The purpose was to deny Israel's access to oil shipments into the port of Eilat on the Red Sea. In disgrace, he resigned shortly after the defeat. However, thousands of supporters marched in Cairo to show their support and he decided to remain in office for another three years.

Israeli Prime Minister Levi Eshkol (1895-1969), a Ukrainian by birth, emigrated to Palestine in 1914. As the first Director General of the Ministry of Defense, he was instrumental in procuring much of the materiel needed to keep the Israeli Army in the field during the Arab-Israeli War of 1948. He became prime minister in 1963. Several days before the outbreak of the Six Day War, he appointed Moshe Dayan (1915-1981) to his former position as defense minister. Levi Eshkol died on February 26, 1969, of an apparent heart attack. He was in office as prime minister at the time. The legacy of that war was that Israel, like Masada, continues to stand but, more than most nations, has had to fight for the right to exist.

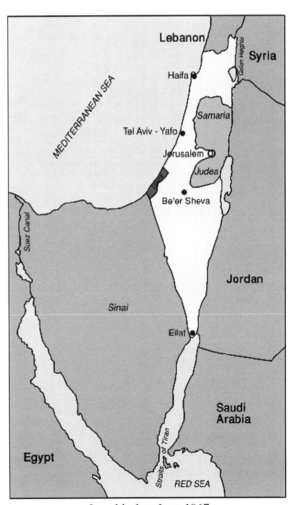

Israel before June 1967

Israel

Capital: Jerusalem (State of Israel)
Population: Over 6 million
Area: Just over 8,000 square miles
Climate: Very dry Mediterranean away from coastal areas. Light rainfall November to March
Topography: Mostly desert or mountains to 3,300 feet and valleys
Religion: Over 80% Jewish, about 15% Muslim, and 5% Christian and other
Surrounded by Egypt, Jordan, Syria, Lebanon and the Dead Sea and Mediterranean Sea
Summary: Israel was formed in 1948 as a major consequence of the horrific events of World War II and the absence of a Jewish homeland for nearly 2,000 years. The siege of the mountain fortress of Masada by the Romans basically marked the end of Jewish occupancy in their traditional homeland along with the Philistines, Hittites, and Canaanites. Israelites are believed to have origins among the Semitic people of Arabia (language group: Arabic, Hebrew, Amharic, and Aramaic) who emigrated to Mesopotamia. The earliest date on the Jewish calendar is 3,760 B.C.E. Approximately 2,000 B.C.E. Israelites migrated from the Euphrates River Valley to Canaan. The approximate time of the Israelite exodus from Egypt was 1,250 B.C.E. By approximately 1,000 B.C.E. the Hebrew Israelites established Jerusalem as the capital of Israel. Their survival as a nation in that historic homeland had to be defended in 1948 and 1967 by going to war with neighboring countries.

164

46
The Vietnam Tet Offensive, 1968

The physical and cultural remoteness of Vietnam to America's strategic interests was long apparent to all. The occupation of Indochina by the Japanese in July, 1941, resulted in little more than intensified embargoes from the United States. One obvious reason was that the U.S. needed several years to restore strategic interests in the Philippines and islands of the Pacific Ocean. The eviction of the French at Dien Bien Phu in 1954 opened opportunities for U.S. assistance and alliances, but Presidents Harry S. Truman and Dwight D. Eisenhower both wanted to avoid involvement in Southeast Asia. It was not until 1963 that President John F. Kennedy expressed real concern about the Domino Theory where one Asian country after another was being forcibly converted to communism. Most of Eastern Europe had been forced into communist control since the end of World War Two. Mainland China came under communist control by the end of 1949. North Korea remained communistic at the unofficial end of the Korean War. The international Cold War continued to gain momentum and international communism was at its peak. It was in Vietnam that President Kennedy decided to "hold back the red tide." After the Kennedy assassination, it was the mission of Presidents Lyndon B. Johnson and Richard M. Nixon to carry out that legacy.

The deployment military advisors and then all branches of the U.S. armed forces increased American personnel in the region from 23,300 in 1963 to 184,000 in 1966. A peak of 542,000 troops were reached by the beginning of 1969 under the orders of President Nixon. It was on the night of January 31, 1968, however, that approximately 70,000 North Vietnamese soldiers launched the Tet offensive. The intended surprise attack in great force commenced at the beginning of the lunar new year truce that had been negotiated. The broad-based attack into rural and urban areas was an all-out push to demonstrate the vulnerability of targets throughout Vietnam and to appeal to anti-war efforts that were building and constantly in the media of both Europe and the U.S.

The aggressive campaign had been planned and orchestrated by North Vietnam's General Giap as far back as 1967. General Giap was a hero of the Dien Bien Phu defeat of the French

Destruction from Tet Offensive, 1968

that ended French colonialism there in 1954. The Tet offensive was entirely different yet intended in some small ways to repeat that earlier success. Mostly, the Tet offensive was intended to show widespread control by the North and break a stalemate situation that had become an extremely costly war of attrition. Additional goals were to press for a halt of the aerial bombardment of North Vietnam and to negotiate a withdrawal of the Americans from a position of strength. The North Vietnamese plan was far more political than it was military.

Due to the American's aerial support that was far superior to the Dien Bien Phu battle, the Tet offensive did far better with its political than its military goals. For the U.S. and South Vietnamese military it was a successful defense against overwhelming odds in many instances and great losses for the North Vietnamese regulars and Vietcong guerrillas. The projected image on U.S. television, however, graphically projected a confusing and gory conflict into the living rooms of most Americans. The non-military impression of the war was suddenly very different from what the politicians were saying. It did not appear to television viewers that the war in Southeast Asia was near its conclusion. The exact opposite image was projected to American viewers that the war would be long and extremely costly in every way. The completely obscure purpose of "holding the red tide" was no longer worth the cost. That war was increasingly seen as a civil war with the intent of uniting an arbitrarily divided country. The televised imagery, to the folks safe at home, was that the war had to be successfully ended with honor, and soon if not immediately. U.S. Secretary of State, Henry Kissinger, acknowledged the watershed effect of the Tet offensive. He reported shortly after the Tet offensive that, "Henceforth, no matter how effective our action, the prevalent strategy could no longer achieve its objectives within a period or within force levels politically acceptable to the American people." Walter Cronkite, one of the most trusted news anchors in American history, on February 27, 1968, described the outcome of the Tet offensive as a stalemate. For the American and South Vietnamese forces it was a military victory with approximately 50,000 of the original 70,000 North Vietnam regulars and Vietcong being killed. U.S. and South Vietnamese losses were estimated to be 6,000.

Perhaps the most shocking single event of the Tet offensive was in the first hours of the attack. Less than two dozen Vietcong Special Forces followed irregular tactics of arriving at the U.S. Embassy in Saigon by taxi. They penetrated the facility by making a hole in the wall, and took control. Attacks were simultaneously launched at the headquarters of both the U.S. and South Vietnamese armies. The sweeping raids throughout South Vietnam stunned most military commanders. The supreme commander of U.S. forces, General William Westmoreland, apparently saw the offensive as a last desperate act such as the Battle of the Bulge. The issue of who was actually in control was placed in doubt.

The battle of Que Sanh was the location of the most intense fighting of the Tet offensive. To the North Vietnamese it may have resembled the tragic mistakes of the French position at Dien Bien Phu in 1954. The surprise attack at that U.S. Marine outpost was mostly unanticipated. The U.S. forces, however, were far better armed than the French at Dien Bien Phu. The biggest difference by far was the superior strength of U.S. aerial firepower. As a result of one of the most intense firefights of the ten year war the North Vietnamese lost up to 10,000 troops and the U.S. Marines lost roughly 500.

It was public confidence that was defeated for a great many Americans after the Tet offensive, not U.S. military forces. Sustained, national pressure to end the war, such as "Hey, Hey, LBJ, how many kids did you kill today?" eroded the president's confidence as well. On March 31, 1968, President Lyndon Johnson made a televised statement to the American people and the world. In part, he said, "I shall not seek, and I will not accept, the nomination of my party for another term as your president." Intensified efforts were made to negotiate a settlement of the war but all efforts broke down without an honorable resolution for all sides. U.S. troop levels remained above 500,000 for some time and the war lasted until the fall of Saigon on April 30, 1975. It was at 8:35 a.m. that the last Americans, ten U.S. Marines from the U.S. Embassy, departed from Saigon by helicopter to offshore carriers in the South China Sea. The Cambodian government was dominated by communist Vietnam for a period of time, but the "red tide" did subside and then did a monstrous reverse with the collapse of the Soviet government in 1991.

Southeast Asia

47
Star Wars vs. the Evil Empire

It was on March 23, 1983, that President Ronald Reagan made his first, televised announcement to the American people of his intention to authorize construction of a nuclear missile shield. The goal was either to minimize or end the costly and wasteful nuclear arms race. The official name for the program was to be the Strategic Defense Initiative (SDI). The quickly popularized name for the program was "Star Wars" because of a skimpy relationship to George Lucas' science fiction films under that name.

President Reagan poised the following question to the American people with the awareness that much of the world was also receiving his message:

"What if free people could live secure in the knowledge...that we could intercept and destroy strategic ballistic missiles before they reached our own soil...?"
Also: "There was a time when we depended on coastal forts and artillery batteries, because, with the weaponry of that day, any attack would have had to come by sea. Well, this is a different world, and our defenses must be based on recognition and awareness of the weaponry possessed by other nations in the nuclear age."

"We can't afford to believe that we will never be threatened. There have been two world wars in my lifetime. We didn't start them and, indeed, did everything we could to avoid being drawn into them. But we were ill-prepared for both. Had we been better prepared, peace might have been preserved."

"...The Soviet Union is acquiring what can only be considered an offensive military force. They have continued to build far more intercontinental ballistic missiles than they could possibly need simply to deter an attack. Their

conventional forces are trained and equipped not so much to defend against an attack as they are to permit sudden, surprise offensives of their own."

The concept of the "defensive umbrella" over the United States was shocking in its simplicity. The image that was so confidently projected to the world and to the Soviets in particular was that such a "science fiction" defense was actually possible. The president, well known as "the great communicator," was thought to have accepted the "drawing board concept" at face value. Concern for extreme complexities, or even researched feasibility, were not expressed. One of the most obvious factors to all who took the notion seriously was that initial research and development would cost billions of dollars. Another issue

President Ronald Reagan

was that the build-up of a new system of defense is typically perceived by an opponent of that system as offensive. It mattered little that President Reagan suggested that he would share the technology with the Soviets, if the Soviets believed the U.S. might launch a first strike and then escape retaliation by using the Star Wars defense.

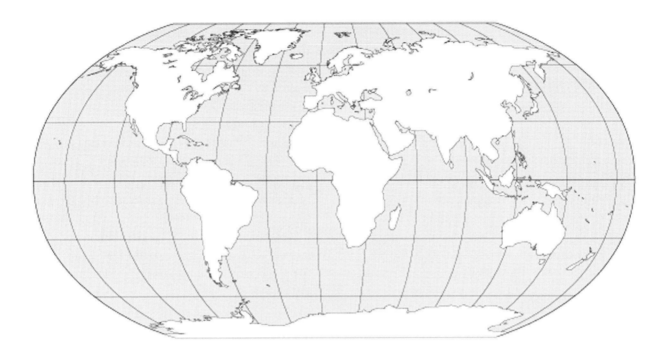

In the Cold War environment of the early 1980's the Soviet Union had already invested a tremendous amount of its total resources in building up a ballistic missile defense system. The enormous size of that defense system was typically perceived by the U.S. as "offensive" in nature rather than defensive. The reality of the times was that within minutes, and perhaps by accident, either side of the Mutual Assured Destruction (MAD) equation might launch a first strike if MAD was no longer a certainty.

Without persuasive documentation of the feasibility of a "Star Wars defense system," the impression apparently settled into the Soviet military establishment that their large numbers of defensive and offensive missiles might soon be obsolete. The projected cost to surpass the Americans would completely bankrupt the Soviet Union. The risk existed that the American Star War defense might well be superior to their own, and, perhaps the Americans would perfect an offensive "solution" to a Soviet "Star War umbrella."

Mikhail Gorbachev was born on March 2, 1931, to a humble family in a rural expanse of the U.S.S.R. near Stavropol. By 1990 he was a recipient of the Nobel Peace Prize for his contributions in helping to end the Cold War. A man of extraordinary humility and perception in a closed society, he rose to the top communist party position in March, 1985. From the beginning of his tenure he implemented a program of cultural openness (glasnost) and internal, societal reforms (perestroika). He was the first younger man in some time to head the Soviet Union and he had a good grasp of

Soviet President Mikhail Gorbachev

169

the hardships on the civilian population to continue hysterical arms races at any cost. The sweeping changes did little to alleviate the massive country's bitter economic crisis. Also, the changes he promoted were either much too radical for some or much too slow for others.

The concept of "openness" helped to set the stage for virtual civil war with independence movements in the Baltic States and other Soviet republics. Eastern Europe (Poland, Hungary, Czechoslovakia, Bulgaria and Romania) began a bloodless breakaway and Germany reunited without Soviet repression as in the past. On June 12, 1987, President Reagan addressed the German people before the Brandenburg Gate. He made the now world famous remark, "…Mr. Gorbachev, open this gate. Mr. Gorbachev, tear down this wall!" By November 11-12, 1989, the Berlin Wall began, in fact, to be torn down. For old-line conservatives in the Soviet Union, the sweeping changes felt like betrayal. A coup d'etat was therefore staged to violently replace Premier Gorbachev in August, 1991. The failed attempt did lead to his pressured resignation by the end of the year, but did not reverse the sweeping changes that he had helped to set in place. A philosophical battle over defense between two world leaders directly contributed to one of the most sweeping political changes in the history of the world. The investment to date has exceeded forty billion dollars. Considering the outcome, who would argue that it was not worth it?

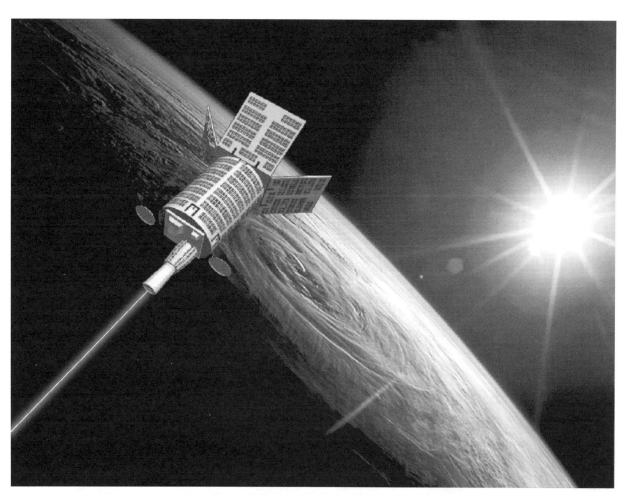

Artist conception of the Strategic Defense Initiative (SDI). or more commonly referred to as the "Star Wars" Defense Shield

48
Desert Storm, 1991

The disastrous conflict between Iraq and Iran (1980-1988) was slowly fading from the public's consciousness as the decade of the 1990's began. The rebuilt Iraqi army was suddenly ranked the fourth largest in the world. The leader of that Middle Eastern country was a known tyrant who had used strongman tactics since adolescence to achieve virtually unrestrained power over his own countrymen. His name was Saddam Hussein. His SCUD missile attacks against Israel marked him as one of the most unstable tyrants in the world.

On the morning of August 2, 1990, President Saddam Hussein's well-equipped Iraqi army and Iraqi Republican Guard invaded the neighboring country of Kuwait under the pretext that the area had once been a province of Iraq. In a very short time the control of that small, oil-rich country was in the hands of the Iraqi dictatorship.

President George H.W. Bush

The response in the United States was prompt and code named "Operation Desert Shield." The objective was to remove the threat to Kuwait and to protect Saudi Arabia from possible Iraqi invasion. By August 7, 1990, a deployment of U.S. troops was initiated under the authority of United Nations Resolutions 660 and 662. On August 20, 1990, President George Herbert Bush signed National Security Directive 45 which was titled, "U.S. Policy in Response to the Iraqi Invasion of Kuwait." That U.N. document called for immediate withdrawal of all Iraqi forces from Kuwait.

A United Nation's ultimatum known as Security Council Resolution 678 was released on November 29, 1990. That ultimatum set the date of January 15, 1991, for Iraqi President Saddam Hussein to completely withdraw from Kuwait or face a U.S-led coalition of armed forces of 33 nations that were internationally authorized to remove them.

The international demands for a peaceful reso-

Saddam Hussein

lution of the crisis were ignored by the Iraqi government. All diplomatic efforts to resolve the crisis and to restore Kuwait's sovereignty without intervention of military force had failed. Thus, on January 17, 1991, the U.S-led coalition commenced intensive and precisely targeted air attacks against select Iraqi positions. The Iraqi military, which had been ranked fourth in size in the world, was soon incapacitated. Radar structures, communication and supply lines, and weapons arsenals were quickly destroyed. Ultimately, there were a total of almost 110,000 sorties flown during the 43-day war. The night attacks, in particular, quickly neutralized Iraqi tanks and missile defense systems. The sophistication of the coalition's weapons reduced the amount of explosive tonnage to levels far below that used in Vietnam, Korea, or World War Two. The televised feedback of guided bombs flying directly into specific targets, and "hardened targets," helped to establish the term "smart bomb" in the world's vocabulary.

The exclusive control of Iraq, within the "Fertile Crescent" of early civilization, has been attributed to the violent use of power by one man—Saddam Hussein. He remained as the president and dictator of Iraq from 1979 to 2003 because he was not removed from power as a condition of ending Desert Storm. His political career is understood to have commenced in 1958 with the assassination of Iraqi ruler Abdul-Karim Qassim. He ruthlessly rose through the ranks of the revolutionary Baath party and became president in 1979 in a *coup d' etat* by the Baath party. He aggressively

American tanks in Desert Storm

pursued a decade-long war against the far more populous nation of Iran. He had long been attributed with genocidal abuses against the Kurdish people and other religious, ethnic, or political "dissenters" within the Iraqi boundaries that were somewhat capriciously established by the British after World War One. He ran Iraq as a one-man ruler police state with great oil wealth.

The nemesis of this charismatic street thug who became one of the world's most vicious tyrants to his own people and neighboring countries was U.S. President George Herbert Bush. On October 15, 1990, the U.S. president described Saddam Hussein in the following manner: "We're dealing with Hitler revisited." That comment was later retracted following criticism that it was disrespectful of what had actually occurred during the Nazi Holocaust. It was President Bush, however, who approved General Norman H. Schwarzkopf (b. 1934) to

be the supreme commander of the coalition forces and to remove Saddam Hussein's forces from the independent nation of Kuwait.

Soon after the Iraqi forces invaded and took control of Kuwait beginning on August 2, 1990, General Schwarzkopf and his headquarters staff were stationed in Riyadh, Saudi Arabia. His assignment was to command the U.S. and allied forces. He made sure that massive concentrations of troops, supplies, and equipment were in place before making his move. He initiated the 42-day war on January 17, 1991. An average of over 2,500 precise bombing sorties were flown over Iraq each day and night for most of the campaign. A 100-hour ground assault was implemented during the concluding days of the brief war. Overall, General Schwarzkopf had effectively utilized a combination of allied air, sea, and land forces to achieve a multinational victory over Saddam's tyranny.

The independent nation of Kuwait was liberated and Iraqi forces were immediately placed on the defensive. It has been estimated that from 8,000 to 15,000 Iraqi forces were killed and over 85,000 combatants captured during the 42-day Desert Storm. Loss of life for the coalition forces was minimal. The severely traumatized nation of Kuwait has since been able to rebuild and retain its independence.

———❖———

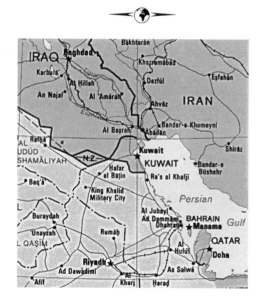

Kuwait

Capital: Kuwait City
Population: Just over 2 million
Area: Almost 6,900 square miles
Religion: Muslim
Climate: Arid desert region with fairly extreme high and low temperatures and idealistic coastal climate along the Persian Gulf
Topography: Mostly sea level and desert terrain up to 650 feet above sea level.
Surrounded by Saudi Arabia, Iraq, and the Persian Gulf of the Arabian Sea

Summary: The nation of Kuwait claims independence as early as 1710, but was governed by the British until 1961 when official independence was granted. This small but oil-rich nation is one of the most affluent nations in the world. Kuwait's key position in the Middle East as well as great harbor facilities on the Persian Gulf assure continued prosperity to the extent the small nation is not overrun such as was done by Saddam Hussein's Iraqi forces in 1990.

49
Afghanistan, 2001

The terrorist attack of 9/11/01 on the World Trade Center buildings of New York City shocked the citizens of America and much of the world. The image of an American passenger airliner being flown into one of the world's tallest twin towers appeared to be a profoundly tragic accident caught on film. Moments later, when a second passenger airliner flew into the other twin tower, it was apparent that the United States was under attack. Innocent people were dying to serve some obscure political agenda.

Subsequent news reporting acknowledged a third hijacked airliner (Flight 93) had crashed in the State of Pennsylvania, and, finally, that a fourth hijacked airliner had been flown into the Pentagon Building. There was no doubt that an immediate national response was required. The response, however, had to be tempered by quick awareness that the cold-blooded assaults had been orchestrated by a terrorist organization with no borders to defend and that it was a fanatical fringe element of the Islamic religion. The actual perpetrators eluded personal consequences for their acts by committing a form of religious suicide as they killed thousands of randomly selected civilians. The scale of the cowardly acts was intended to get international media attention and inflict some sense of vulnerability.

One of the first consequences of the terrorist attacks was an international media response that virtually no one could ignore. Elements of the Islamic media, including *Al-Jazerra*, put their own spin on events. Manipulation of the media was certainly an intended tactic of Islamic extremists. Similar, anti-U.S. media manipulations occurred when Islamic extremists, who had exiled the Shah of Iran, tried to expunge all Western culture from their own, and held U.S. journalists captive for more than

one year. The followers of Osama bin Laden used violent means to gain media attention that has been directed at weakening Western influences.

The attackers were identified as fringe followers of an extremist sect headed by Osama bin Laden, a Saudi Arabian national, and others. Documentation of the group's activities in the

Osama Bin Laden

1998 bombings of American Embassies in Kenya and Tanzania, Africa, and the attack on the *USS Cole* in the Yemen harbor already existed. Tracking of this pro-violence organization placed large numbers of the spin-off sect members in Afghanistan. The al Queda, as they called themselves, had been granted sanctuary in the war torn nation that was ruled by a different extremist sect known as the Taliban.

The remote and typically impoverished nation of Afghanistan had resisted occupation by the Soviet Union (December, 1979 to February, 1989) as a result of massive military assistance from the United States. In the end of that invasion, 115,000 Soviets troops finally withdrew from Afghanistan. The failure of the Soviets to control Afghanistan helped to create the image that no outside nation, including the British and Chinese, could occupy and control that remote and mountainous region of the world. Afghanistan appeared to be the perfect base for international terrorists. Islamic extremism could be exported to Pakistan, Uzbekistan, Turkmenistan, Tajikistan, Kyrgyzstan, Malaysia, southern Philippines, and westward into Middle Eastern nations. The difference from the Soviet experience was the ability of the United States to effectively use air power (including B-1 bombers), smart bombs and missiles, satellite surveillance, night vision, and determined ground forces with state-of-the-art equipment, training, and supplies.

A new president of the United States, George W. Bush, showed a decisiveness that appeared to be lacking when American journalists were held hostage for over one year by Islamic extremists in Iran. President Bush ordered aerial assaults of terrorist camps in Afghanistan on October 7, 2001. The aerial bombing came as a result of the ruling Taliban's refusal to surrender Osama bin Laden and his cohorts without absolute proof of his direct guilt.

Initially there were refugee redistributions, often to desolate high ground, of up to 7.5 million residents of Afghanistan. The hardships imposed by such an uprooting must have been beyond imagination. It was just a matter of time, however, before the exceedingly harsh and extremist government of the Taliban fell.

Taliban fighters on tank

Many weeks of air strikes on cities such as Herat, Kandahar, Kabul, Bhakkar, and Jalalabad resulted in mass exoduses from those cities.

The intent was to surgically focus on known or assumed terrorist positions, especially in caves and areas of resistance. According to a survey in the *London Guardian* newspaper as many as 20,000 Afghans may have lost their lives as a direct or indirect result of the U.S. intervention in Afghanistan. A more precise study by Marc Herold, University of New Hampshire professor, revised the casualty figures to a range of 3,100 to 3,800 (Source: *Body Counting* by Mackubin T. Owens, Professor, Naval War College, 03/25/02). Richard A. Clarke, a former terrorism advisor to the Bush Administration, indicated in his book, *Against All Enemies,* that U.S. Marine ground forces were not sent in to attempt the capture of al Qaeda or Taliban leaders until nearly two months after the aerial assaults began. The border with Pakistan was not sealed. Osama bin Laden was either not there at the time, or managed to escape and remain in hiding.

By December, 2002, U.S. Secretary of Defense, Donald Rumsfeld, reported that the Taliban had been removed from power for more than one year and that Hamid Karzai had been elected as the president of Afghanistan. He did emphasize that Afghanistan needed a substantial amount of reconstruction assistance, but significant aid appears to be slim and slow to arrive in that part of the world. The overall situation following the war in Afghanistan appears to have deteriorated. Well-armed warlords tend to control difficult to access areas as in past generations. President Karzai has been reportedly described as the Mayor of Kabul to reflect the weakness of central authority throughout that geopolitically important nation. The exact whereabouts of Osama bin Laden, Ayman al Zawahri, other al Qaeda leaders, and Mullah Omar, the Taliban leader, may never be established. Cowardly terrorism of the self-appointed "True Believer" variety may never be erased, but sustained vigilance can limit its impact on the world's people.

Afghanistan

Capital: Kabul, U.N. supported president, Hamid Karzai (elected, 2004)

Population: Over 22 million

Area: 250,000 square miles

Surrounded by Tajikistan, Pakistan, Iran, and Turkmenistan

Religion: Sunni Muslim 85%, Sh'a (Shiite) Muslim 14%, other 1%

Topography: Probably the highest and driest landlocked country in the world with elevations to 9,843 feet

Climate: The widest range of any populated country with a range of 50F below to 125F above. Very dry except in mountain valleys.

Summary: A crossroads of the Silk Road in ancient times. Strategically isolated in Central Asia northwest of India and Pakistan and lacking access to any of the world's oceans. It is an impoverished, agriculturally-based area with terrible roads and little modern infrastructure. It has been overrun by Chinese, Mongols, Turks, British, U.S.S.R., Taliban, and U.S.-led coalition forces. In the 1980's it was virtually occupied by the Soviet Union. The Pashtun Taliban came to power in 1996 but were defeated by U.S.-led anti-terrorist forces beginning in late 2001.

176

50
The Iraq War, 2003

The nation of Iraq has been somewhat of an enigma since its "creation" by the British at the end of World War One. Lines on a Mideast map redefined old elements of the Ottoman Empire into a consolidation of Kurds, Shiites, Sunnis, Marsh Arabs, and assorted others in one new nation. It was to be an inland nation with only 35 miles of coastline on the Persian Gulf. Mostly, Iraq was to serve as a buffer between Iran, Kuwait, Saudi Arabia, Jordan, Syria, and Turkey. Little real thought was given to the preservation of antiquities in this "Cradle of Civilization," birthplace of Abraham (father of Judaism, Christianity and Islam), possible site of the Garden of Eden, site of Babylon, and traces of humanities' early development from nomads to agrarian village dwellers. Iraq achieved independence from the British and established a kingdom in 1932. The new nation was declared a "republic" in 1958, but in reality has been ruled by military strongmen (dictators) since that time.

Saddam Hussein, a street thug who came to power as Iraq's dictatorial president-for-life in 1979, turned a territorial dispute with Iran into a profoundly tragic war. From 1980 through 1988, Iraq engaged in an extremely costly war with Iran that finally descended into an inconclusive stalemate. Tremendous numbers of young men were killed on both sides for no appreciable purpose. By August of 1990, the Iraqi leadership used a slim pretext to seize the independent nation of Kuwait. The Iraqis, however, were expelled following a 42-day battle with a U.S. led coalition of United Nations' forces in the first months of 1991. The distinct conditions of that U.N. intervention were that Iraq was to scrap all weapons of mass destruction (WMD), to scrap all long-range missiles, and to allow unlimited U.N. verification inspections.

It was the determination of the second Bush Administration that the United Nations' conditions were not being followed. Inspectors were eventually denied access. U.N. authorized aircraft patrolling the Iraqi "no fly zones" were being fired upon, and it "appeared" that Iraq was stockpiling biological, chemical, and perhaps nuclear weapons of mass destruction in violation of the U.N. agreements. Also, following the terrorist attacks on the United States on September 11, 2001, there was substantial, if unproven, suspicion that hostile elements within Iraq were supporting al Qaeda. The announced concern was that sources within Iraq might provide al Qaeda with weapons of mass destruction to be used on the civilian population of the United States, Great Britain, or others. Therefore, following two years of great tensions between the U.S. and Iraq, President George W. Bush announced an ultimatum to Saddam Hussein on March 17, 2003, as follows: "...The danger is clear: using chemical, biological or, one day, nuclear weapons, obtained with the help of Iraq, the terrorists could fulfill their stated ambitions

and kill thousands or hundreds of thousands of innocent people in our country, or any other." The President had much more to say but essentially he issued an ultimatum for Saddam Hussein and his sons to go into exile within 48 hours or face military conflict. Obviously, Saddam Hussein did not take the requested action and therefore set the stage for military action by a large coalition of nations. On March 19, 2003, President George W. Bush made the following comment in part: "Now that conflict has come, the only way to limit its duration is to apply decisive force. And I assure you, this will not be a campaign of half measures, and we will accept no outcome but victory."

President George W. Bush

In April, 2003, coalition forces led by the United States and Great Britain surprised the world with a stunningly fast military campaign against Iraq. Coalition forces soon occupied Basra, Tikrit (Saddam's birthplace), Mosul, and Baghdad. The Iraqi nation appeared to descend into a state of anarchy as well as euphoria about toppling all images of the mostly detested Saddam Hussein. The exception, once again, was possibly the Republican Guard that was among the most loyal support of Saddam and the most likely to be held accountable for their actions by the Iraqi people.

Were the satellite assisted weapon systems, computer directed firepower, and tactics of the coalition forces totally superior, or was the quick outcome due to the paper tiger quality of Saddam's frequently battered forces? Where were the weapons of mass destruction? The biggest surprise following the war's end was the inability to identify any stockpiles or even obvious facilities for producing stockpiles of biological, chemical, or nuclear weapons.

Also, the suspected linkage with al Qaeda appeared to be lacking.

Defeated Iraqi soldiers were often allowed to blend back into the civilian population and to retain access to stockpiles of conventional weapons. The warlord-like power struggles in that region of the world will no doubt make extensive use of the misplaced arsenal of the world's fourth largest military force. To date more coalition forces have been killed in ambushes following the war than occurred during the war. In the crossroads of both ancient and contemporary influences and between the classic east and west divide, there continues to be strong cultural conflicts and instability. Movement toward the contemporary west promises a life filled with rapidly changing technology. Movement toward the ancient east promises a life of dogmatic religious principles and resistance to change.

Over 8,000 of the world's rarest antiquities from museums in Iraq remain missing because there was not a specific priority to immediately guard such antiquities for the benefit of present and future generations of the world's citizens. To restore the basic infrastructure of a modern, independent nation the investment of billions of dollars will be required for an effective start. Establishing peace in the Middle East with the rest of the world will likely result in more of an uneasy coexistence that could be described as trying to fuse the Bronze-Age with the age of the Internet.

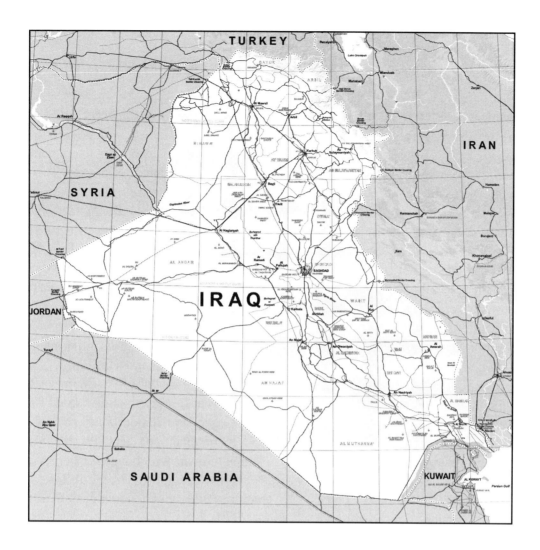

Iraq

Capital: Baghdad (nation formed in 1932)
Population: Over 23 million
Area: Almost 169,000 square miles
Religion: Sh'a Muslims about 2/3rds and Sunni Muslims about 1/3rd
Climate: Hot and dry much of the time. High temperatures often above 100F
Topography: Except for major river valleys tends to be desert with some marshlands in the south and rolling, fertile hills in the north
Surrounded by Saudi Arabia, Kuwait, Iran, Turkey, Syria and Jordan. Iraq has about 35 miles of coastline on the Arabian Gulf.
Summary: Baghdad has been a center for Islamic culture since the year 813. That ancient city was one of the first walled cities in approximately 7,000 B.C.E. and site of one of the first groups of people to use metals and to develop agriculture. Iraq is an oil-rich and history-rich nation that was created by the British following World War I. It was formerly a part of the Ottoman Empire and prior to that a part of the Persian Empire. Archeological history in the area has confirmed that the Tigris and Euphrates River valleys were agricultural settlements for some of the first humans who gave up the nomadic life (about 8,000 B.C.E.). It was the site of biblical cities such as UR, the birthplace of Abraham (father of Judaism, Islam, and Christianity), Babylon, and the "Garden of Eden." It was the site of an almost decade-long war with Iran in the 1980's and the U.S.-led coalition to free Kuwait in 1991 (Desert Storm). Currently it is the site of U.S.-led coalition to confront terrorism in that region of the world.

Epilogue

Carl von Clausewitz, (1780-1831) Prussian general and military theorist, described war in his book *Vom Kriege (On War)* as "…the continuation of policy [i.e., politics] by other means." For well over 5,000 years "civilized" humanity has been associated with and killed or wounded by battles too numerous to count. It's doubtful, in fact, that whatever lessons were learned from previous battles will significantly reduce the number of future battles. One certainty is that technology has moved even the small battle (guerrilla warfare) to a level where thousands and perhaps tens of thousands of non-combatants are likely to be at risk in the opening minutes of the battle. What, then, is the importance of knowing the details of previous battles? One big lesson, and a subjective one at that, is "If you want peace, first you must have justice."

The issue of justice for all sides tends to be a very tortured one. The politically focused American Civil War, for example, often pitted family members against one another and one American against another American until a total of 620,000 Americans had been killed. Where's the justice in that? The "deep, dark, psychological motives," alluded to in the introduction quickly became obscured by the more urgent need to kill or be killed. Confederate General Robert E. Lee, observing the senseless carnage of Union troops assaulting a sunken road near Fredericksburg, Virginia, said "It is well that war is so terrible, else we should grow too fond of it." And near that terrible war's conclusion, Union General William Tecumseh Sherman said, "War is cruelty. There's no use trying to reform it, the crueler it is the sooner it will be over."

One distinction from the past is that huge scale battles did not typically have the goal of manipulating the media and therefore manipulating the minds of both the home forces and the opponents. Battle news historically traveled no faster than a determined rider on horseback, or faster than a ship could sail. The Greek Battle of Marathon was a classic example of a runner, Pheidippides, being sent on foot to warn the Athenians that the Persian forces sailing toward them had already been defeated once. News of the Little Big Horn defeat required many days to reach the American press. Today, Internet and CNN are 24/7.

One of the first of the truly great media-manipulators was a sociopathic, military genius, for brief moments only, by the name of Adolph Hitler. That bigoted fanatic "sold" his murderous agenda to demoralized and bankrupted masses that had been declared the losers in a stalemated war which ended after more than 30 million casualties. In the following generation, Hitler, and henchmen such as Joseph Goebbels, effectively used the mass communication of the controlled radio, newspapers, film, posters, heroic symbolism, and mass rallies to instill his brand of fanatic nationalism and militant solution to "problems" as he saw them. The Fuhrer, as he preferred to be called, wrote in his book, *Mein Kampf,* "Any alliance whose purpose is not the intention to wage war is senseless and useless." In contrast, one of the most responsible persons in ending the Fuhrer's reign of terror, General Dwight D. Eisenhower, said "I hate war as only a soldier who has lived it can, only as one who has seen its brutality, its futility, its stupidity."

The Cold War that immediately followed the Second World War intimidated much of the world for decades, especially during the Cuban Missile Crisis of 1962, and was also a war of propaganda. Technology had raised the stakes of all-out-battle to annihilation of the planet. Mutual Assured Destruction (MAD), the ominous acronym for a true Armageddon, was something each citizen of the world was expected to live with. The potential for escalation of any event, no matter how stupid or accidental, into an uncontrolled spiral was simply out there. Unexpectedly to most, that hopeless scenario was out-bluffed by President Ronald Reagan's projected Star Wars defense. The ideological struggle between communism and democracy was in many ways comparable to wars and conflicts of religion that persist to this date. Conflicts with either a religious or political motivation have been pandemic since well before the darkest days of the Dark Ages. The present conflict between fringe elements of the Muslim religion and the world's other religions and political orientations has roots back to the Talas River, the Christian Crusades, the defeat of the Moors in Spain, the defeat of the Muslim fleet at Lepanto, Gallipoli, the Arab and Israeli wars, Desert Storm, Afghanistan (2001), and Iraq (2003).

Technology, spurred on by wars, is in the process of changing at a far more accelerated rate than the ways in which groups of people work out their conflicts. Human evolution is not keeping pace with the evolution of technology. A satellite in space can now visualize a lone jaywalker, and a different satellite has already traveled outside our solar system. Men have walked on the moon. Scram jets can fly at over seven times the speed of sound. Computers process millions of bits of information in seconds. Nuclear submarines can remain submerged for weeks and possess more hitting power than the combined weaponry of most previous armies and navies combined. Sophisticated missiles are programmable smart-bombs. The Internet links the world. Ideas cannot be suppressed for those willing to risk their lives, if necessary, to seek out reliable information. Battles will continue for the minds of people in addition to all of the rationals that have been conjured up in the past. A Pax El Mundo due to the hoped for defensive shields of Star War technology may not

be a reality, but ending the Cold War was a huge step toward reducing the chances for escalating "an issue" into an all out war. Alternatives have to be found to grisly small wars (guerrilla wars), genocides, famines, disease, and willingness to kill to express a point of view. Changing technology will inevitably be a part of the solution. Lasting solutions will require mutual justice and resourcefulness, not war and indifference.

The final word is in the form of a "parting shot." General Marcus Crassus, Rome's wealthiest citizen-soldier and the man credited with capturing Spartacus' army of slaves, was offered a share in the Roman Empire along with Julius Caesar and Pompey. The event occurred in 60 B.C.E. and was known as the Triumvirate. Crassus received the wealthy province of Syria but wanted far more. He led his army against the Partian Empire (250 B.C.E. to 225 C.E.) with little knowledge of his adversary or the terrain. The Partians were a nomadic steppe culture (i.e., ideal cavalrymen) who could effectively fire their arrows in all directions from a mounted, horseback position. They drew Crassus' dehydrated and exhausted forces into the site that became known as the Battle of Carrhae in 53 B.C.E. The defeat was very one-sided and famous for the Partian's ability to fire arrows even as they departed. Hence, the "Partian shot" became the "parting shot." End.

Appendix 1
Pacific Ocean during World War II

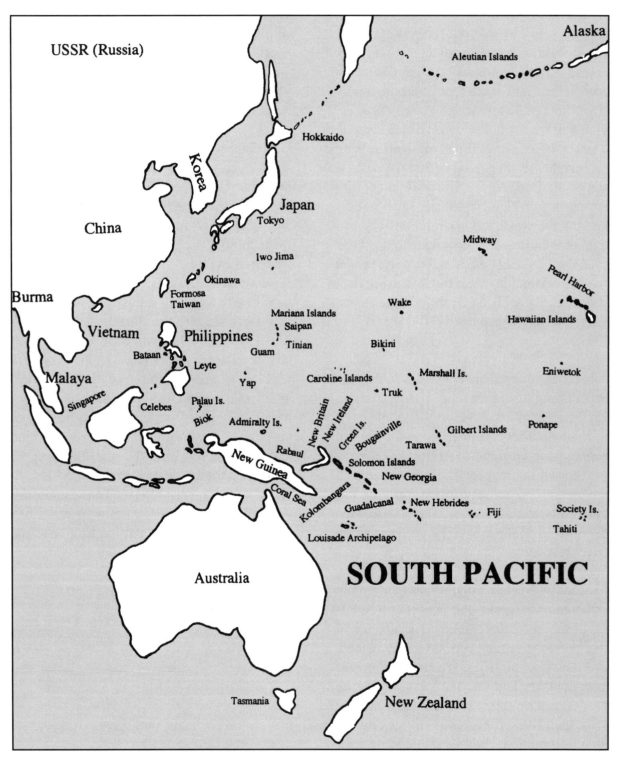

Appendix 2
Korea

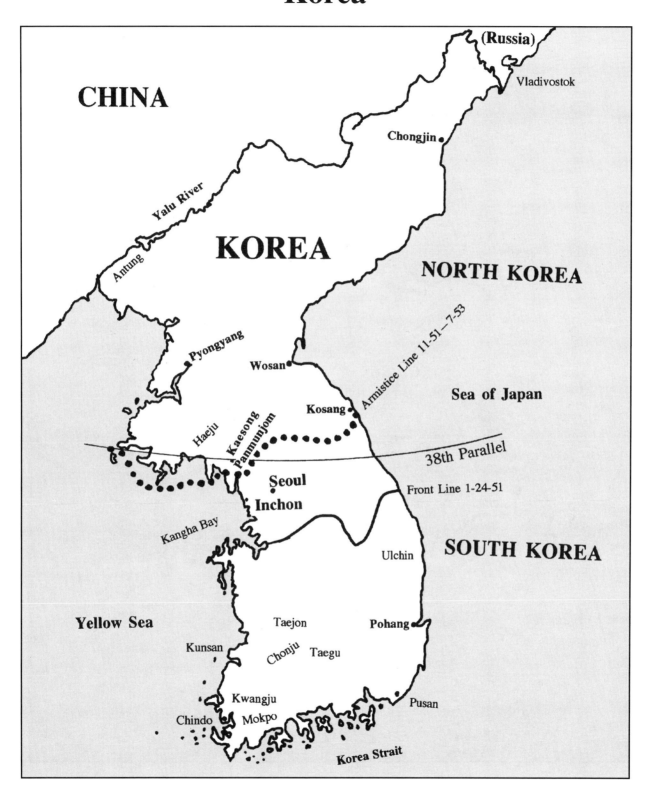

Appendix 3
Vietnam

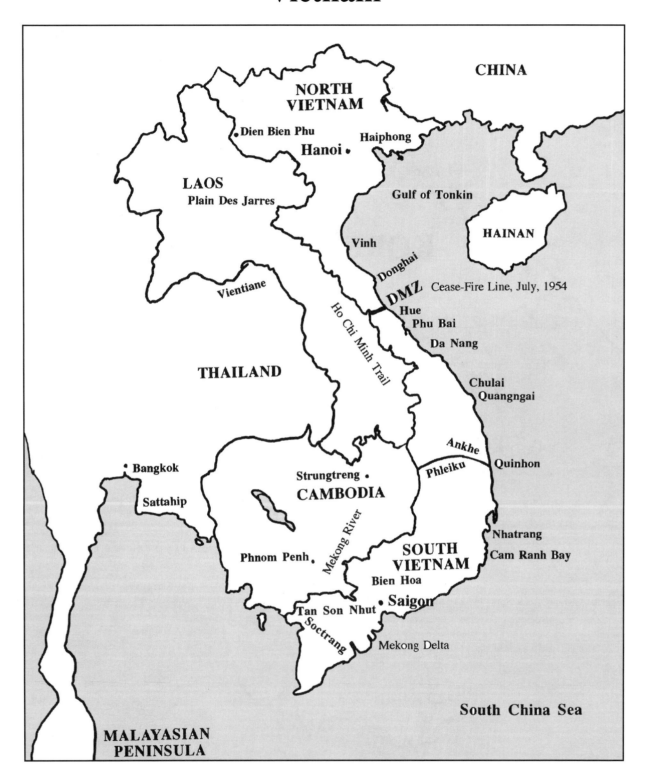

Appendix 4
Desert Storm Area

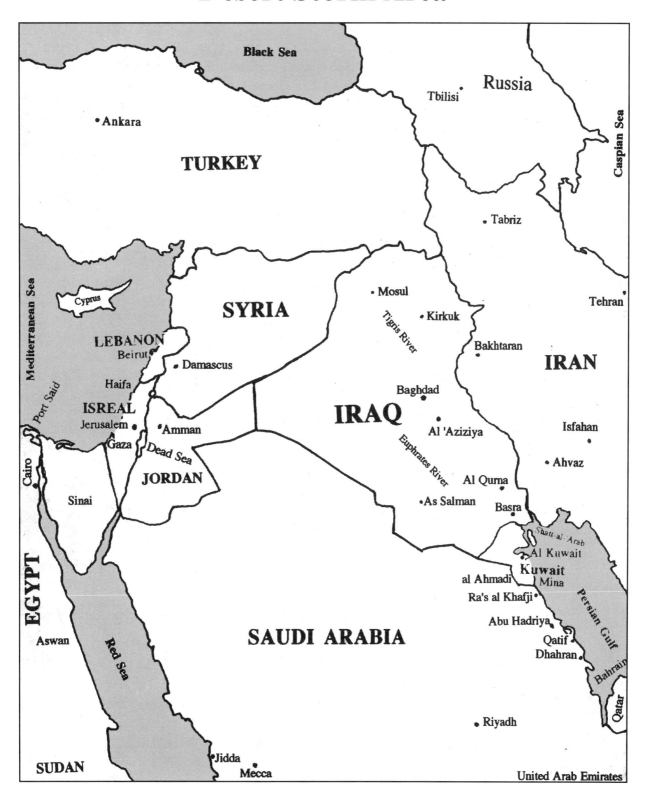

Appendix 5

Afghanistan

Iraq

Battlefield Associations & Resources

American Assn. Military Uniform Collectors
P.O. Box 304
Chardon, OH 44024

American Battlefield Protection Program
1201 Eye St. NW #2255
Washington, D.C. 20005

American Historical Assn.
www.affiliate_news@historians.org

Archaeological Magazine
33-36 33rd St.
Long Island City, NY 11106

Army Air Forces Historical Assn.
www.info@AAFHA.com

Association Militaria Italian
P.O. Box 14402
Huntsville, Al 35815

Battle of Nashville Preservation Society
P.O. Box 190493
Nashville, TN 37219

Cabinet War Rooms
St. Charles Street
London SW1A 2AQ U.K.

Calgary Military Historical Society
www.calgmhis@cadvision.com

Carabinieri Historical Museum
Rome, Italy   Tel: 653-06-96

CEC/Seabee Museum
P.O. Box 657
Gulfport, MS 39502

Central Maryland Heritage League
P.O. Box 721
Middleton, MD 21769

Chute and Dagger
P.O. Box 7201
Arlington, VA 22207

Civil War Preservation Trust
11 Public Square #200
Hagerstown, MD 21740

Civil War Preservation Trust
1331 H. St. NW #1001
Washington, D.C. 20005

Custer Battlefield Preservation
P. O. Box 7
Hardin, MT 59034

Early Middle Ages Museum
Rome, Italy
Tel: 592-58-06

Fondation Napoleon
148 Blvd Haussmann
75008 Paris – France

Franklin Battlefield Preservation
P.O. Box 851
Franklin, TN 37065

Friends of Fredericksburg Battlefield
P.O. Box 3112
Fredericksburg, VA 22402

Friends of Wilderness Battlefield
P.O. Box 576
Locust Grove, VA 22508

Georgia Battlefield Association
2331 Fireside Ct.
Jonesboro, GA 30236

German Historical Institute
www.ghi-dc.org

Gettysburg Battlefield Preservation
P.O. Box 4087
Gettysburg, PA 17325

Glorieta Battlefield Preservation
6324 Beaver Ct.
Rio Rancho, NM 87124

Heritage Preservation Services, NPS
P.O. Box 37127
Washington, D.C. 20013

Historic Hawaii Foundation
P.O. Box 1658
Honolulu, HI 96806

Historical Armed Combat Assn.
www.thehaca.com/

Historical Preservation Group
1603 West Road
Kinston, NC 28501

Imperial War Museum
Lambeth Road
London SE1 6HZ U.K.

Italian Militaria Collectors Club
www.securidata.it/collezio.html

Kubinka Tank Museum
Niibt Collection
Moscow, Russia

Military Museum
Castell de Montjuic
6608038 Barcelona, Spain

Military Museum
Citadel Historic District
Cairo, Egypt Tel: 2025129619

Military Vehicle Preservation Assn
.P.O. Box 520378
Independence, MO 64052

Museum of Archaeology
University of San Marcos
Lima, Peru

N.C. Civil War Tourism Council
P.O. Box 31522
Raleigh, NC 27622

Napoleonic Museum
Rome, Italy Tel: 654-02-86

Nat'l Archives and Records Admin.
7th and Pennsylvania NW
Washington, D.C. 20408

Nat'l Historical Foundation
1306 Dahlgren Ave.
Washington, D.C. 20374

Nat'l Maritime Historical Society
www.seahistory.org/

Nat'l Parks Conservation Assn.
1776 Massachusetts Ave. NW #200
Washington, D.C. 20036

Nat'l Trust Historic Preservation
1785 Massachusetts Ave. NW
Washington, D.C. 20036

National Indian Wars Association
1707 Bates Ct.
Thousand Oaks, CA 91362

National Museum of Rome
Rome, Italy Tel: 488-08-56

National Rifle Association
Washington, D.C. 1-800-672-3888

Naval War College Museum
686 Cushing Road
Newport, RI 02841

Palmetto Conservation Project
P.O. Box 1984
Spartanburg, NC 29304

Pearl Harbor Memorial
Arizona Memorial Place
Honolulu, HI 96818

Pennsylvania Historical
www.phmc.state.pa.us/
Perryville Battlefield Preservation
P.O. Box 65
Perryville, KY 40468

Polish American Historical Assn.
www.polishamericanstudies.org

RAF Museum Hendon
Grahame Park Way
London NW9 5LL U.K.

S. African Military Historical Society
www.rapidttp.com/milhist/index/html

Save Historic Antietam Foundation
P.O. Box 550
Sharpsburg, MD 21782

Sixteenth Century Studies Conference
www.2truman.edu/escj/scsc/

Smithsonian Information
P.O. Box 37012
Washington, D.C. 20013

Society for Creative Anachronism
www.sca.org/

Society for Historical Archaeology
www.sha.org/

Society for Military History
www.smh-hq.org/

Society of Ancient Military Historians
Western Illinois University
309-298-1387

Society of East German Collectors
P.O. Box 2153
Reston, VA 22090

The Civil War Trust
1515 Wilson Blvd. #350
Arlington, VA 22209

The Conservation Fund
1800 N. Kent St. #1120
Arlington, VA 22209

The Great War Society
P.O. Box 4585
Stanford, CA 94309

The Historical Assn (London)
FAX 020-7582-4989

U.S. Dept. of the Interior
1849 C St. NW
Washington, D.C. 20240

U.S. Naval Historical Center
805 Kidder Breese St. SE
Washington, D.C. 20374

U.S. Naval Institute
291 Wood Road
Annapolis, MD 21402

U.S. Navy Seabee Museum
Bldg 99 1000 23rd Ave.
Port Hueneme, CA 93043

USMC Historical Center
1254 Charles Morris St. SE
Washington Navy Yard, D.C. 20374

Vicksburg Convention Bureau
P.O. Box 110
Vicksburg, MS 39181

Victorian Society of America
www.victoriansociety.org/

Vietnam Insignia Collectors
501 W. 5th Ave.

Covington, LA 70433

World History Association
www.thewha.org/

WWII Studies Assn (WWTSA)
www.parillo@ksu.edu

Bibliography

"A Date Which Will Live in Infamy," www.historymatters.gmu.edu

"Remember the Maine," www.cascobay.com

"The Fall of Singapore, February 15, 1942," www.historylearningsite.co.uk

A Brief History of Spain, www.spainview,com

A Brief History of the War in Afghanistan, www.ishipress.com/afghans.html

A Personal History of Ghengis Khan, www.greenwiki.co.nz

A Short History of the Kingdom of Spain, www.abacci.com

Adhemar of Le Puy, www.en.wikipedia.org

After Madrid: A Strange Sort of Solidarity, www.spiked-online.com

Anglin & Hamblin, World History to 1648, NY: Harper-Collins Publishers, 1993

Archaeology in Masada, www.mosaic.lk.net

Aztec Empire, www.mnsu.edu

Battle of Dien Bien Phu, www.en.wikipedia.org

Battle of Lepanto, www.infoplease,com

Battle of Midway: 4-7 June 1942," www.history.navy,mil/faqs/faq81-1.htm

Battle of Okinawa, www.globalsecurity.org

Battle of Talas River, 751, www.campus.northpark.edu

Battle of Talas, www.encyclopedia.the freedictionary.com

Battlefield Detectives, www.historychannel.com

Benjamin Franklin and the New World Order, www.belcherfoundation.org

Berube, Margery, The American Heritage Dictionary, NYHoughton Mifflin Co., 1982

Beshara, Adel, Hannibal Barca: Military Genius, www.dsoln.com

Bethell, Nicholas, Russia Besieged, Chicago: Time-Life Books, 1980

Biography of Hernan Cortez, www.sacklunch.net

Boadicea: Queen of the Iceni, www.enya.org

Boxell, Geoff, The Battle of Stamford Bridge, www.members.tripod.com

Bradford, Ned (Ed.), Battles and Leaders of the Civil War, NY: New American Library, 1984

Brokaw, Tom, The Greatest Generation, NY: Dell Publishing, 2001

Brokaw, Tom, The Greatest Nation Speaks, NY: Dell Publishing Company, 1999

Brown, Francis, The War in Maps, NY, London, Toronto: Oxford University Press, 1942

Buell, Thomas B., Master of Sea Power, Boston: Little, Brown and Company, 1978

Burns, Edward McNall, Western Civilizations, W. W. Norton & Co., Inc.(now 14 Editions)

Campbell, Joseph, The Power of Myth, NY: Doubleday, 1988

Carter, Jimmy, The Hornet's Nest, NY: Simon & Schuster, 2003

Causes of the French Revolution, www.cyberessays.com

Charles XII and the Northern Wars, www.utb.boras.se/uk

Chomsky, Noam, The War in Afghanistan, www.nadir.org

Clark, Kenneth, Civilisation, NY: Harper & Row, Publishers, 1969

Clarke, Richard A., Against All Enemies

Cordesman, Anthony H., The Iraq War, www.csis.zoovy.com

Costello, John, Days of Infamy, NY: Pocket Books, 1994

Courage at Little Round Top, www.nps.gov

Cowles, Virginia, The Kaiser, London: Collins, 1963

Crusades, www.worldhistory.com

CSS Virginia & USS Monitor, www.en.wikipedia.org

Curtis, Edward S., The North American Indian (1890-1930), 20 Volumes

Desert Fortress Overlooking the Dead Sea, www.jewishvirtual library.org

Douglas MacArthur, www.anythingarkansas.com/arkapedia/pedia/Douglas_MacArthur/

Dyer, Gwynne, War, NY: Crown Publishers, Inc., 1985

Early Amphibious Warfare, www.exwar.org

Edwards, I.E.S., Tutankhamun, NY: Alfred A. Knopf, Inc., 1976

EyeWitness to History, Alexander Defeats the Persians, 331 BC, www.eyewitnesstohistory

Failure of a Frankish-Mongol Alliance in Palestine, 1259, www.nyu.edu

Fargis, Paul (Ed.), New York Public Library Desk Reference, NY: Webster's New World, 1989

Faust, Patricia L., Illustrated Encyclopedia of the Civil War, NY: Harper Perennial, 1991

Field Marshall Sir Douglas Haig, www.diggerhistory.info

Fischman, Josh, Digging Up Clues to the Truth Behind the Myth, U.S. News & World Report, 5/04

Ford, Daniel, The Last Raid, www.airspacemag.com

Foss, Daniel A. Third and Sixth Century Crises East and West, www.hartford-hwp.com

Foss, Daniel A., The Koreans of Baghdad, www.listserv.acsu.buffalo.edu

Francisco Pizarro (1471-1541), www.bruce.ruiz.net

Gallipoli, www.paralumun.com

Gangarosa Jr., Gene, Browning: Armorer to the World, NJ: Stoeger Publishing Co., 1999

Gardner, John, The Life and Times of Chaucer, NY: Vintage Books, 1977

Gaugamela, 331 B.C., www.pictorsstudio.com

Genghis Khan (1162?-1227), www.members.tripod.com

Genghis Khan, www.geocities.com

Genghis Khan, www.nationalgeographic.com

Genghis Khan's First Mongol Empire, www.faculty.cua.edu

Ghengis Khan, www.mongolsibir.ch/history.html

Goths, www.27.1911encyclopedia.org

Groove, Eric, Big Fleet Actions, London: Brockhampton Press, 1998

Grunlund, Lizbeth, The "Star Wars" Legacy, www.clw.org

Harald Hardrada, www.itsa.ucsf.edu

Harald Hardrada, www.spartacus.schoolnet.co.uk

Haws, Duncan, Ships and the Sea: A Chronological Review, NY: Crescent Books, 1975

Heritage, Andrew (Ed.), Financial Times World Desk Reference. NY: Dorling Kindersley, 2003

Hernan Cortes Arrives in Mexico, www.pbs.org.

Herr, Michael, Khesanh, www.gonzo.org

Hersh, Seymour M., The Other War, www.newyorker.com

HMS Warrior 1861, www.royal-navy.mod.uk

Hoberman, Barry, The Battle of Talas, www.saudiaramcoworld.com

Hooker, Richard, The Peloponnesian War, www.wsu.edu:8080, 1999

Hough, Richard, Dreadnought: A History of the Modern Battleship, Bonanza Books, 1975

Humble, Richard, Submarines: The Illustrated History, Belgium: Basinghall Books, Ltd., 1981

Incas and Conquistadors, www.dialspace.dial.pipex.com

Inchon Invasion a Turning Point in Korean War, www.cnn.com/2000/US/09/14

Inchon Invasion, www.kmike.com

Iraq: Denial and Deception, www.whitehouse.gov March 17, 2003

Japan Mongol Invasions, www.workmall.com

Jennings & Brewster, The Century, NY: Doubleday, 1998

Kagan, Donald, The Outbreak of the Peloponnesian War, Ithica: Cornell U. Press, 1987

Kimmel, Husband E., Admiral Kimmel's Story, Chicago: Henry Regnery Company, 1955

Kimmel, Jay, Custer, Cody & the Last Indian Wars, Portland: CoryStevens Publishing, 1994

Kimmel, Jay, U.S. Navy Seabees: Since Pearl Harbor, Portland: CoryStevens Publishing, 1995

Kindersley, Peter, DK World Atlas, NY: DK Publishing, 1997

Kolata, Katheryn, The Long March, www.iusb.edu

Kublai Khan Rules China 1215-1294, www.campus.northpark.edu

Kublai Khan, www.infoplease.com

Kublai Khan, www.members.tripod.com

Kuijt, David, Mongol_DBA 154, www.umiacs.umd.edu

La Gloire, Ironclad! www.home.freeuk.com

MacDonald, John, Great Battlefields of the World, NY: Collier Books, 1985

Maddox, Robert, The New Left and the Origins of the Cold War, NJ: Princeton U. Press, 1973

Mansfield, Henry C., The Prince: Niccolo Machiavelli, Univ. of Chicago Press, 1985

Mao Tse-Tung: A Biography, www.geocities.com

Marquis de LaFayette (1757-1834), www.swil.ocdsb.edu

Masada, www.crystalinks.com

Medieval History of Spain, www.medieval-life.net

Mitchell, Gordon R., The Betrayal of Reagan's Star Wars Vision, www.pitt.edu

Mongols Under Kublai Khan Attempt to Invade Japan, 1274, www.campus.northpark.edu

Morelock, Col. J. D., Great Land Battles: From the Civil War to the Gulf War, Berkley, 1994

Muslim Expansion in the West, www.ccat.sas.upenn.edu

Muslim Spain, www.foclark.tripod.com

Napoleon I, Emperor of the French (1769-1821), www.2.lucidcafe.com

Operation Desert Storm, www.globalsecurity.org

Pakula, Andrew, President Reagan's 'Star Wars' Plan, www.peacemagazine.org

Parsons, Marie, King Scorpion, www.touregypt.net

Peter I (The Great) 1689-1725, www.campus.northpark.edu

Phillips, David, Maps of the Civil War, NY: Metro Books, 1998

Pope Gregory VII, www.fact-index.com

Presidency in Taiwan, www.en.wikipedia.org

Queen Boadicea: Leader of the Iceni Tribe, www.stevedunks.demon.co.uk

Queller, Donald E., Crusades, www.worldbookonline.com

Rang, Lee Wha, The Koryo-Mongol Allied Invasion of Japan, www.kimsoft.com

Realm of the Mongols, www.geocities.com

Rough Riders, www.lcweb.loc.gov

Saddam Hussein, www.abcnews.go.com/reference/bios/shussein.html

Samarkand, 751 A.D., www.saudiaramcoworld.com

Shakespeare, William, Henry V

Spaniards v. Incas and the Fall of the Inca Empire ,www.muweb.millersville.edu

Spanish Armada 1588, www.theotherside.co.uk

Speech at Council of Clermont, 1095, www.fordham.edu

Spencer, Robert F., The Native Americans, NY: Harper & Row, Publishers, 1962

St. Pius V: A Dominican Pope, www.nashvilledominican.org

Stephenson, Michael (Ed.), Nattlegrounds: Geo. & History of Warfare, Nat'l Geo., Soc., 2003

Stevenson, William, A Man Called Intrepid: The Secret War, NY: Harcourt Brace, 1976

Stewart, Edgar I. (Ed.) Penny-an-Acre Empire in the West, OK:: Univ. Oklahoma Press, 1968

Stewart, Edgar I., Custer's Luck, Norman: Univerity of Oklahoma Press, 1955

Templar History, www.templarhistory.com

Tet Offensive: A Turning Point in the Vietnam War, www.marxist.com/1968/vietnam.html

The 1967 Six-Day War, www.jewishvirtuallibrary.org

The Battle of Agincourt, www.historychannel.com

The Battle of Cannae, www.barca.fsnet.co.uk

The Battle of Little Round Top at Gettysburg, www.geocities.com

The Battle of Stamford Bridge, www.britainexpress.com

The Battle of the Talas River, 751 AD, www.tse.dyndns.org

The Conquest of the Aztec Empire: Hernan Cortes, www.ucalgary.ca/applied_history,html

The Crusaders Capture Jerusalem, 1099, www.eyewitnesstohistory.com

The Fall of the Aztecs, www.pbs.org

The Fall of the Bastille, July 14, 1789, www.campus.northpark.edu

The Inchon Invasion, www.britains-smallwars.com

The Iraq War 2003, www.mideastweb.org

The Mongol Invasions, www.ic.ucsc.edu

The Naval Battle of Lepanto, www.nafpaktos.com

The Normans, 1066, www.historychannel.com

The Seljuks, www.allaboutturkey.com

The Somme, www.spartacus.schoolnet.co.uk

The Spanish Inquisition, www.bibletopics.com

The Spanish-American War, www.smplanet.com

The Story of Queen Boadicea, www.observatory99.freeserve.co.uk

The Strengths of the Spanish and English Fleets, www.angelfire.com

The Visigoths, www.campus.northpark.edu

Theodosius the Great, www.roman-empire.net

Toland, John, Infamy: Pearl Harbor and Its Aftermath, NY: Doubleday & Company, 1982

Tomoyuki Yamashita, www.spartacus.schoolnet.co.uk

Tsouras, Peter G., Alexander the Great's Most Heroic Moment, www.historynet.com

Ventrella, Jeffery, Practicing Postmillenialism, www.chalcedon.edu/articles/0203

Visigoths (West Goths), www.orbilat.com

Visigoths, www.home.comcast.net

Wars Between the Jews and Romans: Masada (74 CE, www.livius.org

Weir, William, 50 Battles that Changed the World, New Page Books, 2004

William Henry Harrison (1773-1841), www.whitehouse.gov

Winterbotham, F.W., The Ultra Secret, NY: Dell Publishing, 1974

World War One, Somme, www.ragz-international.com

www.World Atlas.com

Yorktown Campaign (August-October, 1781), www.xenophongroup.com

Map Index

Index

Notes

CoryStevens Publishing
15350 NE Sandy Boulevard
Portland, OR 97230
www.corystevens.com